AN UNSUITABLE BOOK

The Bible in the Modern World, 7

AN UNSUITABLE BOOK

THE BIBLE AS SCANDALOUS TEXT

Hugh S. Pyper

SHEFFIELD PHOENIX PRESS

2005

Copyright © 2005 Sheffield Phoenix Press

Published by Sheffield Phoenix Press
Department of Biblical Studies, University of Sheffield
Sheffield S10 2TN

www.sheffieldphoenix.com

A CIP catalogue record for this book
is available from the British Library

Typeset by Forthcoming Publications
Printed by Lightning Source

ISBN 1-905148-32-7
ISSN 1747-9630

CONTENTS

Chapter 11

ACKNOWLEDGMENTS

Many people, friends, colleagues and students, have contributed, wittingly or unwittingly, to the development of the ideas in the following essays through conversation, questions, their own writings and their friendship and support. To them all I give my thanks and of course take responsibility for any errors and omissions in the work. It is hard to single out names, but Tim Beal, Eric Christianson, Alastair Hunter, Stewart Lasine, Tod Linafelt and Yvonne Sherwood may recognize why they are mentioned here specifically; whether they see this as the compliment it is intended to be is another matter. I owe a particular debt to all my former colleagues in the Department of Theology and Religious Studies of the University of Leeds who put up willingly with a rather maverick Hebrew Bible scholar in their midst. Their range of expertise in Theology and Religious Studies and beyond encouraged me, no doubt to their alarm, to explore beyond the normal boundaries of the subject. I also owe thanks to my old friends and new colleagues in the Department of Biblical Studies in Sheffield. After many years as a sort of northern satellite or acolyte of Sheffield, moving to the department has been more of a homecoming than a venture into the unknown and I am glad to be able to thank more specifically Philip Davies for his friendship and support and David Clines, Cheryl Exum and Keith Whitelam for their continued encouragement and the acceptance of this book for the Sheffield Phoenix Press. Thanks are also due to Ailsa Parkin and the inimitable Duncan Burns for their unstinting help in seeing this manuscript through the press.

I owe further thanks to the editors and readers who accepted and commented on earlier versions of some of these essay. Their provenance is as follows:

'Selfish Texts: The Bible and Survival'. This essay was derived from two articles published separately as 'The Selfish Text: Memetics and the Bible', in J.C. Exum and S. Moore (eds.), *Biblical Studies/Cultural Studies* (JSOTSup, 266; Sheffield: Sheffield Academic Press, 1998), pp. 71-90, and 'The Triumph of the Lamb: Psalm 23 and Textual Fitness', *Biblical Interpretation* 9 (2001), pp. 384-92.

'Speaking Silence: Male Readers, Female Readings and the Biblical Text'; slight revision of the article of the same title which appeared in *Literature and Theology* 8 (1994), pp. 296-310.

'Readers in Pain: Muriel Spark and the Book of Job'; revision of 'The Reader in Pain: Job as Text and Pretext', *Literature and Theology* 7 (1993), pp. 111-29; reprinted in R.P. Carroll (ed.), *Text as Pretext: Essays in Honour of Robert Davidson* (*Journal for the Study of the Old Testament*, Supplement Series, 138; Sheffield: JSOT Press, 1994), pp. 234-56.

'Reading Lamentations'; revision of the article of the same title which appeared in *Journal for the Study of the Old Testament* 95 (2001), pp. 55-69.

'Modern Gospels of Judas: Canon and Betrayal'; revision of the article of the same title which appeared in *Literature and Theology* 15 (2001), pp. 111-22.

'The Rebellious Son; Biblical Family Values'; revision of 'The Family in the Bible', in Hugh S. Pyper (ed.), *The Christian Family: A Concept in Crisis* (Norwich: The Canterbury Press Norwich, 1996), pp. 14-28.

'Fleshing Out the Text: Re-reading Circumcision'; previously published as 'Fleshing Out the Text', in Jonneke Bekkenkamp and Yvonne Sherwood (eds.), *Sanctified Aggression: Legacies of Biblical and Post-Biblical Vocabularies of Violence* (*Journal for the Study of the Old Testament*, Supplement Series, 400; Bible in the Twenty-first Century Series, 3; London: Sheffield Academic Press, 2003), pp. 44-59.

Finally, this book is dedicated to two people whose effect on my thought and life continues to be profound: the late Robert Carroll, and Ronald Weitzman, who is sadly now living in the shadow of severe brain damage.

1

INTRODUCTION

In Dame Ivy Compton-Burnett's novel *Daughters and Sons*, the following exchange, so characteristic in its asperity, takes place between Hetta, the lady of the house, and Miss Hallam, the latest in a succession of governesses employed to teach Hetta's niece Muriel:

> 'You do not mind reading the Bible with Muriel?' said Hetta. 'I am afraid that is part of the duty you undertake'.
> 'No, not at all, if you don't mind her reading it. I think it is an unsuitable book for a child, but I like it very much myself. I am glad she is to adapt herself to me, and it is good for children to read unsuitable books.' (Compton-Burnett 1972a: 121)

The spirit of Miss Hallam underlies the following essays. In them I hope that my own liking for the Bible is clear and also that a good deal of what I like about it is its unsuitability. What that in itself rather unsuitable description implies is what this book is about and I hope will be clearer once it has been read. I do, however, wholeheartedly share Miss Hallam's convictions both that the Bible is unsuitable, even scandalous, and that it is good for children, and indeed any of us, to read unsuitable books, especially if we have a Miss Hallam to read with us. I was struck myself when I came to collect these essays how many of them depend on the insights of remarkable women writers and readers: Isak Dinesen, Muriel Spark, Hélène Cixous, Carol Kendall and Dame Ivy herself, among others. The implications of this I leave the reader to decide.

The importance of scandal in approaching the Bible is one of the many insights that I have gained through a long encounter with Søren Kierkegaard. Scandal is a profoundly biblical category. God in the Hebrew Bible threatens on a regular basis to do things that will amaze and confound people and often carries out the threat. The gospels and other New Testament writings almost monotonously record the scandalized response of those who hear Jesus or witness his actions. For Kierkegaard, their reaction is infinitely preferable to the kind of unthinking acceptance of the paradox of God become human, or God's choice of Israel, that was common in the Danish Church of his day. We *should* be scandalized by the Bible — only then, he would argue, is there any chance that we might be taking it seriously. Acknowledging its dangerous offensiveness is the first step to wondering whether the root of the offence lies in ourselves or in the text. Kierkegaard's influence pervades this book.

It will also be apparent that these essays are written by someone who was first trained as an evolutionary biologist before turning to the study of the Hebrew Bible. My experience is that people are fairly neatly divided into those who find this an almost inconceivable leap and those who see it as a natural progression. Not surprisingly, perhaps, I find myself in the latter camp. Where the two areas of study meet, I maintain, is that both are concerned with the interplay between conservation and diversification in the propagation of information over time. The information in question may be encoded genetically and manifested in the diversity of biological organisms, or else it may be recorded in written or spoken language and other cultural productions.

It is out of this meeting that the first chapter 'Selfish Texts: The Bible and Survival' arises. In it, the analogy is drawn between the text and its reading community, on the one hand, and the genome and its surrounding protoplasm, on the other. Here the unsuitability of the Bible is explored in explicitly Darwinian terms, drawing on the work of Richard Dawkins and Daniel Dennett on the idea of the 'meme', a unit of cultural information that is transmitted across time on the analogy of the gene. This is an intriguing but elusive concept which, I would argue, can actually be more usefully employed to understand texts and cultural artefacts, which are structured blocks of information, than in the more vague and notional way that it is usually used.

The useful thing in the present context is that 'unsuitability' has an important place in a Darwinian understanding of evolution. The organism that is entirely suited to its environment or its lifestyle is vulnerable to any change in that environment. It is precisely a seemingly unsuitable variation that will prove to be the one that can cope with the change.

Human beings are a case in point. On almost all grounds, the naked individual human being seems pathetically unsuited to life on this planet. It lacks the strength and the weapons to defend itself or attack its prey; it is uncomfortable both in hot and cold climates; it lacks the specialized digestive systems to make full use of vegetable food; it is much slower than rival animals on land, in water, or in the trees. Its offspring are effectively helpless for several months if not years after birth. The list can continue, but it is precisely because human beings are not 'suited' to any environment that they have been able to exploit such a variety of habitats and foodstuffs. Individual vulnerability necessitates cooperation and the ability to modify the environment. Adaptability has been purchased at the price of suitability.

Analogously, the texts most likely to survive are those not entirely suited to any one reading community and its cultural norms. These norms of suitability vary between groups and across time. The Bible does not survive because it fits the expectations of its readers, but because it refuses to be so confined. In anthropomorphized language, the Bible has little interest in merely serving the interests of any community, however fondly they imagine that it is 'their' book. Communities come and go. To survive, it has to be a 'selfish' text.

This may seem an 'unsuitable', not to say 'scandalous', description. The scandal here is the one that Dawkins exploits in the title of his book *The Selfish Gene*, where he promotes the reductive idea that living organisms can be understood simply as the vehicles through which the blind programme of self-replication by DNA molecules is accomplished. The word 'selfish' is deliberately and provocatively misapplied here to disrupt the anthropocentric and purposive view of evolution that Dawkins is seeking to challenge. To see the Bible as 'selfish' in these terms is equally provocative. The success of the Bible as the most widely disseminated of all texts can be explained in a way that does not depend on any divine intervention, or on its truth, but rather on the text's ability to maintain identity through change and to persuade groups of readers to devote their energies to copying the text. 'Western culture is the Bible's way of making more Bibles' is the deliberately controversial claim at the centre of this paper. It is a claim that can certainly be argued against, but the questions it raises lead to a reappraisal of how texts work and what makes an effective text.

The article was also written, however, as a teasing rejoinder to Dawkins's impassioned stance against religion. Biblical metaphors and language permeate popular writing on genetics, leading to the presumably unintended irony that writers such as Dawkins may contribute to the survival of the biblical text, if only as a necessary cultural reference point. Once again, the Bible escapes the intentions of those who use it.

This essay also introduces another recurrent theme of this collection: the metaphor of predator and prey as way of expressing the relationship between the Bible and its readers. The Bible as predator may seem an extreme and frightening image, but the text itself seems quite prepared to apply the same metaphor to God, either as a beast of prey or as a ravening warrior. Darwinian models remind us that in evolutionary terms, predator and prey are inextricably linked in a constant battle to outwit one another. The specific example of the metaphor of the shepherd in Psalm 23 shows that the ambivalence of the metaphor is a vital factor in the remarkable success of this psalm in permeating religious and secular culture. There is another side to this as well, exemplified by the quotation from Isak Dinesen that ends this essay, which celebrates what is now regarded as a shocking pursuit—the hunting of lions. Between hunter and hunted, as between human opponents, especially when they are well matched, there can be a curious, deep bond of respect and even affection.

It is Dinesen who provides the link to the next essay, 'Speaking Silence: Male Readers, Female Readings and the Biblical Text', where her remarkable short story 'The Blank Page' underlies the discussion. In this essay, too, that outstanding biblical reader, Freud, makes his appearance, the first of several in this collection. Both Dinesen and Freud are masterly guides to the realm in which Dame Ivy Compton-Burnett is so uncannily at home, the realm where silence speaks louder than words. Through attention to silences, the veneer of the outwardly 'suitable' is induced to crack, revealing unspeakable things.

A key part of the Bible's uncanny power over its readers resides in its silences. These induce its readers to make their own utterances to fill the gap, often with unforeseen consequences. The Bible's adaptability depends at least as much on what it does not say as on what it does. Its silences demand to be filled, but are open to being filled in different ways by different readers in different circumstances. In this essay, the suggestion is made that such silences in the text can be construed as peculiarly male silences, symptoms of what I call the 'anxiety of utterance' that shapes biblical poetics and which also manifests itself in the violent and irrational responses to the feminine in the biblical text that scandalize the modern liberal reader.

The disturbing power of divine silence is at the heart of the book of Job, where not only the contexts but also the structure of the book trouble readers who struggle to keep the Bible within the bounds of theological, ethical and even literary reasonableness. In the next essay,

'Readers in Pain: Muriel Spark and the Book of Job', the causes and effects of this distress for readers are explored in the company of yet another formidable woman writer and biblical reader, Muriel Spark. She engages with Job throughout her work, but does so explicitly in her novel *The Only Problem*. Her hero in this book, who is writing a commentary on Job, finds that textual ambiguities, structural problems and unexplained silences conspire to give the modern reader at least a faint echo of the pain that Job undergoes. The scandalous picture of a God who is prepared to gamble on the loyalty of his favourites is only exceeded for many modern readers by the unexpected reversal at the end of the book which seems to trivialize the poetry of its tragic centre. The scandal of this unsuitable ending is that it is not scandalous enough. Stylistic unsuitability can mirror other forms of scandal in the text. Yet the difference between the pain of the reader and the pain of the victim of divine violence cannot be evaded, and the inappropriateness of equating the two itself provokes another sort of scandal that at the least should serve to humble biblical commentators, who, whatever else they may suffer, have the education, the wherewithal and the time to devote to such pursuits.

These problems of scandalous reading are taken up in the next few chapters. Harold Bloom's energetic and provocatively playful engagement with Genesis and Samuel is explored in 'The Bible in Bloom'. Can we take seriously a critic who is prepared to suggest that Bathsheba wrote the J material? That depends on what we judge his serious point to be. His own pseudo-Darwinian emphasis on the competition between texts for the scarce resource of readerly attention and his pseudo-Freudian concept of the anxiety of influence which makes writers turn against, and remould, their precursors so that they are read as precisely that—precursors to the later author, not the originators of whom the latecomer is a pallid epigone— coincide with many of the concerns of these essays. His fundamental argument that all readings are misreadings, his concern with the concept of the canon, and particularly his seminal but underexploited insight that canons are the business of writers rather than readers is also vital. His sense of the suppressed violence but also the sheer vivid intensity of the act of writing is exhilarating, and his distinction between strong and weak readings an important one. He makes it clearer that the point of reading is not to find the most accurate interpretation by some chimerical standard of correspondence to authorial intention, but the most fecund one.

Where Bloom falls short of a full engagement with the strength of the biblical canon, in my judgment, is in evading the ultimate scandal of resurrection in favour of a very personal version of Gnosticism. This is explored more fully in the next essay, 'Modern Gospels of Judas: Canon and Betrayal', which looks at the growth of interest in the Gospel of Judas and the reappraisal of Judas himself in nineteenth- and twentieth-century literature. Judas is seen as the betrayed rather than the betrayer, and the suppression of his version of the gospel as the epitome of the ideological imperialism of the creators of the Christian canon of Scripture. As Kierkegaard argues, the revolt against the cruel paradoxes of the canonical scriptures that this represents is evidence of a far more spiritually and ethically mature response than is the tame acquiescence shown by weak readers. We *should* be scandalized by Scripture. Yet, I argue, the option for Judas itself betrays a choice of death as against life and, once again, ultimately shies away from the true scandal of the Christian canon.

One text that epitomizes the scandal of the Hebrew Bible, and which, for that reason, lies nearer to its core than is usually acknowledged, is the book of Lamentations. Its scandal arises from its implacable commitment to survival: the survival of the community, but above all of God. The next chapter, 'Reading Lamentations', argues that, as in Job, the poetics and structure of the book embody its message. The rigid compression of anguish into the form of the alphabetic acrostic which then breaks down to a chaotic shadow of itself in the last chapter in its own way reveals the deep 'unsuitability' of the book. Here we can see this formal veneer crack, as the survivors turn on the dead to discharge their anguish and purchase the survival of the paternal God who is the author of their distress at the expense of the degradation of Jerusalem, the city as mother. Suppression, silence, anxiety and betrayal all meet together here in the type example of the text of survival.

The paradox of survival is to be met with in the New Testament as well. The family, conceived of as the human structure which ensures continuity in the face of the inevitability of death, is there subject to a scandalous attack. In the next article, 'The Rebellious Son: Biblical Family Values', the claim is made that the gospels could be seen to present Jesus' life as the fulfilment of one of the most disturbing pieces of legislation in the Hebrew Bible, the call for the stoning of the rebellious son in Deut. 20.18-21. This shocking assault of the parents on their child, the hope for their future, becomes a radical challenge to the biological mechanisms of survival of the community which the gospel writers use as a means to establish a new sort of community with a new principle of identity and of survival. The weak misreadings of the New Testament that seek to assimilate the text once more to a more 'suitable' stance on family values, and then seek to shore up those values by appeal to the text seriously mistake the radical strength of these texts.

The danger of such misreadings is explored in the following chapter, 'Fleshing out the Text: Re-reading Circumcision', where an astonishing outburst by Gershom Scholem on the danger of the suppressed violence in the Hebrew language forms the starting point for an exploration of the danger of suppressed biblical metaphors in any modern Western language. The focus of the discussion is the strange domestication of circumcision as a normative practice in the culture of the United States, and a matter of little remark in the theo-logical discourse of Western Christianity. Seen as a deliberate act of sexual violence practiced on infants incapable of protest or consent, it takes on a scandalous connotation as is argued by those men who see themselves as 'circumcision survivors'. The interaction of biblical, social and psychoanalytic discourses here is bewildering, as are the implications for the dialogue between Jewish and Christian readers of the Hebrew Bible. What is clear is that we have here a type-case of the suppression of violence and scandal which may have unacknow-ledged resonances in Western culture and perhaps particularly in its treatment of the child.

The issue of the child, and of children's reading, is the topic of the chapter entitled 'The Bible as Children's Literature: The Metrical Psalms and *The Gammage Cup*'. If even half of what is outlined in the earlier chapters is true, Ivy Compton Burnett's Miss Hallam is quite right in declaring the Bible unsuitable for children. Yet for centuries children have read it, and indeed it has been the text from which they have been taught how to read. The consequences of this are lamen-tably underexplored as an aspect both of the history of biblical inter-pretation and of our wider literary culture. In this chapter, the virtues of encountering this unsuitable text as a central part of a young reader's education are examined. As an example, the maladroit technique of the Scottish metrical version of the psalms opens the reader's imagination to the manifold effects and uses of language far beyond mere factual communication. The biblical text becomes a stimulus to creative misreading of a kind that can produce a new generation of strong readers rather than weakly accurate ones. Carol Kendall's *The Gammage Cup* is used as an intertext with the Bible to illuminate the way in which children's literature serves to free the child to probe the whole notion of suitability, and how the Bible can be a vital part of that education.

That is not to say that everything is safe for a child, of course. There are real dangers to be faced, and the dangerous aspect of the Bible as predator is the topic of the final chapter, a tribute to a particularly bold but canny reader of the Hebrew Bible, the late Robert Carroll. His influence on me as teacher and friend has been profound. His controversial book *The Wolf in the Sheepfold: The Bible as a Problem for Christian Theology* bears witness both to his love and respect for the Bible's dangerous power and his scorn for its weak readers. The metaphor of the Bible as wolf is the binding thread of this chapter, which makes explicit the ambivalences over predator and prey, speech and silence, wild and tame, suitable and unsuitable, that have been the recurrent themes of these essays.

It will be no secret by now that my sympathies are with his call for a recovery of the wildness of the Bible, but, as with the call for the reintroduction of the wolf into the now tamed wildernesses of Europe and America, it does raises important philosophical and practical problems. How wild can the Bible now be and what would be the cultural consequences of uncaging it, even supposing this were possible? A final great woman reader and writer, Hélène Cixous, offers an answer in her remarkable meditations on the wolf and love. To love and be loved is to be open to being prey, and also to acknowledge that one can be predator. Risk is at love's heart.

I do not claim that these essays offer clear answers — uncertainty is part of the exhilaration of taking the unsuitable seriously — but I do hope to have made the point that, whatever the future risks, there are present dangers in keeping the Bible caged and rewards in letting it run free. The Bible is an unsuitable book, which will turn against those who think they can control and manipulate it, sometimes in ways devastating not only for them, but also for innocent bystanders. That is the secret of its survival and the vital contribution it makes to our culture; 'vital' here means not simply essential but also, as its root implies, 'life-giving'.

It is very good for us to read unsuitable books with the power of the Bible. It is not safe, or comfortable, and may be profoundly shocking and painful, but it is an encounter with life. These essays are offered in that spirit.

2

SELFISH TEXTS: THE BIBLE AND SURVIVAL

According to the collective authors of *The Postmodern Bible*, it is a 'truism' that the Bible has exerted more influence on Western culture than any other book (The Bible and Culture Collective 1995: 1). In art, literature, politics and religion, biblical thought-forms, narratives and quotations are all-pervasive. As Western culture becomes globalized, so does the Bible. It is said that between a quarter and a third of all Japanese households possess a Bible, in a country where only one or two percent of the population have any Christian adherence. This is because it is regarded as essential background for a proper understanding of Western culture. One effect of the spread of Western culture through trade and conquest as well as missionary activity has been the spread of a collection of ancient Hebrew and Greek texts to every corner of the globe. Where Western culture goes, the Bible goes too.

Simply in terms of the number of copies currently in existence, the Bible represents one of the most successful texts ever produced. Whereas other great texts of the ancient world have either been lost or else exist only in a relatively small number of copies, the Bible is ubiquitous. It exists in over two thousand different languages and in many of those languages it exists in multiple translations. Something identifiable with the Bible in its present form has existed for nearly two millennia and some of its components for much longer. If 'survival of the fittest' has any validity as a slogan, then the Bible seems a fair candidate for the accolade of the fittest of texts.

How have the biblical texts achieved this remarkable success and what does this reveal about the cultures in which they are embedded? It will be obvious that the model by which I intend to do this is a Darwinian one. Indeed, I propose to turn for this to one of the fiercest contemporary critics of the biblical world view, Richard Dawkins.

His book *The Selfish Gene* (1976 [rev. 1989]), itself a runaway best-seller, has popularized the admittedly controversial idea that human beings, indeed all living organisms, can be construed as the 'survival vehicles' for their genetic material.

This claim is a variant on Samuel Butler's well-known description of a hen as 'an egg's way of making another egg'. An organism is a gene's way of making another gene. More pertinent to our purposes is Dawkins's further claim that there is a strict analogy between the processes of biological evolution and the development of human culture. This idea has been taken up by Daniel Dennett who adapts Butler's epigram to read 'A scholar is just a library's way of making more libraries' (1991: 202). It is the following further adaptation of this slogan that forms the background to this chapter: Western culture is the Bible's way of making more Bibles.

In an attempt to see if and how far this rather bold assertion can be defended, I will analyse in more depth the nature of the analogy that can be drawn between biological and culture evolution and in particular the usefulness of Dawkins's concept of the 'meme' in this context. In the process, however, it will become apparent, I hope, that the literature of popular Darwinism is itself a cultural product, affected by the very phenomena, including the prevalence of the Bible, that it tries to analyse. My contention, overall, will be that any attempt at a reductive reading of the Bible in terms of some metanarrative of biological determinism or a postmodern analysis of cultural relativism may find itself hoist with its own petard.

Genes, Memes and Texts

In *The Selfish Gene* (1976), Dawkins contends that just as biological evolution can be studied at various levels — the gene, the genome, the individual, the gene-pool or the species — so cultural evolution can be looked at in multiple levels, from the spread of the simplest catch-phrase to the rise and dominance of the great civilisations of China or the Islamic world. In terms of evolutionary biology, the main point he argues in the book is that the clearest way to think about evolution is to work from the point of view of the smallest replicating entities, in the case of genetics, the gene. By analogy, studies of cultural evolution in Darwinian terms will proceed best by examining the smallest replicating units in culture. It is these that he designates as 'memes'.

He illustrates the concept as follows:

Examples of memes are tunes, ideas, catch-phrases, clothes-fashions,
ways of making pots or building arches. Just as genes propagate
themselves in the gene pool by leaping from body to body via sperm
or eggs, so memes propagate themselves in the meme pool by leaping
from brain to brain via a process which in the broad sense, be called
imitation. (1976: 206)

Later, however, Dawkins becomes concerned to distinguish between
a meme as a unit of information lodged in a brain and the phenotypic
effects of that meme, such manifestations as the tune or the idea
(1982: 109).

Definitions are difficult, to say the least, in these areas. What
exactly constitutes a meme or a culture defies classification and the
recent literature on memes is bedevilled by shifting definitions and
unsupportable generalizations and comparisons. Extravagant claims
for the explanatory power of this concept have been made, including claims that the key to human self-understanding is in the new
'science' of memetics. As the originator of the concept, Dawkins has
been far more modest in his assessment of its value. Dennett, who as
a philosopher has written with more rigour on the subject than most,
elaborates the concept of the meme in Chapter 12 of his *Darwin's
Dangerous Idea* where he defines memes as 'self-replicating complex
ideas which form distinct memorable units' (1995: 344). Even so, the
concept remains notoriously fluid and therefore liable to abuse. How
could it be applied to the Bible? The Bible if anything seems more like
a repository of memes than a meme itself or even a 'meme complex'.
In the ensuing argument, we will at times be using the term 'meme'
for its convenience and its heuristic power in applying Darwinian
insights to cultural developments, but always with a weather eye on
its slippery nature.

The Bible as Replicator

At this point, however, I want to turn to a more fruitful line of
enquiry provided by Dawkins's later, more rigorous discussion of
another concept, that of the 'replicator'. This he defines as follows: 'A
replicator is anything in the universe of which copies are made'
(Dawkins 1982: 83). At a banal level, that is a claim that can undeniably be made for the Bible, and so it may be of interest to explore the
ramifications of this analogy.

Note, first of all, that Dawkins carefully does not say that the replicator must be self-replicating. There is a fundamental point here
which has often been missed. DNA is sometimes described as a

'self-replicating' molecule. In one sense this is true. Given the right environment, a molecule of DNA is capable of acting as a template so that an exact copy of itself is produced. The important point is that it needs the right environment. DNA on its own cannot reproduce itself; it needs a complex of enzymes which will guide and manage the process. In fact, it is only at the level of the cell that we find a replicating structure which can produce copies of all its parts from raw materials in a simple environment.

In that sense, the Bible is no different from DNA. Shut a Bible, or even two, in a cupboard and you will certainly not find more Bibles when you come back. Leave a jar of DNA on a shelf, and it will not increase either. Only in the context of a cell, of a 'survival machine', will we find DNA reproducing. Likewise, Bibles can only reproduce through the agency of a human reader who then takes steps to ensure that more copies are produced.

The crucial point which lifts all this from the level of a truism is the way in which Dawkins then refines the concept of the replicator. He distinguishes between an active replicator, the nature of which has some influence over the probability of its being copied, and a passive replicator, the nature of which is immaterial. DNA, the replicating molecule which encodes genetic information in cells, is an example of the first, in that it exerts phenotypic effects on the environment through the protein synthesis it enables, which in turn influence whether it will be copied.

Active replicators modify their environment in such a way as to enhance their own reproductive capacity. To illustrate this, Dawkins makes a particular study of the interactions between parasites and hosts. For example, at a simple level, a gall wasp larva will carry genes for the synthesis of chemicals that mimic the growth hormones of an oak tree, inducing the tree to grow an unusual structure which serves to protect and feed the wasp larva. Here the wasp genes are acting on the phenotype of the oak tree, not the wasp, in a way that enhances the wasp's reproduction but which may have a deleterious effect on the tree. The relevance of this parasite/host model for the consideration of the Bible will become clearer as our discussion develops.

Unfortunately for our purposes, Dawkins's example of a passive regulator is a sheet of paper which is Xeroxed. On the face of it, this undercuts any analogy between the genetic material and the Bible. He goes on, however, to concede that some pieces of paper are much more likely to be copied than others because of what is written on

them. They then become active replicators as they convey information which acts on readers and their environment in such a way as to
induce them to copy the text. The argument we will pursue is that in
this sense the Bible is indeed an active replicator, one which alters its
environment so as to increase its chances of being copied. The
intriguing questions then become how the Bible does this and why it
has been so conspicuously successful.

Dawkins goes on to discuss other aspects of active replicators. It is
a fundamental point in his argument that no process of replication is
infallible. Strikingly, a favoured metaphor to illustrate this in popular
genetic texts is the variability of the biblical text in different translations or through processes of copying. Robert Pollack in his *Signs of
Life*, for instance, sets out six English versions of Jas 4.5 to illustrate
the phenomenon of alleles, the existence of variant forms of the same
gene within a population or indeed an individual genome (1994: 38).
Dawkins himself uses the 'mistranslation' of the Hebrew for 'young
woman' as 'virgin' in the Septuagint version of Isa. 7.14 as an example of the potentially enormous phenotypic effects of a small change
in DNA. He also provides a footnote explaining the Hebrew and
Greek texts complete with citations in Hebrew, remarking that 'I
suppose the scholars of the Septuagint could at least be said to have
started something big' by this (1989: 16). This infiltration of biblical
examples into the texts of popular genetics is an intriguing phenomenon to which we will return.

The crucial consequence of this variation is that when it occurs
some replicators may turn out to be less efficient than others at replication and so will tend to be replaced by the more successful replicators. For active replicators, whose nature affects their success in
achieving replication, such variation may have a remarkable effect on
their reproductive ability. Those which replicate most efficiently will,
if all else is equal, come to predominate in the population.

Yet variability in itself is not enough; it must be coupled with
stability. If 'successful' variants are to survive and out-compete the
others, they must be conserved over time. Dawkins sets out the conditions for a successful replicator in the following slogan: longevity,
fecundity and fidelity. The replicator must last long enough to reproduce, it must be capable of producing a sufficient number of copies,
and these copies must be accurate. To ensure accuracy, the genetic
material has a whole complex of 'editor enzymes' which repair and
correct copying errors in DNA. So too the biblical text has become
sacrosanct with a premium put on its accurate reproduction. The

great complexes of the Masoretic apparatus and the libraries of biblical criticism which have sought to preserve the text in its 'original' form are the evidences of this.

The stability of a particular text or a particular DNA sequence, what Dawkins calls its 'longevity', is an important factor. The replicator must maintain its identity over time. Equally important, however, is its capacity to throw up variants which, when conditions change, may confer an advantage on the organisms which bear them. It is this balance between the ability to reproduce faithfully a particular variant but also to be able to produce variation if the circumstances favour it that confers reproductive success on any replicating system.

The Cell and the Community

The Bible, then, operates as a replicator in a way analogous to DNA. Like DNA, it stores information which can be read and translated and which contributes to its own reproduction. This reading, however, requires the action of another level of agency. In the case of DNA, this agent is the cell where the information contained in DNA is translated into proteins which both structure and control the host of chemical processes which are necessary to sustain the life of the cell, and therefore the reproduction of DNA. In the case of the Bible, the agency is a human community which will recopy and disseminate the text.

The crucial question now becomes how the active effect of the cellular DNA on the constitution of the cell or organism which is its 'survival vehicle' is paralleled in the case of the Bible. That a case can be made is evident from the fact that the analogy has been pursued in the opposite direction, notably by Robert Pollack. In his *Signs of Life*, he explicitly embraces the analogy of DNA as text:

> I have organised this book around the notion of DNA as a work of literature, a great historical text. But the metaphor of the chemical text is more than a vision: DNA is a long skinny assembly of atoms similar in function, if not form, to the letters of a book, strung out in one long line. The cells of our bodies do extract a multiplicity of meanings from the DNA text inside them, and we have indeed begun to read a cell's DNA in ways even more subtle than a cell can do. (1994: 5)

The vocabulary of molecular biology is shot through with metaphors of reading: translation, transcription, reading enzymes and the like. Pollack extends the metaphor by suggesting that the genome is like

an encyclopaedia, where the volumes are represented by the chromosomes, the articles by the sets of genes encoding for a particular
character, the sentences by the genes themselves. Words are domains
and letters are base pairs (1994: 21).

Nor is he alone in drawing such comparisons. Dawkins himself
speaks of the tempting analogy of seeing DNA as a 'family Bible'
(1995: 39), a record of our ancestry slightly different for each one of
us, although he quickly goes on to point out flaws in this metaphor.
Dennett makes the point that the strict analogy between genes and
memes can be maintained on the ground that they are both 'semantic
entities', by which he means that they constitute information which
can be variously encoded. A gene is not simply a piece of DNA,
although to be effective it has to be expressed as such. It could equally
be encoded in a sequence of letters on a page, just as a meme may be
contained in the pages of a book.

But as texts, both DNA and the Bible have to be read. In the case of
DNA this is a matter of the synthesis of RNA and through it of particular amino acid sequences in cellular proteins. In the case of a text
such as the Bible, the analogous process, in Dennett's view, is that its
memes influence a human mind and so influence a common meme-
pool as to ensure the physical survival of the text. Dennett expresses
this as follows: 'memes still depend at least indirectly on one or more
of their vehicles spending at least a brief pupal stage in a remarkable
sort of meme nest; the human mind' (1995: 349).

Mere reproduction of a text as a physical artefact is not enough to
ensure its continued survival, as Dennett makes explicit. Individual
copies of books will only endure for a finite period. The relative
youth of even the earliest complete manuscripts of the Bible bears out
the truth of this. Dennett quotes an analogy from Manfred Eigen who
points out that a Mozart symphony cannot be said to survive as a
living cultural entity unless it is played and replayed and checked for
continuing value against other compositions. In the same way, the
Bible must be read and must make itself read if it is to be reproduced.
Its success in achieving this is what makes it an example of a highly
adaptive active replicator.

On this analogy, then, the biblical reader acts as the site of transfer
of the information contained in the text to the meme-pool in which he
or she operates. The book itself encodes memes which once active in
the mind lead the human agents of that meme-pool to produce more
examples of the text. But like all memes, in Dennett's view, they
encounter competition. People have a lot of other things to do with
their time and energy besides copying Bibles, indeed a lot of other

texts to read. What has lead to the particular success of the Bible in this competition for mental space?

The Viral Bible

Controversially, the Bible's success can best be looked at under the rubric of its 'infectivity'. In a paper entitled 'Viruses of the Mind', Dawkins gives an account of the propagating power of what he calls a 'mind-virus' (Dawkins 1993). By this term he means a piece of information which ensures its own duplication without regard to the survival of the system its exploits. Viruses are propagated differently from the genes of their hosts. For instance, influenza viruses spread by coughs and sneezes rather than by being incorporated into a viable embryo for the next generation. This means that, unlike host cells whose genes will only be propagated by the reproduction of the organism of which they are part, viral genes and viruses have no vested interest in the reproductive success of their host.

So, how would a successful 'mind-virus' operate? The problem for a virus is that it must be incorporated into the replicative machinery of its host. What is the parallel mechanism among viruses of the mind? Such a meme will have to instil in the host a mechanism of conserving the meme, and a mechanism for propagating it. It would ideally act like the gall wasp, which diverts the host's energies to its own reproduction. It would also, however, be well advised to have a mechanism of conserving its variability so that any changes in the environment, including the intrusion of other foreign memes, and in particular any developments in the host's own immune system, can be either countermanded or outflanked.

My tentative suggestion is that the Bible instils a meme in its readers which aligns its own survival with that of the reader and his or her community. 'Your survival depends on mine' is the message that the Bible gives. If the primary evolutionary drive is for survival, then a virus or a meme that 'persuades' its host that it is necessary to the host's own survival and therefore conveys a reproductive advantage will have an instant welcome into the replicatory machine. The virus becomes a symbiont, an organism which co-operates to mutual benefit with its host, rather than a parasite.

Of course, it is only in hindsight that the nature of the association can be known with certainty. It is quite possible that an organism will live quietly as a symbiont and then suddenly turn on its host at a later stage. Images of John Hurt and the parasitic alien busting out through his body wall are only too apt in this connection, but the process may be a much quieter one. It may be that a false offer of reward to the host is never cashed out. From the invader's point of view, this matters little as long as it achieves its goal of its own reproduction.

Strategies of Survival

What the Bible has to offer the communities it needs in order to reproduce is the unique variety of powerful strategies of survival it enshrines. Dawkins and other writers on memetics frequently cite the example of the 'God-meme' as a meme which has a powerful record of propagation across time and space. From a theological point of view, of course, the reduction of the complexity of human accounts of God to a single meme is a gross oversimplification. What seems to be implied is rather a meme which predicates human survival on something other than purely biological grounds, which offers a space not only for bodily survival but for memetic survival.

This has resonances with the account that Zygmunt Bauman offers of the whole enterprise of human culture (Bauman 1992). Culture, he claims, is a human construct designed to fend off the threat of death. It is a survival mechanism which finds a way of promising a form of survival in the face of the inevitability of individual death. For Bauman, the Jewish tradition is the clearest case of the subsuming of individual death in communal survival. The individual may die but his or her genes and memes will carry on. The duty of the individual, then, in the sense of his or her best survival strategy, becomes one of ensuring the survival of the group, not of prolonging his or her own life. Christianity has adopted the alternative strategy of a promise of immortality, in that the believer's death is caught up in the context of the resurrection of Jesus. Both genetically and memetically, the after-life of the believer is strictly irrelevant except in so far as belief in personal immortality acts to sustain the continuity of the meme pool.

Both of these strategies are offered to the reader of the biblical text, together with stern warnings of the likely outcome of failing to abide by the word of the text. This is also aligned to a particular set of strategies which reinforce the integrity of the biblical text. In order to maintain continuity and identity, any organism or any gene-pool has to be able to filter out undesirable interlopers.

Again, a cunning usurper will both penetrate these defences but also quickly turn them to its own advantage, keeping out competitive genes and installing itself as the object of the host's attention. At the scale of the individual organism, the efforts of a baby cuckoo to throw the host species' own eggs and chicks out of the nest combined with its success in subsequently subverting the host's nurturing instincts to its own development are a classic case. The cuckoo succeeds in deflecting to its own benefit the mechanisms of rearing young which have evolved for the vital task of reproducing the host species.

The Bible contains powerful instructions as to its own unique worth and the limits to be placed on the infiltration of foreign information or texts into the communities which propagate it. Transgression of these limits will lead, so it warns, to communal disaster which must be avoided by rooting out any alternative ideology. The whole process of canonization reveals a complex interaction between text and community which serves, for example, to oust the fledgling apocrypha and turn the community's attention to the ever-growing task of copying and commentating on the biblical text with an increased sense of its importance and of the need for its conservation.

The propagation of the text and the founding of new communities are also linked to the survival of the reader and his or her community, or meme-pool. The Hebrew Bible is full of admonitions about the duty to hand down its teaching, and by implication the text, to the next generation. In addition, the text contains a strong message of evangelization which encourages the recruitment of new transmitters of the tradition. The survival of the reader's community, so the Bible intimates, depends on the production of new copies of the texts and new communities. This complex of memes and of strategies forms a powerful ensemble to ensure the accurate transmission of the text.

Biblical Variation
If the Bible thus encodes strategies to ensure its longevity and accuracy, what then of biblical variability? Superficially, of course, Bibles show variation. The physical appearance of the Bibles on our shelves is very different from that of the scrolls found at Qumran, an evolution that has something to do with ease of reading, portability and changes in the mechanics of reproduction. In another obvious sense, the Bible has evolved out of its component parts which themselves have undergone a long process of development. It now exists in a number of forms: the Tanakh, and the various canons of the Christian Churches.

Despite this variation, it might be argued that within each community it has on the whole developed a fixed form. However, that form itself preserves a great variety of strategies of survival. There is an analogy here perhaps in the way in which variant genes can be maintained in a population even if they have no particular advantage, or are perhaps deleterious.

In many organisms, chromosomes and the genes they contain are carried in pairs. This means that an individual may carry two different variants of any gene, such variants being termed 'alleles'. In most cases, one of the alleles is dominant, so that in an individual that carries two copies of the gene only the dominant characteristics are expressed. The consequence of this is that the individual may carry without any disadvantage another allele which could if expressed have a deleterious effect, but which might also, in changed circumstances, turn out to confer an advantage. The sexual process leads to the constant reassortment of alleles, which means that the population will be able both to express the alleles of the gene but also to carry them under the cloak of the dominant phenotype.

It is tempting to speculate whether some of the redundancies and doublings in the biblical text may have a similar function in that they can preserve maverick readings. These can be ignored by the mainstream interpreters, especially if an interpretative parallel to the dominance mechanism is in play, whereby an anomalous or redundant verse or passage can be 'corrected' by appeal to other verses in scripture or the perceived overall theological thrust of the material. The day may come, however, when the suppressed alternative reading may prove of interest or use to a particular interpretative community which then propagates the Bible on the basis of that alternative reading.

Furthermore, even in its canonical form the Bible can still generate variety. The information contained between the covers of any given edition the Bible varies and develops, especially in terms of marginalia and commentary, which may, at times, have outweighed the biblical text in terms of importance. It is only necessary to count the number of editions of the Bible currently available to realize how in adapting to the needs of different communities, cultures and age groups, the contents of the physical entity called the Bible can vary widely. These variations serve to widen its appeal, or in other words to enable it to gain entry to and propagate itself in a whole variety of new environments.

In this connection, one of the most obvious sources of variation and adaptive strategies that the Bible is its translatability. Translation is a good trick for increasing the number of Bibles — I certainly possess at least 17 versions of the scriptures and I suspect that most regular biblical readers, let alone scholars, possess more than one version, something which would be unlikely for many other books in their libraries. From the blindly functional point of view, there is para-doxical advantage for a text in being written in a dead language once it has achieved a cultural dominance in another language group. It can potentially always be re-translated because the precision of the match between the words and the meanings cannot be guaranteed in the way that the text itself insists is important. Such a text is more open to revision than one inscribed in the native language of a culture, except in rare instances where a text preserves an older form of the evolving tongue. It is possible, for instance, to find modern language paraphrases of Shakespeare, but there is a great resistance to producing new English versions of his works, whereas, once the interesting conservatism over the Authorized Version was broken, the floodgates of new biblical translations in English were opened. Additionally, there is implicit permission for the text to be translated into the vernacular language of any community which uses the book, again increasing both its diversity and adaptability but also the sheer numbers of copies in existence.

This is by no means a one-way process. The success of the Bible in reforming the communities into which it moves through translation is also striking. As Carroll and Prickett observe in their introduction to the World Classics edition of the Authorized Version:

> What we can observe is that it was not just the Bible that was trans-formed in the course of successive reinterpretations. The Vulgate, a single, authoritative, monolingual instrument for the entire Western Church, was the instrument of the new imperial power of the Roman Church. Luther's Reformation translation of the Bible was to change the German language for ever; his commentary on Romans to set the agenda of theological debate for centuries. Tyndale's translation of the New Testament, on which the Authorised Version was to be so closely modelled, did the same if not more for English. (Carroll and Prickett 1997: xiv-xv)

Communities based on the Bible may have a strong interest in con-serving it unchanged. From the point of view of the Bible, however, its ability to adapt to new communities is an essential part of its success. The fact that much human ingenuity has been expended on ensuring that the Bible does not change and that such mutations have at times been physically rooted out merely goes to show the strong pressure on the text to mutate and its potential for evolution. As I noted before, the interests of the text and those of its nurturing com-munity may not coincide.

As a result, when another champion of scientific realism, the astronomer Carl Sagan, lays into the Bible in his attack on what he conceives of as superstition in his book *The Demon-haunted World* (1996), he in fact reveals one source of the Bible's reproductive success. Contrasting the love of one's enemy enjoined in the Gospels with the celebration of holy war of Joshua, he writes, 'The Bible is full of so many stories of contradictory moral purpose that every generation can find scriptural justification for nearly any action it proposes, from incest, slavery and mass murder to the most refined love, courage and self-sacrifice' (1996: 275). Indeed, and this has surely contributed to its survival. A book to which both the Apartheid regime in South Africa and its most fervent opponents can turn to justify their position may not offer unambiguous moral precepts, but it does ensure that both sides will own their own copies. For the survival of the book, its amazing capacity to sustain opposing camps is a very successful strategy.

Part of the Bible's success is its very diversity, but also the fact that the elements of that diversity can be differently enacted in different communities or in novel circumstances. As is well known, every cell in the human body contains the same genome, but this is differently expressed in different tissues to give cells which vary radically in form and function. The difference is the particular portions of the genome which are read. So too the Bible contains more information than any one community can readily assimilate, especially as it may seem mutually contradictory or impossible to apply in a given situation. What then happens so often is the formation of a canon within the canon, where the community opts to read and follow a particular smaller set of instructions, read with a particular interpretative slant. This may change over time, giving a flexibility and yet continuity to the community. Biblical communities themselves show a capacity for survival which consists in a knack of maintaining continuity through change.

Biblical Advantage
It was allegedly the physician to Frederick the Great who when asked by that monarch to give a proof of the existence of God replied 'The continued existence of the Jews' — an existence bound up with the identity, adaptability and continuity that the Bible confers. In a more theoretical vein Sir Peter Medawar attributes the biological success of human beings as a whole to a new form of inheritance — exogenetic or exosomatic heredity: 'In this form of heredity, information is

transmitted from one generation to the next through non-genetic channels — by word of mouth, for example, and by other forms of indoctrination; in general by the entire apparatus of culture' (1977: 14; quoted in Dennett 1995: 342). Henry Plotkin in his *Darwin Machines and the Nature of Knowledge* (1994) cites the Bible and the Koran as just such devices of exosomatic storage. He speculates on the selective advantage of such texts to the cultures which retain them by drawing on Bartlett's work on the degradation of oral narratives, which implies that over time any group will retell a tale in such a way as to bring it into line with accepted norms. Plotkin argues that the 'exosomatic storage of memes' in the Bible may have preserved 'richness, subtlety and beauty' in cultures which possess the book (1995: 220).

That continuity is bound up with the continued existence of the Bible. The community of readers sees it as its duty to ensure the survival of the book. More than this, it sees the book as the guarantor of its own continuity and survival. The book itself contains a whole plethora of strategies for survival, and in particular, is the record of an amazing feat of cultural continuity as the diaspora communities of Jews manage to retain a sense of themselves as Israel, as members of one 'meme-pool' of cultural exchange, protected by firm filters from external memetic contamination. The fact that historians might take leave to differ over the actual continuity of the community and its immunity to outside infection is surely a proof of the power of the meme complex in question. Despite the available evidence of all that might have led to its dissolution and disappearance, the community is maintained, and the text is preserved.

Even more amazing is the development of communities of those supposedly excluded by the text, the Gentiles, who find ways of identifying themselves as Israel and arrogating to themselves both the promises and the duties imposed by the text, chief among which is the duty to ensure the perpetuation and dispersal of the text. Here the 'gene-pool' of Judaism, with its claim of descent from Abraham's seed, is replaced by a 'meme-pool', a claim of descent from Abraham's faith, a line of argument already presaged in the Old Testament itself.

This is an astonishing success and one of crucial importance to the propagation of the text. The consequence of its incorporation into the canon of the Christian Bible is an exponential leap in the number of copies produced. However, it may also be true that the text turns against the communities that have sustained it if that is to its advantage.

The horrid record of Christian anti-Semitism shows the consequences of the reappropriation of the filter mechanisms for memetic purity being turned against the original host community as the Bible takes on a new existence as Christian Scripture. The mechanisms that originally served to exclude 'Canaanite' memes from the biblical community now act to exclude Judaism. A prime exemplar of such 'selfishness' of the text might be seen in the Reformation, where the text operates to cause a major breach and disruption in the community which sustained it in order to take advantage of the new technology of printing. It achieves this through the propagation of a meme that removed the authority of interpretation from the institution to the individual and to the possibilities of reproduction within vernacular language communities. The peril of too close an association with the host community may be that the text will fall with the community that guards it. The success of the Bible has been predicated on its ability to 'jump ship' when necessary.

The paragraph above is an obviously self-parodic example of the prevalence of the intentionalist fallacy in the discussion of Darwinian replicants. It is patently a fallacy to argue that the Bible provoked the Reformation in order to increase its own population, but the facts remain. Whatever damage the Reformation did to the Church and to the victims of the religious wars that accompanied it, it was certainly good for the Bible.

The Triumph of the Lamb

For a concrete example of this phenomenon in action, let us turn to one of the most successful and widely propagated of all biblical texts, Psalm 23. The Northern Irish poet Louis MacNeice attests to its success in his poem 'Whit Monday', in which he recorded his reactions as he walked through the ruins of war-torn London one morning in 1942. He writes:

> The Lord's my shepherd—familiar words of myth
> Stand up better to bombs than a granite monolith. (MacNeice 1979: 201)

MacNeice not only expresses but demonstrates the power of survival of this phrase and the psalm from which it is drawn, although his reading of it in the poem continues with an increasing cynicism. No matter; from the point of view of the text, MacNeice himself has added to the stock of citations and through his reputation contributed to its persistence. It would indeed be hard to think of another text which has lasted as long and which has penetrated so deeply

into so many cultures. In their anthology of versions of the psalm —
and how many texts of such a size could sustain their own anthology? — Strange and Sandbach (1978) record some 87 translations and
paraphrases in English which represent only a small selection of
those extant. Not only in longevity and ubiquity, but in its capacity
for diversity, the psalm seems a prime candidate for a preliminary
foray into the question of textual fitness. In a sheerly Darwinian
sense, Psalm 23 is one of the most successful of texts.

What is there about this particular psalm, however, which has
induced its readership to ensure its survival so long and so widely?
My answer, as outlined above, is that this psalm clearly demonstrates
the way in which it aligns its own survival with that of the reader
and his or her community. 'Your chance of survival is enhanced by
ensuring mine' is the message that it gives. What the psalm has to
offer the communities which it needs in order to reproduce is the
variety of powerful strategies of survival it enshrines. It offers rest,
food, consolation, protection and permanent living quarters — all that
one could wish for and all under the guarantee of a God who is
identified as a shepherd. A community which reproduces the psalm
retains a resource which will help it to retain its communal identity in
times of crisis and to celebrate its continuity with its ancestors and its
descendants in times of plenty.

Yet that offer holds an ambiguity which is enshrined in the second
part of the first verse: *lo' 'ehsor* ('I shall not want [or lack]'). In Hebrew
as in English this may imply either 'I now lack nothing and will continue to do so', or 'I am now lacking, but will not in the future'.
Throughout the psalm and its reception history, these two basic interpretations, one which sees the psalm as an expression of gratitude for
present content and the other which interprets it as a more or less
anguished affirmation of, or plea for, reassurance in a time of trouble,
account for part of its adaptability. It has found its way into the
rituals of both weddings and funerals, two major loci of what we
might term 'the anxiety of survival', where the community gathers to
celebrate transition and the handing on of the task of survival to a
new generation in continuity with the old. Its ability to cover a broad
emotional range is evident, although which emotions apply to which
occasion may not always be so clear-cut.

Neither, when we look at it, is the first phrase, 'The Lord's my
shepherd' quite as unambiguous as it seems. In Hebrew, of course,
the words are in apposition, answering both the questions 'Who is
my Shepherd?' and 'Who is the Lord?', or perhaps 'In what relation
do I stand to the Lord?' The references to God as shepherd in the

Hebrew Bible take us to God as the defender, but also may remind us that others who are described as shepherds, for instance the leaders of the community in Ezekiel, prove to be disastrous.

Yet there is another consequence of this phrase which is arguably the most important feature of this psalm's particular success, its extraordinary coup in the evocation of what can only be called the 'virtual lamb'. Peter Craigie makes my point succinctly when he argues that 'The psalm is written consistently from the perspective of the sheep' (1983: 209). In actual fact, no sheep is ever mentioned in the text. What is interesting is how powerfully despite this the psalm is drawn into the resonances of the words 'sheep' and 'lamb' and what it means for it to insert the reader into an implicit 'ovine' role.

To be a sheep in the biblical world is an ambiguous fate. Shepherds, after all, do not keep sheep for the love of it. Shepherd and sheep are bound in a mutual bond of survival. The young David may kill bears and lions to protect the flock,[1] but when Samuel arrives and a feast is in order, the same sheep may find their shepherd a rather less agreeable visitor. Sheep are a shepherd's way of making more shepherds.

David Clines has drawn attention to another such ambiguity implicit in the psalm:

> Even the twenty-third Psalm lays itself open to deconstruction when the worshipper as sheep is comforted by the thought of returning to, or dwelling in, the Lord's house for ever; for our knowledge of why sheep go to the Lord's temple — their destiny as lamb chops — undermines the image of security the poem has been at such pains to establish. (1997: 20)[2]

This is a typically provocative observation, but there are several comments that could be made. First, the fact that such things as mutton pie and rack of lamb exist may be regrettable for the individual sheep, but being reared to be slaughtered at least means that one is reared in the first place. We need only compare the world population of domestic sheep with that of their wild cousins to realize that to make the trade-off of mutual survival between sheep and human in the process of domestication may succeed as a strategy. To evoke

1. We can find here another level of mutual co-implication in survival. The psalm's survival is not hurt by its link with Israel's poet-king and with the canonical book of Psalms. At the same time, David, the ambitious upstart of 2 Samuel, is redeemed by the attribution of the soul of a romantic adolescent harping to his innocent charges in all too many misty-eyed commentaries and biographies.
2. See also his article 'Varieties of Indeterminacy' (1995: 19).

Butler yet again, the claim that a shepherd is a sheep's way of making more sheep is as true as its converse.

Secondly, Clines's comment takes us into the comparable economy of sacrifice where the need for sacrificial victims means that lambs aplenty will be bred. In the story of the origin of the Passover ceremony, the paschal lamb is slaughtered in order to provide the sign which persuades the angel of death to pass the household by. Quite explicitly, a lamb ensures the survival of the community by its death, but paradoxically the result of this is the nurture of lambs for the key annual festival which recalls the central myth of survival and renews the community's sense of identity.

Thirdly, the lamb may be turned into chops, but in the long run the temple itself is reduced to rubble. It is the psalm which survives, with its ambiguous loyalties. On the face of it, the psalm's promise in its final verse of a permanent dwelling in the temple is patently broken, but the psalm survives, as does Judaism, this otherwise catastrophic event by its ambiguous capacity to be re-read. The 'house of the Lord' is a phrase which has proved capable of sustaining any number of spiritualizing interpretations. The psalm, indeed, becomes the vehicle for the temple's survival, rather than the other way round.

Finally, the shepherd and the virtual sheep are the hook by which the psalm reinserts itself into other communities. The New Testament gives us a whole range of references to Jesus as the shepherd, with the result that this psalm can swiftly be reinterpreted as Christological by the young Church. It can also resonate with the New Testament's metaphor of Jesus as the lamb which draws in all the resonances of the paschal sacrifice. This culminates in Revelation 22 where the lamb, triumphant in its wars, is enthroned as Lord and light of the New Jerusalem, the city without a temple because the Lord is its light. In this reading, the lamb decidedly has the last laugh on the temple and its pretensions of security, itself representing the house of the Lord. Here, too, the lamb turns writer and determiner of the reader's survival, as the inhabitants of the city are only those who are 'written in the book of the Lamb'.

Yet this is all predicated on a phrase whose ambiguity allows the text to survive beyond the era of the Christianity of convention. In Christian communities, the christological reference in the Lord as Shepherd is absolutely clear, yet for those with little or vestigial Christian commitment, the psalm can slip back into a more open unitarian-universalism without effort. The image of shepherd resonates far beyond the Christian interpretation. Successful texts, as with successful genes, have to be able to jump ship between communities of readers. The text makes the transition from Judaism to Christianity with noted success, but is not bound to a Christian interpretation.

Indeed, in the passage from David Clines we see it make another such move. How clever of the text to insert itself into the discourse of postmodernism. For the survival of the text, the fact that another generation of readers with very different agendas can still find something to say about it is entirely to the point. That this text can be discussed in Darwinian terms, for instance, is another tribute to its extraordinary resourcefulness.

Yet another possibility is open to this text which dispenses with the lamb altogether. There exist an enormous number of paraphrases of the psalm which fit it to the needs of particular communities, especially modern urban communities which have less empathy with the metaphor of the shepherd. Here are some examples:

The spaceman's version:

> The Lord is my controller, I shall not deviate;
> He places me in true orbit around my planet Earth.[3]

The street kid's version:

> The Lord is like my Probation Officer,
>   He will help me
> He tries to help me make it every day.[4]

The so-called Japanese version

> The Lord is my pace-setter, I shall not rush;
> He makes me stop and rest for quiet intervals.[5]

These are all recognizable as variants of Psalm 23 even though they have no linguistic correspondence with it. Instead, they reinscribe what their writers take to be the force of the psalm's metaphors for their particular readership. By doing so, however, the danger is that they become bound too closely to one cultural subgroup and its dialect, and these may prove not to last. The particular form of the text will die with the culture. It will lose the readership which might transmit it, becoming at best a museum piece. This danger is wittily pointed out in a parody of the psalm written as a riposte to the Church of England's Alternative Service book:

3. Attributed to E. Hayman by Strange and Sandbach (1978: 116).
4. Attributed to Carl Burke from his *God is for Real, Man* (1966) by Strange and Sandbach (1978: 115).
5. Attributed to Toki Miyashina (trans. Eric Frost) by Strange and Sandbach (1978: 112).

> The Lord and I are in a shepherd/sheep situation and I am in a posi-
> tion of negative need. He prostrates me in a green-belt grazing area; he
> conducts me directionally parallel to non-torrential aqueous liquid.

This continues in the same vein with the memorable line:

> My beverage utensil experiences a volume crisis.[6]

It is this very ambiguity and malleability which contributes to the
psalm's success. A particular form of the psalm may have only a
short and restricted life, but these versions may serve to turn readers
to the original which still persists because its central metaphors have
a universality which these lack. As Jonathan Magonet writes, 'This
way of expressing both security and danger within the same composition may explain the secret power of this Psalm — that it can comfort without being dishonest to disquieting realities… It is at one and
the same time affirmation, consolation and prayer' (1994: 68). That is
one way of putting it. Another might be to say that the psalm has the
knack of offering promises which evoke, and yet can never be faulted
for not assuaging, the anxieties of survival that undergird all human
communities.

As MacNeice indicates in the poem quoted at the start of this
chapter, the psalm survives because it is seen by succeeding generations of readers as an aid to their own survival.

The Survival of the Bible

What then of the Bible in the twenty-first century where the traditional communities of interest in the Bible may be thought to be in
danger of collapse? Selection is a cruel business as many species and
their DNA find out every day. Surviving intact for a hundred million
years is no defence when your habitat is suddenly filled with indus-
trial pollutants. The best that can be said for any replicator is that it
has survived *so far*. Tomorrow is another day and will perhaps bring
an insurmountable challenge.

Even if the worst comes to the worst in terms of a diminishing community of biblical readers, the important thing for the text regarded
as a meme is not that it be read but that it be copied. By achieving an
iconic status within a culture, the text can relieve itself of the pressure
of seducing readers. The baptismal Bible or wedding Bible may be a

---

6.   Quoted by Jonathan Magonet (1994: 54-55) from a cutting from the *Daily
Telegraph* supplied to him by Father Robert Murray in which it is attributed to
'five clever young men at Christ Church, Oxford.'

gift that is never read, and no one is likely to open the pages of the court room Bible on which oaths are sworn, but they must be complete as the community is well endowed with reverence for the canonical text that is either all or nothing: an incomplete Bible is not a Bible. This mechanism may work more powerfully for the New Testament than the Old in Christian or post-Christian societies as the New circulates independently, but it nonetheless still allows for the reproduction of redundant, unread material within the New Testament. For the sake of iconic completeness, it may even extend to the replication of the even less appealing Old Testament. Bibles contain not only Psalm 23 but also Chronicles and Nahum, for instance.

This too has a biological analogy. One of the more unexpected findings of molecular biology is that a large proportion of the DNA in any genome is seemingly also redundant, consisting of simple repeating sequences which do not encode any gene. Opinion is still divided as to the function of this material. It may have structural or geometrical implications. This redundant DNA is, however, copied and transmitted to the next generation as faithfully as any other. Analogously, the Bible carries a great deal of seemingly redundant information: the detailed instructions for the construction of the tabernacle, for instance. As long as there is some commitment to a notion of completeness, however, this seemingly irrelevant material will be replicated. This means that the Bible can survive to a remarkable extent even on the vestiges of a culture which valued it.

However, the situation for the Bible is by no means as gloomy as that. As I was finishing the original version of this chapter, by coincidence two documents arrived together in my pigeonhole. One was a copy of a review of several modern popular debunking biographies of Jesus which finished by quoting Lord Gowrie's admission that A.N. Wilson's version 'sends us scurrying back to the gospels' (Stanford 1997: 3). The second was a leaflet from the National Bible Society urging donations for the despatch of Bibles to the displaced and starving population of Zaire.

Whatever one thinks of the anti-biblical polemics of an A.N. Wilson and the response of the Bible Society to the disasters of war, there is a common feature to these documents; both seem to serve to increase the sale and distribution of the Bible. The Bible Society can still launch an appeal to increase the number of Bibles in the belief that the Bible will contribute uniquely to the survival of the people of Zaire. Wilson, who seeks to debunk it and would no doubt pour scorn on the Bible Society's work, finds himself both propagating biblical memes in his own texts and sending his readers back to consult the original text. The biblical text is not affected by the fact that the person who reads it is only doing so to refute it as long as there is a sufficient cultural community or meme-pool to maintain the argument and therefore sustain the need for the text.

Yet the Bible has always shown an astonishing facility in generating communities that will see it as worth transmitting. Has the Bible 'succeeded' in making a bid beyond its native environment of the religious communities which may be severely threatened in a new memetic ecology? Is it now able to persuade communities of readers to consider it as a cultural artefact, using the same memetic appeal as Homer and Plato? If so, what a tribute to the extraordinary staying power of the particular combination of memes which the text and the communities it builds around itself enshrine. Having formed communities about itself for two thousand years, often by co-opting its enemies, is the Bible proving able to do this again by infiltrating not religious but cultural discussion?

Ironically, a telling example of this ability of the biblical text to infiltrate the most unlikely communities is the very genre of popular genetic writing of which Dawkins is the most celebrated practitioner. For someone who evinces such a suspicion of the influence of the Bible, he makes a surprising number of references to it. His main rival, both as a best-selling writer of popular genetics and as advocate of what to Dawkins seems a 'heretical' view of Darwinism, is Stephen Jay Gould, whose books are shot through with biblical allusions. The book *In the Blood: God, Genes and Destiny* by another populist geneticist, Steve Jones (1996), is an interesting case in point. In it he covers such topics as the Lost Tribes of Israel and the concept of Armageddon, in the process alluding to a large number of biblical texts and outlining many biblical stories. It would be ironic, would it not, if we were to conclude that Dawkins himself has become a 'survival machine' for the Bible, a 'meme nest' for its dispersed memes which may induce readers who would otherwise leave their Bibles unread to go back to the text.

Dawkins, however, is merely one articulate representative of a much wider conversation in a global gene pool which could loosely be designated as 'Western culture'. Insofar as we have seen that the survival of the Bible seems to be predicated on the persistence of its peculiarly effective set of memes which induce reading communities to propagate it, it is Dawkins inescapable cultural environment which is in evidence here.

But are we then simply the victims of the Bible? Dawkins ends *The Selfish Gene* with a rallying cry: 'We are built as gene machines and cultured as meme machines, but we have the power to turn against our creators. We, alone on earth, can rebel against the tyranny of the selfish replicators' (1976: 215). Is he actually a witness that we may think we can rebel against biblical memes but that such replicators have an uncanny power to survive all our efforts? The revealing passage in his *River Out of Eden* (the title itself needs no comment) on the 'ravishing' poetry of the Authorized Version of the Song of Songs, and the 'lifetime's repetition' which has given it its own haunting appeal despite the possible inaccuracy in translation (1995: 40) argues that aspects at least of the Bible have succeeded in inserting themselves into the 'meme nest' of Dawkin's mind in such a way that they are transmitted, if not replicated.

Dennett comments on Dawkin's challenge to the power of the memes, 'This "we" that transcends not only its genetic creators but also its memetic creators is…a myth' (1995: 366). His own writings show also the power of persistence of the biblical tradition. He ends his 1995 book with an ambivalent plea for the preservation of meme complexes such as religions for their cultural enrichment. 'I love the King James Bible', he declares. 'My own spirit recoils from a God Who is He or She in the same way in which my heart shrinks when I see a lion pacing neurotically back and forth in a small zoo cage. I know, I know, the lion is beautiful but dangerous; if you let the lion roam free it would kill me; safety demands that it be put in a cage' (1995: 515).

This is a rather extraordinary paragraph which is somewhat baffling in its uncharacteristic ambiguity and its implications. What is it that distresses Dennett so much? Is it the use of gendered language of God, rather than the idea of God? Is the King James Bible the cage, in which case what is the love he bears it, or is its place in the cage with the lion because of its dangers?

My own view, and no doubt I here manifest symptoms of my own freight of memetic viruses, is that the Bible has so firmly entrenched a place in our culture that it is ineradicable. It is not a parasite but a constituent part of the great complex of meme complexes that can be designated 'Western culture', part of the exosomatic genome of that culture's members. More than that, I see it in Plotkin's terms as an indispensable source of what might be called 'memetic diversity'. In agricultural genetics, one of the most worrying trends has been the loss of diversity from the appellations of food plants and animals.

There are obvious superficial gains, not least to seed companies and fertilizer manufacturers in growing vast tracts of pure stands of the 'best' varieties, the judgment of 'best' depending on the particular values of the grower or the market. Ease of marketing may well win out against nutrition. However, there is a potential disaster looming if the super-variety is suddenly attacked by a pathogen or if there is a major climatic shift. A variety may be fit for the purpose and the conditions of the moment, but what if conditions change?

Here it becomes vitally important to maintain a 'gene pool' of wild relatives of the crop plants which may themselves have all sorts of drawbacks from the point of view of the technology of farming, but which have shown themselves able to fend for themselves in this competitive world over time. Such wild populations contain a huge diversity of genetic material maintained over time and a vast potential for diversity and for change. Can we view the Bible as a sort of cultural 'memetic reserve'? Parts of it may seem irrelevant, redundant, even detrimental to our survival, but it has kept going and may therefore contain clues as to how we might keep ourselves going. As Medawar and Plotkin indicate, it may serve to maintain a memetic richness and complexity, a inexhaustible source of variety which may contain the unexpected counter to forces that threaten to impoverish our cultural lives.

But Dennett's rather inarticulate declaration of love for the Bible suggests other possibilities. This chapter has, of course, taken a slightly wry look at a provocative re-reading of the dynamics of cultural development. Nothing in the theory of memetics can help us to establish the truth or falsity of a meme, it can only deal with its frequency and prevalence. Questions of reference are not raised. Indeed, the practitioners of memetics have erected some pretty formidable filters to debar any such questions. Methodologically, this may be necessary to prevent muddled thinking, but methodology is not truth despite its strong tendency to become so. The easiest way to filter out a proposition is to declare it to be either meaningless or false. A very different account could have been given on the premise that the Bible reflects the encounter of God with the complex web of human culture and individuality, a premise which methodologically Darwinism cannot entertain. The attempt, however, to follow through such a methodology is a discipline which I hope has brought to light intriguing connections which any account of the relations of the Bible and culture might need to take on board.

The point is made by Harold Fisch in his *Poetry with a Purpose*:

> ...if Hebrew poetics looks to history and the survival of a people, it
> would also be true to say that it is the word that bears the people,
> enabling it to survive. Poetry is in an important sense that which
> makes historical endurance possible. In spite of the lapse of time and
> the decay of memory, the words remain potent. (1988: 64)

So, community and text are bound together in the struggle for survival. The text survives if the community propagates and recopies it;
the community coheres because it can see its continuity in the text.
Yet in its infinitely deferrable promise of eternal security, the text
may yet have the last laugh on all of us.

A more radical question could be asked, however: Is survival, as
Darwinism must have it, really the primary value, or is this perception in turn the product of a methodology which has become a truth?
The lion may be dangerous, and human culture, as Bauman argued,
may well be a device to keep it caged and to ensure survival, just as
the wild lion has been confined practically to game reserves. The
beauty of the cage, then, is in some sense engendered by the lion.
Letting the lion out would have disturbing implications for culture as
well as for scientific method.

Yet there are other models of co-existence between human and
beast, between human beings, the Bible, and the God which it cages
and displays. Here I want simply to recall that Isak Dinesen has a
wonderful account in her book *Shadows on the Grass* of the mutual
respect between the hunter and the lion which grows from the fact
that each knows that the other is hunter as well as prey: 'a lion hunt
each single time is an affair of perfect harmony, of deep, burning,
mutual desire and reverence between two truthful and undaunted
creatures on the same wavelength' (1985: 305). Somewhere in this
may be a dynamic that can lift us beyond the mechanisms of the
meme and into true encounter.

3

SPEAKING SILENCE:
MALE READERS, FEMALE READINGS
AND THE BIBLICAL TEXT

> Here then, where the story teller is loyal, eternally and unswervingly
> loyal to the story, there in the end, silence will speak. Where the story
> has been betrayed, silence is but emptiness. But we, the faithful, when
> we have spoken our last word, will hear the voice of silence. (Dinesen
> 1986b: 105)

Such is the claim of the old woman, the story-teller, in Isak Dinesen's
short story 'The Blank Page' (Dinesen 1986b). My purpose in this
chapter is to explore the idea of the silence which speaks by relating
Isak Dinesen to another story-teller whose silences continue to speak,
the writer of the book of Job, through the mediation of a master
reader of biblical silences, Søren Kierkegaard. In this way, I want to
examine the relationship between speech, silence and gender which
has formed an important element of the feminist reading of texts, not
least the reading of the Bible. Feminist readers have sought to let the
voices of the silenced speak, to read out the suppressed stories of
women from the patriarchal language of the biblical text.[1] I will argue
that the nuances of textual silence are more subtle than such readings
sometimes allow and their critique of the human condition more
radical than the undoubtedly valid critique of the more limited if
pervasive tyranny of patriarchy. It is in the dangerous dynamic of
betrayal and faithfulness that speech and silence, man and woman,
text and reader interact. In particular, my aim is that the role of the
male reader of the biblical text is illuminated by rehearsing the
complex series of gendered readings which will unfold below.

1.   There is now a considerable body of work on this topic. Two works which
have contributed significantly to my thinking for this paper are I. Pardes's
Countertraditions in the Bible: A Feminist Approach (1992) and Danna Fewell and
David Gunn's *Gender, Power and Promise: The Subject of the Bible's First Story*
(1993). Both books are also useful sources of further references on this topic.

The old woman in Dinesen's story goes on to recount the tale of the blank page — a page where, she says, one may read 'a still deeper, merrier and more cruel tale' (Dinesen 1986b: 100) than any written by the most royal and gallant pen. She tells of a convent in Portugal where, ranged in gilt frames, hang the fading witnesses to the honour of royal brides: the central portions of the royal wedding sheets where the imaginative can find traced in the stains whatever sign they look for. But one frame is different. It contains a portion of a pure white sheet, which in 'unswerving loyalty' to the story has been cut out and hung up. It is before this blank sheet that princesses and nuns alike pause and ponder the longest.

The tale that this unsullied linen proclaims in its blankness is more potent than any that can be inferred from the marks on the other sheets. In her reading of Dinesen's story, Susan Gubar[2] (1981: 259) draws attention to the fact that this blank sheet might represent a number of alternative scripts for women: Was the princess not a virgin? Did she flee the marriage bed? Was she abandoned by her husband? Whatever its meaning, the sheet testifies to a disruption of the expected course of events. It proclaims the unusual which is the impulse for storytelling. Its purity implies impurity and sets in train a whole narrative of concealment and revelation, a narrative dependent on its context. It suggests somewhere a betrayal. The events of a night of shame and confusion are betrayed, and that confusion itself implies a prior betrayal or unfaithfulness between man and woman.

Yet, of course, the blankness of the sheet only becomes suggestive in the context in which it is hung, framed as a picture beside the other tokens in the gallery. A virginal sheet straight from the hands of the nuns who lovingly wove it would suggest no such reading.[3] The silence of the blank sheet only evokes its narratives in the gallery of marked sheets, where sulliedness bears witness to the unsullied and the stain proclaims an unstained reputation. Meaningfulness is a product of context, of creating a speaking silence out of the dumbness

2.   I am indebted to Gubar's work in many ways less easy to acknowledge specifically than this citation. The present chapter could be seen as a counterpart to Gubar's from the perspective of a male reader, particularly as it was at a relatively late stage in the development of the argument that I was made aware of it. Her particular concern is with the way in which the silence of the women in the tale is a form of resistance which is echoed in the wider dynamic of female creativity in a patriarchal culture.

3.   Gubar notes that the blank sheet itself silently testifies to female creativity in the patient communal labour of the nuns, who provide, metaphorically, the sheet necessary as a precondition for writing (1981: 260).

of blank paper. It is only framed in the convent's gallery that the unremarkable blankness of the sheet becomes pregnant with story. But what story does it tell?

Quite by chance, as I was pondering Dinesen's 'The Blank Page', I happened across a casual reference in a letter by Virginia Woolf to one of Freud's case histories:

> ...we are publishing all Dr Freud, and I glance at the proof and read how Mr A.B. threw a bottle of red ink on to the sheets of his marriage bed to excuse his impotence to his housemaid, but threw it in the wrong place, which unhinged his wife's mind—and to this day she pours claret on the dinner table. We could all go on like this for hours; and yet these Germans think that it proves something—besides their own gull-like imbecility. (Woolf 1989: 187)

This is a lively anecdote, but one which takes on a special significance in relation to Dinesen's story. Indeed, it leapt to my attention because I had been re-reading that story. Rather as the blank sheet itself attains significance from being framed and hung in a gallery, this anecdote from Woolf attains a significance from the frame that Dinesen's story provides. It becomes an answer; one of many possible answers, but an answer only insofar as Dinesen's story has brought to mind the question: Why is the sheet blank?

In Woolf's narrative, the blankness of the sheet is not primarily the evidence of a woman's story, the story of a royal princess who is not a virgin on her wedding night, of feminine betrayal, but rather testifies to a story of male impotence. The sheet remains blank as a result of a man's inability to utter sexually. In response to this, it is the male who stains the sheets with ink for, be it noted, the eyes of a female reader, the housemaid. The reaction of the woman in Virginia Woolf's account is to stain the table with claret. She re-enacts her husband's performance. Yet, intriguingly, the very edition of Freud's works to which Woolf is referring reveals that in repeating his story, she herself has added to it.[4]

The crucial difference between Woolf's account and Freud's is in the report of the symptoms that the woman displayed. This is particularly significant because, as a case study, the whole *raison d'être* of Freud's account is to provide a reading of the anomalies that are perceived in the woman's behaviour. It is these anomalies which betray the fact that there is a story to be told and which have so disquieted

---

4. The incident is recounted in Freud's 'Obsessive Acts and Religious Practices'. The reference in the edition to which Woolf is alluding is to Freud's *Collected Papers II* (1924): 25-35 (31).

those around her that she is brought to Freud's attention. For his part, Freud records that the woman used to run into a room to rearrange a stained tablecloth so that the stain was visible and then to summon her maid, only to dismiss her on a trivial errand. Note, however, that, in contrast to Woolf's version, there is no mention of her pouring claret on the table. The woman merely displays a stain that was already concealed, rather than creating her own stain. So, Freud concludes, she is enacting a repetition of the original traumatic revelation of a stained cloth to her maid.

This does not complete the series of readings of this incident. Freud later returned to this case history and gave a new and fuller reading of the situation in his *Introductory Lectures on Psychoanalysis* (1973: 300-303). He revised his original account by concluding that the woman was seeking not to repeat, but to correct, the original scenario. The adjustment of the tablecloth signals to the maid that this time the stain is in its right place, and so there is now no need for shame before the maid. The woman seeks to conceal the secret of her husband's impotence. Freud expands this interpretation further to argue that the whole phenomenon of the patient's illness performs the same function of concealment. It hides the shame of her husband's impotence which, he tells us, had eventually led to the couple's separation. The woman's illness, rather than the sexual failure of her elderly husband, becomes the ostensible cause of the separation of the couple. Just as he attempted to conceal his impotence from the maid, she by her madness conceals the true reason for the breakdown of their marriage from the eyes of the world. Yet her effort at concealment is itself an occasion of revelation for the sophisticated eye of Dr Freud. He, the male reader of her fiction, spies its roots in a failure of male utterance.

This brings us back to the question as to why his female proof-reader, Virginia Woolf, introduces the idea of the deliberate spilling of claret in her retelling. Here, the connection of this motif with the work of the female writer is suggestive. In Margaret Drabble's novel *The Waterfall*, the heroine, a poetess, has the sensation as she writes that 'the ink was pouring onto the sheets like blood' (Drabble 1969: 114-15).[5] The ink stain on the sheet of paper perhaps invites the same questions about revelation and concealment as the stained or

5.   I owe this reference to Susan Gubar, who explores more fully than I have space to do here the role of the woman artist's body and specifically her blood in the metaphors and strategies that female artists adopt. See, in particular, Gubar 1981: 256 n. 45, and her wider discussion (1981: 255-59).

unstained sheet may reveal. What then of the role of two feminine retellers: the old story-teller and Isak Dinesen herself? Dinesen spills ink on her sheet to tell us the story of the blank page. To pursue this fascinating example of a presumably unconscious rewriting of Freud's text would take us even further from the immediate relevance of recounting this incident, which is this: in it, we have an unequivocal example of what could be called a 'male silence', a silence of impotence, which is concealed behind the cryptic utterance of the woman.

The connection between this case and Dinesen's story runs yet deeper. What if Freud's patient were to turn out to have been the notorious princess of the blood royal?[6] Dinesen's story, then, would have yet another reading. In this case, however, it is precisely female silence, the fact that the princess, like the wife, does not stain the sheet, either the marriage sheet, or the notepaper that might betray her or her husband's secret, that can be read as betraying male impotence. A chain of gendered readings of the unstained sheet has unfolded here. The husband's impotence prevents him from writing the evidence of his virility on the sheet in the blood of his wife and leads him to the attempt to deceive the eyes of another female reader, the housemaid. This is compounded by the wife's misreading, her attempt at concealment, Freud's redoubled reading of her symptoms, and then Woolf's revision of Freud. Yet this chain starts from silence, a text where a woman does not 'make her mark'.

For whatever reason, Woolf's account of this shows a woman responding to this silence by writing, by spilling ink, by attempting to make her mark belatedly. Freud, however, reads through the woman's symptoms and her silence to a tale of male impotence. Isak Dinesen, the male pseudonym recounting the story of an aged sybil, leaves the reader, with the young girls and the nuns, pondering.

In order to explore the implications of these differing readings more closely, I propose to look at another series of gendered readings and re-readings, this time explicitly rooted in the biblical text. If, as many feminist scholars have argued, the poetics of the biblical text are predicated on the silencing of women, we have here a prime site to explore the dynamic of betrayal and faithfulness which the blank page, the silence of women, may represent.

---

6.   The story might run as follows: utterly humiliated by the incident which her unbending family insist on blazoning to the world, the ink having left the crucial portion of the wedding sheet unstained, she and her elderly husband have fled from Portugal and sought refuge in Vienna, where her bizarre behaviour draws attention.

Any narrative, as Pierre Macherey has indicated,[7] is a means of creating silence — the dumb silence of the speaking page is transformed into the speaking silence of inference. This can clearly be seen in the biblical story of Job, which is framed in silence. The narrative is set in motion by the attempt of Satan to break an implicit silence by forcing speech from Job, to induce him to curse God. At the end of the second chapter, assailed on every side, Job sits in silence with his friends until he breaks out into the great lament over the day of his birth in ch. 3. If he had been unborn, he cries, if his tale had not begun, if his page had remained blank, then there would be no prospect of final silence. Job would not be faced with the terrifying silence of God, a silence which impels him to speech. At the end of the book, Job is reduced to silence again in the face of the unanswerable speech of God who breaks his own silence. In the epilogue of the book, Job never utters.

Yet in a metaphorical sense he does utter. He may not emit words, but he does produce three daughters. His story and his line have an outcome. This recalls to us another silenced voice in the book, that of Job's wife. We read her speech only once, when she tells Job to curse God and die. Immediately Job silences her, telling her that she 'speaks as one of the foolish women speak' (Job 2.10) Thereafter, she disappears from the story. But the epilogue testifies to her silent presence. There is no word that she is taken from Job, and he is presented with three daughters in the epilogue. Someone must have been their mother, but her silence is absolute. Yet her existence is testified in what Kierkegaard was to call Job's 'repetition', his regaining of what had been lost.[8]

The book Kierkegaard entitled *Repetition* can be read as an attempt to come to terms with the paradox of the ending of Job which has puzzled commentators, the fact that Job receives a reward for his faithfulness in denying the link between reward and faithfulness. Job himself appears in Kierkegaard's book as the 'faithful confidant' of

7. See Macherey 1978: 154-55: 'The work exists above all by its determinate absences, by what it does not say, by its relation to what it is not. Not that it can conceal anything: the meaning is not buried in its depths, masked or disguised; it is not a question of hunting down with interpretations; it is not in the work, but by its side: on its margins, at that limit where it ceases to be what it claims to be because it has reached back to the very conditions of its possibility…we should question the work as to what it does not and cannot say, in those silences for which it has been made.'

8. See further the discussion of Job's wife in Pardes (1992: 145-51) and the discussion in the chapter entitled 'Readers in Pain', below.

the lovelorn young man whose letters form the bulk of its second part.

It is no accident, moreover, that on the same day that *Repetition* was published, Kierkegaard's *Fear and Trembling*, his extended meditation on the story of Abraham's sacrifice of Isaac, also appeared. This juxtaposition points up the shared dynamic of the two biblical stories. Abraham is forced to make an impossible choice between his duty of obedience to God and the life of his son, but in the moment of making the choice, he receives both; God intervenes to give him both a blessing and his son. In this, he is like Job, who was forced to choose between faithfulness and prosperity and yet received both in the end. For Kierkegaard, Abraham is the greater: Job's losses are inflicted on him by God through Satan, whereas Abraham has to surrender his son freely.

What is noteworthy in the present context, however, is that Kierkegaard in this work is fascinated by the motif of Abraham's silence. This, he insists, is not a simply a lack of utterance, but results from the impossibility of being understood: 'Abraham remains silent--but he cannot speak. Therein lies the distress and the anxiety. Even though I go on talking night and day without interruption, if I cannot make myself understood, then I am not speaking' (1983: 113).

Even if Abraham had spoken of his dilemma, no one would have understood him. Yet to concentrate on Abraham may obscure the fact that there are other silent figures in this story. There is Isaac himself, who after this story is never represented as having any converse with his father. It is telling that Karen Blixen chose the name 'Isak' for herself, screening her own feminine identity behind the mask of one whose name means 'he laughs'. Susan Aiken in her discussion of this pseudonym (1990: 22) argues that Blixen also inserts herself into the great litany of patriarchal succession, 'Abraham, Isaac and Jacob', part of what Aiken elsewhere sees as her comic and subversive 'revisionist biblical hermeneutic' (1990: 182).[9]

---

9.   Aiken's argument is that Dinesen ironically adopts the trapping of a 'masculist' narratology in order to subvert it in her role as a mocker. By donning masculinity and feminity as masks, she reveals the constructedness of both positions. Aiken quite specifically links the revisionist narratology of Dinesen's *Seven Gothic Tales* to the undercutting of a biblically rooted patriarchal narratology. One of the purposes of this chapter is to explore the consequences of that insight more fully. Aiken does not note that Isaac here hardly signifies the easy inevitability of the patriarchal order. On the contrary, he is the one who nearly was not, the symbol of the potential rupture of the patriarchal flow. The additional fact that Dinesen chose to write under the surname of her beloved father,

More germane to the present discussion, however, in a position somewhat analogous to that of Job's wife, is Sarah, Isaac's mother. Her reaction to this story of God's apparent betrayal of his promise of progeny and Abraham's apparent betrayal of the protective role of fatherhood is never alluded to. This silence is filled in some measure by Kierkegaard himself in the 'Exordium' of *Fear and Trembling* (1983: 9-14). Here Kierkegaard has written out of this silence in the form of four 'midrashim' on this text. Strikingly, each of these short pieces which offers a contrasting motivation for Abraham's silence towards Isaac ends with the same image: that of a mother weaning her child. Strikingly, too, this moment of weaning is one which the feminist writer Dorothy Dinnerstein has seen as the crucial point of rupture of the bond between the infant and the mother.[10] The refusal of the breast, of the nourishing utterance of milk, is a necessary disjunction, but one which the infant experiences as a profound act of treachery. This, she argues, is at the root of the hostility to women in which both men and women are complicit.

In the light of this, it is intriguing to look at another of Dinesen's tales, 'Babette's Feast' (1986a), as an example of the new Isak drawing on, complementing and subverting Kierkegaard's *Repetition* and thus indirectly but not unimportantly giving voice to silences in the biblical text, silences signposted by the nature of Kierkegaard's own utterances.[11]

At the heart of Dinesen's story is the great feast cooked by the French maid of two pious Norwegian sisters, a feast where speech and silence mingle. The sisters and the fellow members of their dead father's little sect resolve to ignore what they fear as the demonic luxuries of what they are eating. The thought that their demure puritanism and indifference to food represents a silent acceptance through repression of the infant's anger at the deprivation of the maternal breast may occur to us here. Also present at the feast,

who had, however, committed suicide when she was a young girl, while in real life insisting on being addressed as Baroness Blixen (even though, strictly speaking, her title lapsed on her divorce from Bror Blixen) reveals the level of complexity in her relationship to the patriarchal structures implicit in the act of naming women.

10.   See her *The Rocking of the Cradle and the Ruling of the World* (Dinnerstein 1987: especially 91-114). Dinnerstein is drawing on and elaborating Melanie Klein's notion of the 'good' and 'bad' breast as set out in Klein's short work *Envy and Gratitude* (1957).

11.   The link between Kierkegaard and Dinesen is made specific by Robert Langbaum in his study of her writings. 'Babette's Feast' is, according to him, 'an answer to Kierkegaard' (1964: 274).

however, is a famous general. As a young man, he had loved one of the sisters, but made his decision to live the life of a courtier. Only he realizes what he is eating, and in the glow of the marvellous food and wine, which the good sectarians experience as the healing grace of divine love, he makes a speech in which he gives voice to his discovery of 'repetition'. Babette, of course, has dedicated her life to the satisfaction of that great maternal role, the accomplishment of plenitude and satisfaction of appetite which the weaned child can never quite recapture. The blessing of the feast is the fullness of the sated infant at the breast.

It is this that allows the general to express to his uncomprehending but accepting audience the great insight of his life. He has been with the woman he loved in spirit every day in a way which marriage to her could never have brought him, different as they were. Like Abraham, like Isaac, he made his choice, but ultimately, unexpectedly, impossibly, has gained both prizes; his glittering career and the woman he loved. So he can say:

> We tremble before making our choice in life and, after having made it, tremble in fear of having chosen wrong. But the moment comes when our eyes are opened and we see and realize that grace is infinite, see that which we have chosen is given us, and that which we have refused is also and at the same time, granted us. (1986a: 61)

The bond broken by the refusal of nourishment, by the breast withheld, is remade.

What Dinesen has done here is to give voice to the female in this context of repetition. Babette speaks for Job's wife, who is his provider and the faithful companion, the woman who has also lost all her children and all her property and is left only with a sick husband who refuses her ministrations. Babette too is displaced alone and childless. But for Job, it is this silent woman who is the material source of his renewed family and his continued prosperity.

Such a reappraisal of sexual roles and of speech and silence is seen even more clearly in Dinesen's novella *Ehrengard* (1986c), an explicit response to Kierkegaard's 'Diary of a Seducer' (Kierkegaard 1987).[12] Ehrengard, the eponymous heroine of the tale, is a young noblewoman of unassailable honesty and simplicity who is chosen to

12.	The 'Diary', sometimes published as a separate work, records the elaborate deceptions plotted by a young man to ruin and abandon an innocent girl called Cordelia. In the context of female silence, there is much to ponder on in Kierkegaard's choice of the name of the daughter of King Lear who will not answer his demand that she articulate her love for him.

nurse the baby who has been born out of wedlock to the local ruling family. The fact of the birth has to be kept silent until a proper interval has elapsed after the hastily arranged marriage of the child's royal mother and father. In the entourage which is brought together to ensure this secrecy is also the court painter, Herr Cazotte. He conceives a desire to seduce, not physically but spiritually, the hitherto invincibly innocent Ehrengard, by bringing to her cheek a blush which will represent her 'full triumphal consent to her own perdition' (1986c: 109). This he sets out to do by secretly painting her as she bathes in the lake at dusk each day. It is the revelation of this painting to her which will be the occasion of her seduction.

Of course, the deception over the heir is discovered by the enemies of the prince and Ehrengard and Cazotte have to flee with the child until they are cornered in an inn. Forced to reveal who the child is, Ehrengard without shame announces that it is hers, and, pointing to Herr Cazotte, declares that he is the father. 'At these words', Dinesen writes, 'Herr Cazotte's blood was drawn upwards, as from the profoundest wells of his being, till it coloured him all over like a transparent crimson veil. His brow and cheeks, all on their own, radiated a divine fire, a celestial, deep rose flame, as if they were giving away a long kept secret' (1986: 109).

In this moment the great artist, who has sought to reveal the most hidden secret of Ehrengard's womanhood to her, is himself silently betrayed by the blush: the witness of blood spreading, as it were, over the blank page of the skin. The shameless innocence with which Ehrengard fathers her child on Cazotte names the primal desire for procreation which has lurked unuttered under the rococo elaborations and misdirections of his supersubtle devices. It is not the hidden desires of Ehrengard which are made visible, but the artist's desire for paternity, a desire figured and sublimated in the recreative nature of his calling. This is made more pointed in the coda to the tale, where Dinesen reveals that his name is altered in his subsequent career to Casanova. He is thus identified with a figure who, like Don Juan and Kierkegaard's seducer, reveals the desperate attempt to smother the desire and dread of fatherhood in an excess of sterile sexual adventure.

The desire which is silenced speaks through the body, through the stain of blood on the cheek. The root of the desire to evoke such a sign is traced once again to the male, to the complex of power, and impotence, of potency and sterility. Once again, a man is silenced by a woman's power of revelation.

The silencing of the woman in the text is, of course, a central tenet of feminist criticism. So, for instance, Deborah Cameron can entitle a chapter of her book *Feminism and Linguistic Theory* 'Silence, Alienation and Oppression' (1992: 128). In an early section of this chapter, she looks at the way in which the work of the social anthropologists Edwin and Shirley Ardener on 'muted' and 'dominant' groups has been taken up by various feminist theorists. The Ardeners' argument is that in any society, subordinate groups have to express their own reality in terms set and controlled by the dominant groups. To be 'muted' is not to be prevented from speaking, but to be unable to encode one's reality in the dominant language. Such is the predicament of women.[13]

This has clear resonances with Kierkegaard's claim that the most fearsome form of muting is to be effectively silenced by the incomprehension of others. Abraham represents for him a phenomenon of male muting. Such a silence, however, can be interpreted as the result of a failure of reception, a failure of the hearer to understand. Male silence can be construed as the responsibility of the unresponding listener. In the gendered terms of this discussion, the male can blame his silence on a female refusal or inability to hear, itself further confirmation of the male sense of betrayal.

Cameron acknowledges, but has little time for, the argument that men are as disadvantaged as women by being silenced. She quotes the work of Jack Sattel (1983) who argues that men's inexpressiveness is actually a powerful determinant in maintaining dominance. To be silent is to forbid discourse, to stifle questioning, to restrict the possibilities of the other, especially of those who are subordinate to you. Male silence is thus a condition of male dominance, and therefore male acculturation forbids certain speech to other men. In order to disempower women, men have to silence each other, to ensure solidarity. To blame this silence on female unreceptiveness is to add insult to injury.

This argument is a forcible counter to the attempt to lay the responsibility for male inarticulacy at the feet of women. The point surely is, however, that the fundamental premise of Sattel's account is male powerlessness. It is the dread of impotence, the knowledge of dependency, that leads to the self-inflicted emotional muting that characterizes masculinity and enforces the subordination of women.

---

13. Cameron (1992: 140-46) discusses Shirley Ardener's two edited collections, *Perceiving Women* (1975) and *Defining Females: The Nature of Women in Society* (1978).

The wife in Freud's case-study who is forced into madness to connive in the illusion of her husband's manhood is plainly a victim; but a victim of a system of discourse where her husband cannot confess his impotence.

For a further investigation into the phenomenon of male silence, we can turn to Jonathan Rutherford (1992[14]) who makes a suggestion which ties in with a theme we have alluded to above. In his analysis, male silence, the emotional muting of men, is a product of the need to deny certain kinds of intimacy which he traces back to that rupture of the bond with the mother which Kierkegaard and Dinnerstein both light upon. It is in reaction to what is interpreted as a fundamental betrayal that men construct their masculinity, and impose it on each other, in order to fend off any possibility of such deep betrayal being repeated. Here we have a dread of repetition rooted in the fear of betrayal. Men thus take on the burden of silence between themselves in order to silence the women who have betrayed and may betray their impotence. And yet the paradox we have explored is that it may be that very female silence which in the end betrays that impotence most tellingly.

Nowhere is the male claim to power based on the silence of women which lies at the heart of Judaeo-Christian civilization made more manifest than in its canonical texts. Not only is the speech of women suppressed, as many critics have demonstrated, but it is explicitly forbidden by Paul in his first letter to the Corinthians. Once again, we find Kierkegaard in his inimitable way insisting on rather than excusing or glossing over the seeming scandal of Paul's prohibition against women's speech in 1 Cor. 14.30. Kierkegaard takes Paul's pronouncement as in fact an acknowledgment of the power of woman. She is able to do what man finds almost impossible: she is able not to speak. In his *For Self-Examination*, Kierkegaard claims that the most urgent need for the cure of the present state of the world is the need to create silence (1990: 47). This is a woman's especial talent, as he sees it, her silence which reveals that she truly treasures the word preached to her. This silence then becomes the source of her power, as opposed to the noisy bluster which characterizes the male claim to power.

Kierkegaard's own position in regard to this topic is complex to say the least. He it is who sought to rupture his bond with Regina Olsen by allowing her tacitly to assume that he was a reckless roué,

14. See especially Chapter 4, 'Silence, Language and Psychoanalysis' (1992: 199-222).

only to be dumfounded by her faithfulness, and devastated by her marriage to another man. He it is who in the vast corpus of his often intensely autobiographical writings never so much as once mentions his mother, the servant whom his puritanical and guilt-laden father had impregnated only months after his first wife's death.[15] It is hard to see this as anything other than a framed silence, one which invites the question: Why is his mother is not mentioned?

In this context, it is easy to read Kierkegaard's tendentious endorsement of Paul as a kind of bribe to women in order to maintain the conspiracy of silence that shores up male claims to power. If representing women's silence as their strength ensures that they will keep silence, then perhaps it is the best defensive move that men can make. Yet one of his female readers, Birgit Bertung, has argued that Kierkegaard is carrying the argument to the point of absurdity in order to shock women out of their complacent acceptance of a more subtly worded but equally repressive patriarchy in nineteenth-century Denmark. Indeed she specifically sees him as anticipating Dinesen's feminist revision of his work (Bertung 1984).[16] The point remains, however we read him — that silence itself speaks and speaks women's stories about men.

Kierkegaard himself provides a fascinating text which can be taken as oblique but powerful confirmation of this. It so happens that the very discourse where Kierkegaard most clearly expounds the Pauline prohibition on women's speech is itself structured so as to confront us directly with the nature of silence in the biblical text.[17] He begins the piece with a discussion of the most fitting approach to the reading of scripture. After dismissing several alternatives, he settles on the metaphor of the 'letter from the beloved' which the lover as reader must treasure and obey even without full comprehension. Yet,

15.   A fuller discussion of these issues, which also brings out their relevance to the matter in hand, can be found in Pattison (1990). Pattison ends his discussion pointing to Kierkegaard, not as a feminist, but as 'perhaps the first major Christian thinker whose thought reveals the impact of the revolution which the assertion of feminine consciousness was to bring with it' (1990: 90).

16.   Bertung's thesis is discussed by George Pattison, who is not persuaded: '*We* may choose to read Kierkegaard in this way if we want to, but when we do so we are not really reflecting *his* most persistent thinkng on the matter' (1987: 437). This response itself raises interesting hermeneutic questions. Suffice it to say that the mere fact that a female reader does choose to read Kierkegaard in this way is of interest in the context of our discussion.

17.   The discourse forms the first section of *For Self-Examination* and is entitled 'What is Required in Order to Look at Oneself with True Blessing in the Mirror of the Word' (1990: 7-51).

in the gendered world of Kierkegaard's discourse, it must be a woman who writes this letter. If the reader of the love letter is male, then the writer must be female.

By the logic of the metaphor, the biblical text thus becomes a female utterance. Though this is a bizarre conclusion to draw, perhaps, it evokes the figure of that neglected biblical woman, the prophetess Huldah in 2 Kgs 22.14-10, who ultimately gives the imprimatur, to use a felicitous anachronism, to the book found in the temple during Josiah's reign. Insofar as it exerts power on male speech and silence, the biblical text itself, and the silences which it is its business to frame, can be framed as female silences. As female silences, they betray male impotence. The silenced voices of the women in the Bible speak what men are unable to hear or cannot utter.

God's silence represents this impotence to Job, and it is this betrayal against which he protests at length, his own inability to control his circumstances. His human sense of betrayal has its counterpart in such passages as the Lord's angry railings over the treacherous and unhearing masses of Israel in the figure of the faithless wife which ring through the pages of Hosea. Notoriously, throughout the Hebrew Bible, it is the faithlessness of women which is legislated against and fumed against with the appalling anger and violence of those who feel themselves impotent and betrayed. That anger is the anger of impotence.

And, further, it can operate in the reactions of the reader of the biblical text. Betrayal is of the nature of the experience of reading. The text which seduces the reader into bringing it into imaginative life, which feeds the imagination by so composing its silences that it evokes the reader's effort of inference, at the last must betray the reader by its ending, must inevitably withdraw its offer of fulfilment unfulfilled. The biblical text in particular claims to offer a kind of fullness which makes its inevitable finiteness either a spur to rejection, to the reining in of desire or to the concoction of a feast of plenty in the interpretive creativeness of the tradition.

But perhaps also the great texts, the enduring classics, are those which effect a continuity between the silences within the text and those which reverberate in the reader after the text is finished. By reframing the reader's silence, that silence can be construed as a question which evokes the reader as answer, and which provides a context for reframing the unyielding silences of the world that confront the reader. The silence which seems to forbid speech invites it, as Job testifies. The betrayal which withdraws the nourishment of the breast also marks the possibility of independence, and the opportunity to develop as a provider as well as a consumer of both silence and speech. Those faithful to the story, as the old woman says, will hear silence speak, because they will be able to provide a frame for their own silences that may evoke speech from those silenced by repression or betrayal.

This complex story of gendered readings brings us to the final point of this chapter. It is this: there is a need for the male readers of the biblical text to find their way to confront its revelation of their impotence. It is for the female readers of the Bible to speak on behalf of their sisters, to spill claret on the laundered tablecloths of the establishment in their attempt to give the muted a voice. For its male readers, there is a different task: the need to listen to the way in which those very silences betray that silent conspiracy which prevents man speaking to man. One of its consequences has been the emotional muting of the theological and academic enterprise. Is there, could there be, an adequate theology of the emotions, let alone male emotions, or a literary criticism which can handle the emotional responses evoked and provoked by a text—a poetics of the wrath of God?

The feminist readers of the Bible can open our eyes to the fact that the male conspiracy is already betrayed in the text, betrayed both in the sense of being laid bare and of being rendered impotent. The task that the text then lays upon its male readers is to take on in faith the risk of utterance, through hearing the voice of silence. It is that faith which in the end lies behind the possibility of repetition, faith in the healing work of grace. Abraham, Job and Kierkegaard are struck dumb by it, but Karen Blixen enables her general to testify to it in 'Babette's Feast'. He concludes his speech after the meal with the following resounding biblical cadences on the subject of the rejected voice which can reconcile the irreconcilable: 'Ay, that which we have rejected is poured upon us abundantly. For mercy and truth have met one another, and righteousness and bliss have kissed one another!' (Dinesen 1986a: 60-61).

Beyond betrayal lies the possibility of trust.

4

READERS IN PAIN:
MURIEL SPARK AND THE BOOK OF JOB

Muriel Spark's *The Only Problem* (1985) is a long-considered novel which takes the book of *Job* as its pretext. In it, she offers a reading of *Job* on two levels.[1] Her hero, Harvey Gotham, is a wealthy recluse who is writing a monograph on Job in an effort to come to terms with 'the only problem' of the title: the problem of human suffering in a world created by a good and all-powerful God. Through Harvey's reflections and conversations as he wrestles with his reading of *Job*, Spark is able to engage directly with the critical and exegetical problems of the biblical text. At the same time, the plot of the novel brings events more or less analogous to those recorded in *Job* into Harvey's life. The play of harmony and dissonance between Harvey's

---

1.   Following Muriel Spark's own practice, I italicize *Job* when referring to the biblical book and revert to Roman type for the name of the character. The very fact that in certain cases there is otherwise ambiguity over which is meant is suggestive. The novel is the culmination of a sustained fascination with *Job* on Muriel Spark's part. Peter Kemp (1974: 17) quotes an interview from 1953 which implies that she was already at work on a book on *Job*. In 1955 she published a review of Carl Jung's *Answer to Job* (see below nn. 8 and 9, and the discussion in the main text). The title of her first novel *The Comforters* (1957) is an allusion to Job's comforters. In it, the heroine becomes aware that she is a character in a novel while her 'comforters' try to persuade her otherwise. This is an interesting analogy to Job's situation. The reader is aware that Job is the subject of a divine experiment. Job has an inkling of this which his comforters try to argue away. He is aware of an 'author' with some creative jurisdiction over his life. Spark and Job raise the huge question of the freedoms of the character and the author. On the face of it, the character is entirely at the author's mercy. However, authors can also find that the character takes over and demands that the plot follow a particular course. Such analogies between world and text are central to Spark's interest in Job as expressed in *The Only Problem* and to the argument in this chapter.

critical reflections and his response to the events in the world around him gives the novel its characteristically deft and provocative irony.

On the back cover of the paperback edition of the novel the following quotation from a criticism in *The Guardian* appears. It picks up a sentence from Harvey's reflections on his work: '"To study, to think, is to live and suffer painfully." To read, though, is another matter, especially when the craft is as flawless as Muriel Spark's'.[2]

The Guardian critic's remark raises some intriguing questions: Is the quotation from the novel Muriel Spark's own view, or the view of a character in her novel? If the latter, is Spark endorsing or satirizing that view? Is it a view which can be defended? Leaving these questions aside, how valid is the critic's extension of the quotation to exclude reading from the experience of suffering? Is pointing out the painlessness of the reader's experience as complimentary to Spark as might at first appear? Not if we are to take seriously the advice which Franz Kafka gave in a letter to his friend Oskar Pollak:

> I think we ought only to read the kind of books that wound and stab us. If the book we are reading doesn't wake us up with a blow on the head, then what are we reading it for? So that it will make us happy, as you write? Good Lord, we would be happy precisely if we had no books, and the kind of books that make us happy are the kind we could write ourselves if we had to. But we need the books that affect us like a disaster, that grieve us deeply, like the death of someone we loved more than ourselves, like being banished into forests far from everyone, like a suicide. A book must be the axe for the frozen sea within us. (1977: 15-16)[3]

For Kafka, reading has little point if it is not a painful experience. But in what sense does the reader feel pain? Certainly there is a commonly attested experience of finding something 'too painful to read'. Most of us find reading accounts of torture, for instance, deeply distressing. But how does this distress relate to the physical anguish of the victim? Is it merely a vicarious experience with a tendency to lapse into voyeurism? Is there a valid pain for the reader?

One indication that there could be a kind of suffering of the reader can be seen in the phenomenon of experimental neurosis. A classic experiment by Pavlov illustrates this (Pavlov 1927: 290-91). He trained dogs to discriminate between a circle and a flat ellipse by offering them food consistently with the display of the circle and

---

2.   The quotation on the book cover is unattributed. It derives from a review of the novel by Carol Rumens in *The Guardian* (13 September 1984).
3.   Letter to Oskar Pollak, 27 January, 1904 (Kafka 1977: 15-16).

withholding food when the flat ellipse was displayed. By monitoring the saliva flow of the dogs, it could be demonstrated that a consistent link between the sign and the dogs' expectations had been established. The dogs were then shown shapes intermediate between the flat ellipse and the circle. They displayed a profound change in behaviour, becoming wild and snapping angrily, straining to get free. At the same time, they lost the ability to discriminate between clear signs which they had previously demonstrated. If the experiment was continued, the dogs evinced an abnormal listlessness and ceased to react to any signs whatever.

This is a well-attested phenomenon in many experimental animals. It only occurs when the animal is in a situation where it can perceive both that a problem exists and that it is being offered a potential solution. Frustration builds up when the animal is capable of seeing the potential rewards of solving the problem and yet is thwarted in its attempts to discern a replicable pattern in the results of its response to stimuli.[4]

It would be possible to draw a parallel here with Job's situation. He is unable to correlate his experience of suffering with his expectation of blessing, but he is beset by the tantalizing conviction that he should be able to make sense of this contradiction. He is bombarded with contradictory stimuli, both in the tragedies which beset him and the arguments to which he is subjected. The final straw is the overwhelming assault of the divine speeches to which Job responds in a way very reminiscent of the dogs in Pavlov's experiment. After the snapping and straining of his complaints in the dialogues, he is reduced to an abject and listless silence. That may be stretching the point, but the fact remains that even dogs can feel this frustration of the failed attempt to make coherent sense of conflicting signs to the extent of exhibiting physical symptoms of distress.

Human beings can be distressed by the inability to find an interpretation of the world that will enable them to make consistent predictions within it. That world can be the world evoked by a text. Reading is a process of inference, and a text may not provide sufficient clues, or provide ambiguous clues, and thus defer a coherent interpretation. Up to a certain point, this can be stimulating and enjoyable. The popularity of crossword puzzles and detective novels is evidence of this. Beyond that point, it becomes frustrating; the unpopularity of some modern verse arises from its resistance to inferential processes. This either leads to boredom and an abandon-

4.   For further discussion, see Polanyi 1962: 367.

ment of the effort at interpretation, or else to frustration and anger. The reaction will depend on the perceived rewards of deciphering of the text. If the readers are merely seeking entertainment, they will quickly seek it elsewhere. If, however, the text encodes the only way of escape from a perilous situation, then the reader will persist perhaps to the point of extreme rage and despair.

Somewhere between these positions, however, is the idea that a text can by its difficulty produce emotional states in its readers which lead them to share the frustration of the protagonist. Such an interpretation is put forward by Longinus in his *On Sublimity* as he praises the use of what he calls 'hyperbaton', the distortion of the sequence of words and thoughts, in Demosthenes:

> His transpositions produce not only a great sense of urgency but the appearance of extemporization, as he drags his hearers with him into the hazards of his long hyperbata. He often holds in suspense the meaning which he set out to convey, and introducing one extraneous item after another in an alien and unusual place before getting to the main point, throws the hearer into a panic lest the sentence collapse altogether, and forces him in his excitement to share the speaker's peril, before, at long last and beyond all expectation, appositely paying off at the end the long due conclusion... (Longinus, *On Sublimity* 22.3-4)

Thus the emotional excitement of a narrated incident is conveyed to the reader through his distress at the possibility that he will not be able to salvage a coherent reading from the narrative. Though Longinus is here concentrating on the syntax of a sentence, such an effect can be prolonged so that the text as a whole may induce this 'panic' that it will in the end prove irresolvable.

I would argue that the suffering of the reader is a central issue in Muriel Spark's novel. Using the book of *Job* as her pretext, she composes a work which plays upon the processes by which readers try to evade, assuage or endure the pain of reading. Her method is mimetic, not diegetic, in keeping with the techniques of the book of *Job* itself. The biblical Job is a man who is unable to read his world and who suffers from that inability. It is not his physical plight which is the cause of his greatest anguish but his need to make sense of his situation. He is caught in the contradiction between his expectations and his experience while being offered authoritative readings of his situation which only add to his sufferings. Muriel Spark's hero, Harvey Gotham, is also a man who cannot make sense of the contradiction between his belief in a loving God and the obvious suffering of the world. But he is also caught up in the difficulties of making sense of the contradictions of the book of *Job*. The parallels between Job's attempts to argue his way to an understanding of his plight and the modern reader's attempts to come to grips with the strangeness of the book of *Job* coalesce as themes in Spark's novel. Both are metonyms for the wider problems of the attempt to wrest meaning from world or work.[5]

Arguably, it was Spark's own pain as a reader, not of Job but of its commentators, which goaded her into writing on the book in the first place. In 1955 she wrote an article for the *Church of England Newspaper* on 'The Mystery of Job's Suffering' (1955) in which she responds to the recently published interpretation of the biblical book in C.G. Jung's *Answer to Job*.[6] She castigates Jung for his disregard for the so-called epilogue to the book, which, however, she admits is the 'stumbling-block for most intelligent readers of *Job*' (1955: col. 3). Jung overcomes this problem by ignoring the epilogue completely. He even praises the author of *Job* for what he calls his 'masterly discretion' in drawing the book to a close at the point where Job is prostrate before God, blithely disregarding the fact that the book does not in fact close with this scene. Jung's truncation of *Job* spurred Muriel Spark to write her article in which she insists on the importance of the epilogue to the understanding of the book. The issue of the reading of the book's epilogue resonates throughout *The Only Problem*. Reading Jung's interpretation has pained her as a reader sufficiently to evoke a cry of protest.

This epilogue, Job 42.7-17, has been a bone of contention in the history of interpretation of the book, as Spark's description of it indicates. In the words of David Clines (1990: 70), it has been a source of 'discomfort' to many of the book's modern interpreters.[7] After the

5. In his essay 'The Book of Job in its Time and in the Twentieth Century' (1972), Jon D. Levenson reviews several modem English adaptations of the story of Job, concluding that a successful re-creation must await a time when 'the tension that informs the Book of Job is again real in the lives of most people'. By making her hero not simply a Job figure, but a reader of *Job*, Spark is able to circumvent the modern lack of engagement with God that Levenson sees as a problem for the contemporary recasting of the story. The problem Job has with God, Harvey Gotham and the modern reader have with the biblical book.

6. C.G. Jung's *Antwort auf Hiob* (1952) was published in an English translation in 1954 (Jung 1954). It is this translation to which Muriel Spark's article refers.

7. Clines accounts for this as follows: 'I suspect that the discomfort is the psychological registration of the deconstruction that is in progress, though until recently we did not have this name for the process, and so did not perhaps properly appreciate its character' (1990: 70).

sublime poetry of the dialogues between Job and his friends and the awesome picture of a universe completely beyond human grasp which God reveals in his climactic speech, we have the banality of the restoration to Job of his livestock, his social standing and, most disconcertingly, of a surrogate family: 'And the Lord blessed the latter days of Job more than the former', as we read in Job 42.12. Not only does this ending seem to trivialize Job's sufferings, but it seems to vindicate the very theology of retribution and reward which Job so vehemently rejects in the dialogues. Job is apparently rewarded for his righteous refusal to link righteousness and reward. In Job the resolution of the conflict for the reader is so long delayed that the 'panic' which the epilogue of the book must allay is intense. No wonder it is the subject of the reader's wrath when it is felt to fail in this task.

The most usual response from biblical critics is to regard the epilogue as the product of a different and by implication inferior strand of material. Usually the epilogue is taken to be the remnant of an earlier folk-tale which the author of the dialogues used as the basis for his poetic masterpiece, perhaps deliberately to expose the crudity of its retributive theology.[8] Alternatively, it is seen as the work of a pious later editor who is concerned to tone down the radical theodicy of the poetic dialogues by giving Job his just deserts.[9]

Both these solutions dissect the work into text and pretext. A later author has used a pretext whose theodicy demands a refutation, and produced a text which undermines the theology of its precursor. The discomfort which the reader feels is alleviated by the critic in an act of violence on the text, dismembering it into earlier and later portions. In either case, as David Clines points out, these historico-critical solutions betray 'a curious but commonly entertained assumption

---

8.   For a concise summary of the historical-critical debate on Job, see Samuel Terrien (1954). In the fifth century, Theodore of Mopsuestia regarded Job as an ancient story blasphemously distorted by a person of literary pretensions, as Urbrock (1981) discusses. The modern 'folk-tale' theory derives from Wellhausen (1871) and Budde (1876: 27-62). Georg Fohrer (1968: 325) speaks of 'almost universal acceptance' of the theory which sees the framework of *Job* as an independent and earlier narrative.

9.   This position is argued for by Robert H. Pfeiffer (1952: 668-71) who traces it to Schultens in 1737. Pfeiffer sees the folk-tale as a later addition by a Jewish redactor to an Edomite poem, drawing on a Judaean version of the traditional material which is also behind the poem. See also K. Fullerton (1924: 126) who writes, 'From my point of view this closing restoration ruins the book artistically'.

that to understand the origin of a discrepancy is somehow to *deal with* the discrepancy, to bring about a new state of affairs in which the discrepancy does not exist' (1990: 70).

We are still left with a biblical book which presents us with a painful clash of interpretations of Job's predicament. If this is not interpreted as the inept result of some editor's attempts to unite different traditions under putative constraints which prevent him from harmonizing the components of the book, what solution can we offer? How does Muriel Spark suggest we cope with the discomfort these clashes cause?

When, in her 1955 article, Spark reproves Jung for his textually indefensible disregard for the epilogue, especially in view of the interpretative weight he gives to the transactions between God and Satan, she writes: 'If Dr Jung wants the prologue (and his whole theory hangs upon it), he must have the epilogue...' She adds this very suggestive phrase: '...no less than his hero Job had apparently to *suffer his reward*' (1955: col. 4 [my emphasis]).

Earlier in the same article she asks: 'Can we really imagine our hero enjoying his actual reward?' (1955: col. 3). For Spark, the ending of *Job* is 'not merely a conventional happy ending'. It transforms the ironic clash between the prologue and the dialogues into what she calls 'that type of anagogical humour which transcends irony and which is infinitely mysterious' (1955: col. 4).

Given these comments, we might suspect that Spark is aligning herself with those who argue that Job is formally a comedy. It certainly ends with restoration and reconciliation, but with a question mark over the status of Job himself. Northrop Frye, who does consider that *Job* should technically be classed as a comedy, nevertheless remarks of the epilogue:

> In its conventional comic form of renewal, this kind of conclusion is seldom very convincing: people who lose their daughters are not really consoled by new daughters; conditions that cause suffering can be changed but the scars of suffering remain... Perhaps if we were to see Job in his restored state we should see, not beautiful daughters or sixteen thousand sheep, but only a man who has seen something that we have not seen, and knows something that we do not know. (Frye 1983: 197)[10]

10. See also Whedbee (1977), who regards Job's suffering as leading him to a sharpened sense of comic awareness. *Job*'s 'happy ending' demonstrates the irony of the book by leaving its incongruities unresolved.

Something of this unknowable quality is perhaps what Muriel Spark means by the 'anagogical humour' of the ending, by which even the concern for the balance of justice in the universe, which Job so desperately seeks to maintain for his own sake, and also for the sake of God's honour, comes to seem, not petty, not unimportant, but incongruous in the way that can only give rise to a self-deprecating smile once we realize that we have totally misread the scale and implications of such a concern.[11]

Turning back to *The Only Problem*, we find that the structure of the novel itself reflects the importance that Spark places on the epilogue in achieving a coherent reading of *Job*. It falls into three sections, the final part being much the shortest and forming an epilogue to the tale of Harvey's tribulations over his wife's escapades. Early in the novel we find a report of a conversation where Harvey and his brother-in-law discuss the ending of *Job*. Harvey decides that Job probably suffered more after his restoration than before it because suffering had become a habit for him. In the epilogue to the novel, Harvey, having completed his monograph, reflects once more on Job's final state: 'And Harvey wondered again if in real life Job would be satisfied with this plump reward, and doubted it. His tragedy was that of the happy ending' (1985: 186).

This reading seeks to accommodate the epilogue by seeing it as continuing the theme of the suffering of Job rather than introducing an incompatible restoration. Harvey, and Spark in her own voice, reject the kind of textual emendation many critics advocate. As Harvey says when explaining the textual problems of Job to a friend:

11.　There is an affinity here with another disputed epilogue, the epilogue to Shakespeare's *The Tempest* (see also n. 15, below). At the end of the play, Prospero has had his kingdom restored to him, yet the last scene and epilogue to the play do not depict a man overjoyed at regaining what is rightfully his and his triumph over his enemies. What he has suffered and what he has learnt about his own nature and the nature of those around him both exhaust him and leave him with a profound sense of the unimportance of his triumph. Compare, too, the Oedipus of Sophocles' *Oedipus at Colonnus*. Oedipus in this play bears some resemblance to Job: a figure who sees himself as set apart from the rest of humanity by the cruel interventions of the gods, yet fundamentally innocent. The appalling crimes that he committed were done in ignorance, and indeed resulted from his efforts to escape committing the crimes which prophecy laid at his door, he protests. Oedipus achieves a death unlike that of any other mortal, a mysterious translation to the world of the shades. The actual moment and mode of his passing is hidden in the play, but it becomes a secret source of blessing to Athens. The strange interaction of blessing and curse in the experience of being singled out by the gods bears distinctly on our picture of Job.

> The scholars try to rationalise *Job* by rearranging the verses where
> there is obviously no sense in them. Sometimes, of course, the textual
> evidence irresistibly calls for a passage to be moved from the
> traditional place to another. But moving passages about for no other
> reason than they are more logical is no good for the *Book of Job*. It
> doesn't make it come clear. The *Book of Job* will never come clear. It
> doesn't matter; it's a poem. (1985: 132)

The implication is that the discomfort that the text causes the reader
by its seeming incoherence is part of its status as a poem. It is a
deliberate device, an example of Longinus's hyperbaton. There is, of
course, a danger that this could be seen as arguing that any illogical
text could be defended on the grounds that it was really a poem.
Neither Harvey nor Spark make clear how we are to make the prior
decision that the text is to be engaged with as a poem and thus is
permitted such logical aberrations. There is no doubt, however, that
the critic who decides to dissect the text has already made judgments
on the criteria of coherence which the text ought to but does not
display. At least the approach in *The Only Problem* allows for the
possibility that the text might expand the reader's categories rather
than have to be pruned to fit them.

Spark does not merely leave us as readers to face the stark contradictions of the text. She does offer a way of alleviating the reader's
discomfort at Job's restoration, but at the price of prolonging Job's
suffering. His happy ending is not so happy after all. The Job of the
epilogue is still scarred by the events of the prologue and dialogues.
If the reader is to be more comfortable, Job must be less so.

Such a reading, though unusual, is not unique to Muriel Spark.
Robert Carroll also points out forcibly the impossibility of any compensation for Job, and the continued suffering which this must mean:

> For Job whose eyes had dwelt on the past there can have been no
> thorough restoration but a terrible sense of loss and perhaps even of
> impotent rage against a power that had so casually discarded his life
> to settle a wager… Job was left to live out the next 140 years brooding
> on the injustice he had suffered. The epilogue neither suggests this nor
> rules it out. (1976: 165)

Is there, though, any justification for such a reading other than the
need to integrate the text by establishing a continuity of pain between
the Job of the various poetic and prose sections of the book? After all,
there is no getting past the plain statement in the epilogue that 'God
blessed the latter days of Job more than the former'. Once we begin to
examine this more closely, however, we find that it is by no means so
straightforward a statement after all.

There is a strange relationship in Job between blessing and its antonym 'cursing' which depends on the mechanism of euphemism. The Hebrew root *brk,* usually translated as 'bless', is used several times in the prologue in contexts where it is clear that it must be translated as 'curse'. This ambivalence must raise a question about the meaning of the word in other contexts in *Job.*[12]

We can tabulate the nine uses of the root *brk* in *Job* as follows, paraphrasing the RSV's translation of the verses in which it appears:

1.5	Job sacrifices lest his sons have *cursed* God in their hearts.
1.10	Satan reminds God that he has *blessed* the work of Job's hands.
1.11	Satan alleges that if God touches Job's possessions, Job will *curse* him to his face.
1.21	Job *blesses* the name of the Lord.
2.5	Satan alleges that if God touches Job's person, Job will *curse* him to his face.
2.9	Job's wife urges him to *curse* God and die.
29.13	Job was *blessed* by those about to perish.
31.20	Job swears to his being *blessed* by the poor man's loins.
42.12	The Lord *blesses* the latter days of Job more than the former.

It is noticeable that six of the appearances of the root occur in the first two chapters of the book, which form its prologue. Though the connection between them is not uncontroversial, the prologue and epilogue are often seen as answering one another. Meir Weiss (1983: 81) argues that the root *brk* functions as a *Leitwort.* The epilogue provides the seventh instance of this root in the prose framework and the completion of this perfect number serves to bind together prologue and epilogue.

There is also a noticeable pattern in the translation of the root as either 'bless' or 'curse'. In every case where *brk* is translated as 'curse', the object of the verb is God. This euphemistic use of the root, which avoids the name 'God' having to appear as the object of the verb *qll* ('to curse'), is known from other biblical passages and from Rabbinic writings.[13]

Once the root has been taken as conveying these two antithetical meanings, albeit in defined contexts, there is obvious scope for

---

12.   In a coincidence of interests, which has happened on other occasions, Tod Linafelt published an article on exactly this topic at much the same time as the original form of this chapter first appeared. It is recommended to the reader (Linafelt 1996).

13.   For a discussion of the phenomenon of euphemism in biblical and Rabbinic literature in general and particularly in relation to the root *brk,* see Christopher Wright (1987: 163) and also Carmel McCarthy (1981: 191-95).

playing on this ambiguity. One striking example is the way that the reversal of meaning makes it possible to read Job in 1.21 as fulfilling the Satan's prediction in 1.11 literally — Job does *brk* God as the Satan said he would — while interpreting his speech as vindicating God's faith in his integrity — Job actually blesses God rather than cursing him. Both God and the Satan are correct in their prediction of Job's response, Satan literally and God functionally.

This reversibility of meaning needs to be borne in mind as we look critically at the two occasions where God is represented as blessing Job. In 1.10, it is the Satan who raises what becomes the fundamental question of the prologue: 'Does Job fear God for naught?' What is the relation between Job's righteousness and God's blessing? Is Job righteous because he is blessed by God? Or does God bless him because he is righteous? Or is there in fact no relation between Job's prosperity and his standing before God?

Already in this verse we meet the paradox that it is God's blessing of Job which becomes the point at issue between God and the Satan. If Job had not been saddled with this blessed status, he would never have figured in the conversation in heaven. God's blessing is what lands Job in trouble. The point at which curse and blessing coincide is that the bearer of either is singled out, differentiated from the mass of humanity.[14] It is that singular status of God's blessing which fits Job for his role as the subject of the experiment which the Satan carries out with God's permission.

If we then turn to the use of the root *brk* in the epilogue, we cannot simply read God's latter 'blessing' of Job as an unmixed affirmation either. All uses of the root *brk* in this text carry with them a shadow-side of curse. Job has to live on in the epilogue after the experience of his utter humiliation before God. Before the divine speech, Job is secure in his right to challenge God and demand justice before him. Afterwards, he has to live knowing how utterly dependent he is on God's grace. His restored prosperity can be no comfort as its precariousness has been made so abundantly clear to him. Wealth and position offered no security against disaster the first time round. The comfort of his friends and family must ring rather hollow given their earlier desertion of him when he actually needed their support.

His new children are a different matter. There is almost a fairy-tale unreality about them in their perfection and the whimsy of his

14. This common element of isolation from the community under both curse and blessing is discussed with reference to Abraham by George W. Coats (1981).

daughters' names.[15] The fact that he makes the unique provision for his daughters to inherit a share of his property along with their brothers may reflect the way in which his material possessions have also become in some way unreal to him. To top it all, he has to survive under these ambivalent circumstances for a hundred and forty years, twice a normal life-span. Even the words which end the book carry an ambiguity. Job dies 'full of days' (Job 42.17). This is usually taken as expressing the satisfaction of having completed a rich and rewarding life surrounded by his descendants, but no less a figure than Friedrich Delitzsch translates the phrase as 'weary of life' (1869: 392). Given all this, in what sense has Job been blessed by being the object of God's special attention?

The Only Problem picks up on this central ambiguity of cursing and blessing, albeit in a rather oblique fashion. We find this in the consideration of a remarkable painting which figures prominently in Harvey's researches into Job. In the novel, Harvey is living near Epinal in Central France in order to be near the picture by Georges de La Tour which was identified in 1935 as depicting *Job visited by his wife*. Harvey is struck by the contrast between the sweet and solicitous grace of the wife in the picture and the angry impatience of the biblical character who incites her husband to curse God (Job 2.9). Commentators have argued whether Job's wife in this verse is urging him to provoke God into striking him dead and thus ending his sufferings or implying that as he is to die anyway, he might as well relieve his feelings. The serenity of de La Tour's picture belies either interpretation. In the novel, Harvey's interpretation of this serenity is that de La Tour is idealizing the deep love between Job and his wife (Spark 1985: 78).

Frank Kermode (1986) interestingly pursues the ambivalence which Muriel Spark has noticed in de La Tour's painting. He puts forward a speculation that de La Tour may have been influenced by the Vulgate translation of Job's wife's speech. Translating the Hebrew literally, St Jerome has her say *benedic Deo* — 'bless God'. De La Tour may be illustrating this moment of blessing. The woman's expression of pity had often led to the painting being tentatively described as the visitation of an angel to some biblical character. Kermode points out, however, that the standard work on the painter written after 1935 when the woman in the picture was identified as Job's wife speaks of

---

15.   Anthony and Miriam Hanson (1953: 118) make this point by translating Job's daughters' names as Swansdown, Lavender, and Mascara. The Hansons describe the epilogue as *The Tempest* tacked on to *Lear*.

the anger and cruelty of her expression. So interpretation reveals its circularity. Kermode see this as an insoluble interpretative problem but he does at least offer the possibility that 'blessing' could be a workable interpretation even within the biblical text:

> …the painter and his patron may really have read the words *benedic Deo* quite literally, and seen Job's wife as tender, however foolish she might be; she may be saying that death is the only way out of such misery and that he should seek it, and make a good end. (1986: 428)

Kermode makes allusion to Freud, among others, as having called attention to the widespread phenomenon of the antithetical meanings of primal words such as the Hebrew *brk*. He ends his paper thus:

> So I think there is a peculiar truth in Job's wife when we cannot decide whether she is tender or cruel, blessing or cursing… We bring ourselves and our conflicts to words, to poems and pictures, as we bring them to the world; and thus we change the poems and pictures, or perhaps it is ourselves we change. (1986: 431)

The same truth lies behind the ambivalence of our reading of the epilogue to *Job*. Here, though, the ambivalence is not in the attitude of Job's wife, but in God's attitude to Job. The question that this reading circles round is 'What is it to be "blessed" by God?' It is remarkable that this ambivalence over the meaning which so profoundly affects the reading of the epilogue arises from the attempt to preserve God's holiness through the use of euphemism. Do we change the text of the book to dispel that uncanny ambiguity between blessing and cursing which contributes to making the epilogue so disturbing, or do we allow the book to change our notions of how God relates to human beings?

It is this alternative of change in the text or change in the reader which the history of interpretation of *Job* illustrates. Whether as historical critics, commentators or novelists, we rewrite the text. The mechanism of counterpoising text and pretext is one that can be used in different ways to accommodate the ambiguity. Either we see *Job* itself as a composite text and thus deal with the ambiguity in terms of conflicting layers of textuality, or, as Muriel Spark does, we take the book itself as a pretext and write out of the conflict of our experience of reading it.

The crucial question remaining is whether, in either case, we are seeking to avoid or to express the alteration the text can effect in us. Do we seek to alleviate the suffering of the reader or, as Kafka would urge, to embrace its potential to shock us awake? The critical method may be used to disarm the text, but it is also possible to see the text itself as much as its retinue of interpretations as the product of a history of deflections of its assaults upon us. The interpreter's role in this approach becomes the stripping away of these accretions in order to restore the text's power to change us.

This is certainly the approach of René Girard (1987). His reading of Job is in keeping with his theory of mimetic rivalry which leads to the unifying act of the victimization of a scapegoat. Girard's Job is the Job of the dialogues, the innocent victim of communal persecution who refuses to play the game that his society demands. He will not be silent about his innocence. For Girard:

> All the additions to the Dialogues do violence to the original text; they are victorious acts of persecution in that they have succeeded, until now, in neutralizing the revelation of the scapegoat…the epilogue drowns the scapegoat in the puerile acts of revenge of a Hollywood success story. (1987: 143-44)

Yet even for Girard the prologue and epilogue are pragmatically indispensable in that they have concealed the implications of Job's protestations from the eyes of those readers who would have suppressed the book entirely if they had been aware of its subversive revelation of the underlying victimage mechanism:

> By concealing Job's subversive power, the mystifying additions have made the text accessible to ordinary devotion and at the same time prevented it from being rejected in horror, or so completely censored, changed and mutilated that its meaning would be lost for ever. By protecting the texts from too rough a contact with a hostile world and serving as shock-absorbers, these additions and commentaries that falsify have made possible the preservation of the texts that no one reads, since they are meaningless within the context given them. If the extent of their subversiveness had been more visible, they might never have survived for us. (1987: 143-44)

So in Girard's account this sugar-coating of prose which is designed to make the book palatable has paradoxically preserved the drastic and bitter medicine of the Joban revelation of the poetic unmasking of the scapegoat mechanism. Girard's metaphors of persecution and mutilation could, of course, be turned against his own reading. It is only by an act of violence, a dismemberment of the text as it has survived that he can wrest out the heart of its meaning. It is the text as survivor, however, which has such fascination as an enactment of its contents. Job survives, and *Job* has survived. Girard wants to strip away the features which have led to the book's survival, and thus must deny Job his survival within the text by discarding the epilogue.

The strength of the kind of reading we have been tracing in *The Only Problem* is that it depends on this ambivalent status of the survivor as both blessed and cursed, preserved from death to live a life of pain, outliving the beloved only to have to endure the knowledge of their absence. Girard's account of the function of the scapegoat focuses entirely on the unifying effect of communal murder of a victim who is reviled and then sanctified to conceal the fact that the blessing of unity is based on innocent bloodshed. The biblical tradition, however, works with a *double* mechanism, perhaps most fully explored by Karl Barth in volume II/2 of his *Church Dogmatics* (Barth 1957: 357-65). In the ritual of atonement in Leviticus 16, the sins of Israel are actually borne not by the goat which is killed, but by the goat which survives to be driven out into the desert. Barth points out the strange relationship between the elect and the rejected in the biblical text. The rejected, or the cursed, are often the ones who live out their lives under a special protection. Cain and Esau are paradigm examples. Contrary to the common perception, which sees length of life as the sign of God's favour in the Old Testament, there is a strand of the tradition which sees prolonged existence as something to be shunned.

One story that illustrates this very clearly is the story of the death of Abijah, the son of Jeroboam, in 1 Kings 14. When his child falls ill, Jeroboam dispatches his wife in disguise to seek out the prophet Ahijah. The prophet tells her that her son will die 'because in him there is found something pleasing to the Lord, the God of Israel' (1 Kgs 14.38). The child is to die, not as a sign of God's displeasure with him, but as a mark of divine favour. He alone of Jeroboam's house will be properly mourned and buried. Jeroboam's wife has to return to her husband bearing this message, knowing that the prophet has said that her son will die as her foot crosses the threshold of the palace, as indeed happens.

Can we draw a parallel here with the experience of the reader? The reader approaches the end of any book with the same knowledge as Jeroboam's wife. As soon as we cross the threshold of the last word of the text, the world we participate in within the book will end. Like her, we have the option of flight. We can close the book and thereby in one sense prevent its ending. Yet for her to flee might be to abandon her child to an infinitely prolonged suffering. It would be to abandon her responsibilities as wife, as mother, and as the bearer of God's word.

I can recall how as a child I would anxiously count the pages left in a book, torn between the desire to reach the end quickly in order to know how things turned out, and a desire to prolong the pleasure of life lived in the world of the book. Coupled with this was a real sense of bereavement with which I would part from the characters as I closed the last page of the book. A re-reading could never quite recapture the sense of discovery, of uncertainty, surprise, and growth in understanding which I and my 'paper friends' had shared. This parting was as painful as partings with real friends. As a reader I survived beyond the end of their story in a world which they could never enter even though the book they inhabited might well outlast me.

Job's anguish is that of the survivor. Even in the prologue to the book, God makes it clear that Job is entirely given over to the Satan's power, except that he is to be kept alive. Of course, like any experimental animal or torture victim, Job must be maintained alive if there is to be any validity to the heavenly experiment to determine the ground of his loyalty. The theme of survival is reiterated in the grim comedy of the impossibly coincident disasters that befall his property and at last his children. Each one of the procession of messengers who bring the awful news ends his proclamation with the phrase, 'And I alone escaped to tell you'. Job is left to outlive his children and in 19.13-19 he bewails his total abandonment by his wife and relatives. Job himself is left alone to tell…whom? — a God whom Job knows must be intimately involved with him for his life to be sustained, who yet abandons him to his suffering and solitude without a word of explanation or comfort. Job is left inextricably in the grasp of a God who has become absolutely alien to him.[16]

It is now a commonplace to trace the development of literary criticism through the twentieth century as a movement from the stress on the author as the guarantor of meaning to the autonomy of the text and then to a re-awakened interest in the reader as the site of the generation of meaning. Illuminating as the insights of reader-response criticism have been, there is a tendency to make the reader a stable centre, the replacement of the author as the authoritative judge of meaning. This can lead us to miss the transactive nature of the act of reading, a process by which the reader undergoes change as a result of reading. Indeed, this is what is involved in describing the process

---

16.   For a profound examination of this aspect of Job's experience, see Karl Barth (1961: 400-404).

involving author, text and reader as a communicative one; the whole point is to achieve a change in the reader.

Job creates us as readers as we seek to create a coherent reading of *Job*. We are left in the grip of a book which has made us its readers and yet refuses our demands that it lay bare its meaning. The book of *Job* makes great demands on the resources which enable its readers to survive as readers. We can survive our reading of *Job* by denying its capacity to change us, or otherwise defending ourselves against the possibility of being changed by it. If, however, we decide to open ourselves to it, we will be left bearing wounds, the mark of Kafka's axe.

Harvey Gotham does survive his engagement with Job and the loss of his wife, but he is not unchanged by the end of Spark's novel. Spark is reticent about his reactions, but she does explicitly mention his sadness at coming to the end of his monograph. Obliquely we infer from Harvey's doubt over Job's happiness that he does not end the book contentedly. He has suffered as a reader and in his daily existence. Yet how real is this suffering? Is it not to say the least tasteless to suggest that the suffering of the reader is in any way comparable to that of the victims of disease, misfortune and human evil?

This problem is also at the heart of Muriel Spark's choice of a reader of *Job* as the protagonist of her novel. Granted that there is a sense in which we can suffer as readers, is this not just a retreat from the real suffering of the world? Is the attempt to justify it as anything more serious not just the illusion which the academic has to believe or at least promote?

Harvey's assertion of the reality of the suffering of thought and study which prompts the quotation from *The Guardian* is part of his musings as he waits in a police station for news of his wife, Effie, who has been accused of terrorist crimes. He becomes fleetingly aware of a man whom he surmises to be a Balkan immigrant:

> Patience, pallor and deep anxiety: there goes suffering, Harvey reflected. And I found him interesting. Is it only by recognising how flat would be the world without the sufferings of others that we know how desperately becalmed our own lives would be without suffering? Do I suffer on Effie's account? Yes, and perhaps I can live by that experience. We all need something to suffer about. But *Job*, my work on *Job*, all interrupted and neglected, probed into and interfered with: that is experience too; real experience, not vicarious, as is often assumed. To study, to think, is to live and suffer painfully. (Spark 1985: 153)

Are we to read this as a valid self-justification by Harvey or as an ironic revelation of the self-absorption which allows him to treat suffering as an intellectual problem? Harvey's response to the world's suffering is to wrestle with the theology of an ancient and obscure text. If, as Alan Bold (1986: 115-19) suggests, Spark is here satirizing Harvey's intellectual detachment, characterizing him as a virtual solipsist, what are we to make of Spark herself, writing a novel based on this problem, or ourselves as readers either of *Job* or *The Only Problem*, or indeed of such a chapter as this?

But is Spark here being as one-sidedly satirical as Bold would have it? In its turn, the very different response to human suffering shown by Harvey's wife Effie's in her involvement in terrorist activity is certainly ironized in the novel as a childish but murderous revolt. The only result of her attempts to redress the sufferings of the world's oppressed is the death of a French policeman, the suffering of whose family is graphically depicted by Spark in a speech given to Harvey's police interrogator.

Elsewhere in the novel, Spark gives ambivalent signals about the reality of Harvey's suffering. She speaks of Harvey as being 'tormented' by his belief in God which leads him to have to confront the problem of undeserved suffering. His brother-in-law Edward, not always a reliable observer in the novel, notes undeniable anxiety and suffering in his face. But towards the end of the novel, Harvey writes in a letter to this brother-in-law:

> ...'no-one pities men who cling wilfully to their sufferings' *(Philoctetes* — speech of Neoptolemus). I'm not even sure that I suffer, I only endure distress. But why should I analyse myself? I am analysing the God of *Job*. (1985: 180)

Earlier in the novel, Harvey uses the opportunity of a press conference eager to know of his involvement with his wife's illicit actions to deliver a lecture on the meaning of *Job*. In a subsequent attempt to placate his aunt who is outraged by his reported blasphemies, Harvey says: 'Auntie Pet, you've got to understand that I said nothing whatsoever about God, I mean our Creator. What I was talking about was a fictional character in the *Book of Job*, called God' (1985: 135).

Harvey's distinction between the God he sees at work in the world around him and the fictional character represented in the text of Job reveals the kind of distancing which allows him to examine suffering dispassionately. Even the etymology of the word 'dispassionate' shows the problem of the discussion of suffering. Those who suffer do not have the luxury of enquiring into their experience as a problem. Job, by contrast, is not at all interested in the question of evil in general. He does not want to know 'Why is there suffering?' He cries out, 'Why *me?* Why am I singled out?'

Harvey exemplifies the problem of those to whom the question of suffering presents itself as 'Why *him?*' In its turn this question can reflect back on the questioner in the form 'Why *not* me?' This is the question every survivor asks. However appalling the events which the readers bring into being as they attempt to synthesize the world of the text, they will walk away from them physically unscathed. Psychologically, they may find it harder to shake off the effects. What we read, we read as survivors.

It is the survivor who feels pain, the body's outraged cry at the assault of death upon it. Even without physical injury, to survive can lead to a kind of suffering: the phenomenon of 'survival guilt' testified to among those seemingly privileged to live after an accident and seen in a peculiarly intense form among many survivors of the Nazi concentration camps. The blessing which survival seems to represent may turn into a life sentence of physical and mental anguish, both as a legacy of the appalling experiences the survivor has undergone, but also through the feeling of unworthiness at being singled out when so many other people with as much or more claim to life perished miserably.[17]

To write a monograph like Harvey's, or a novel like *The Only Problem,* or indeed this chapter, argues a level of privilege, of freedom from the causes of suffering which may prompt the question: 'Why *not* me?' Perhaps like Harvey we have to persuade ourselves that suffering the guilt of privilege is sufficient to give us some inkling of what it might be like to be without that privilege of protection. Part of the pain of the reader is the knowledge of the vicarious nature of the reader's pain.

---

17. For discussions of the phenomenon of survivor guilt, see Anton Gill (1989: 95, 223-24) and Bruno Bettelheim (1979: 26). Bettelheim makes the point that the survivors of the Holocaust were left having to live through psychological traumas unimaginable to those who had not shared their experience. Surviving one set of horrors in itself cruelly laid them open to others.

5

The Bible in Bloom

I begin with an apology to all those who expect from the title of this chapter a discussion of plants of the Holy Land or who hope that we might be spending a fascinating and possibly slightly risqué time exploring the biblical influences in the Dublin of James Joyce's most ebullient creation. We are, in fact, concerned here with the work of the eminent, perhaps notorious, and prolific critic Harold Bloom, who has written extensively on the Hebrew Bible, much to the alarm of those from all other camps. Bloom's work, however, hardly figures in the extensive literature produced by literary critics of the Bible. It is telling, for instance, that despite his record of publication on the subject, there is not so much as a single reference to Bloom in a standard work on contemporary critical theory such as *The Postmodern Bible*.

One reason for this silence may be easy enough to understand. After all, why should responsible biblical scholars spend time on a man who asserts Bathsheba wrote the book of J (Bloom 1994: 5)? What kind of a statement is that and just what is Bloom saying about the vexed questions in this postmodern age of authorship, textuality and critical judgment? In attempting to elucidate this bold and, on the face of it, unprovable claim, I hope that we can shed some light both on why the Hebrew Bible is important to Bloom, and on the questions which his work poses to those who gain their livelihood from reading that set of texts.

Bloom's claim is made in the opening section of perhaps his best-known book, *The Western Canon*, a substantial, controversial and idiosyncratic attempt to call attention to what it is that makes a book 'canonical' — why the works of Shakespeare, Dante, Milton and Whitman, to name four examples, are indispensable. Read as an attempt to prescribe a reading list which becomes a shibboleth of culture, it is easy to dismiss this endorsement of the big guns of the canon, but that is to misrepresent Bloom's project. For Bloom, canons are not the concern or the creation of readers or critics but of writers. So, for instance, when he prefaces his list of contemporary canonical writers in *The Western Canon* with an explanation of his omission of Larkin, he says that it may be that poets will confirm Larkin as canonical by finding him an unavoidable influence.

Those books and writers are canonical which other writers find inescapable. To use that word, however, at least suggests that escape may be desirable. Here we approach a key concept for Bloom, one that is summed up in the title of one of his books which has gained the status of a sound bite: *The Anxiety of Influence* (1973). Put simply — something he quite consciously avoids much of the time — Bloom has a vision of the creation of texts as an agonistic process, a process of struggle. Every text and every writer has to overcome the sense of 'belatedness' — the sense that all has been said — and this manifests itself in a struggle against his or her precursors. In order to clear a space for the new work the writer makes a 'swerve' from his or her precursors by misreading them and therefore both weakening them and assuming their power. Those who succeed, sometimes to the point of suppressing their precursors altogether, he calls 'strong' writers.

The history of the formation of the literary canon, then, becomes a history of struggle as texts jostle and elbow each other to claim the attention of the reader. More particularly it is a struggle to escape the overmastering discourse of one's predecessors. It is a jungle out there. Texts and, through texts, authors fight for their place in the sun, a claim on the ever more overloaded reader's attention and time. In the process thousands if not millions of texts are trampled under- foot. In the battle to survive, each text clamours, 'Read *me*! Read *me*, not him!', elbowing out its rivals so that it may be copied and recopied.

In this respect, Bloom, although not explicitly, is a proponent of a Darwinian view of literature such as I outline in 'Selfish Texts'.[1] More than that, his view is explicitly Freudian in its focus not simply on the competition between sibling texts, the hundreds of titles released in any one month jockeying for position on the bookshop shelf, but on the rivalry with older established texts which represents the turn against the father. Indeed he reads Freud as in some ways an arche- typal strong writer — not in any valid sense as a scientist — but pre- cisely a writer who in the late twentieth century has made his

1. See Chapter 1, above.

metaphors, his way of seeing the world, inescapable and who has at times succeeded in the battle with his precursors. After Freud, it is impossible to read even so strong a text as Sophocles' *Oedipus* without the shadow of Freud's reading falling across it.

This agonistic view of texts extends to the reader. For Bloom, what he calls the 'alert reader' is engaged in a battle with the text that is trying to change him or her. Readers and critics who are adequate to the task must themselves be poets, creating a new text in the act of reading. In his view, we never know a text, we only know a reading of it. Rather, as he prefers to put it, we only know a misreading of it. All reading is misreading, he claims, as a provocative way of making the less controversial point that any given reading is only a partial reading and cannot encompass all the possible meanings of a text (see Bloom 1975). The only difference is whether that reading is a strong or a weak one. Of course, every writer is also a reader and the strong writers are those who can articulate their misreading in such a way as to oust the alternatives, which may include the precursor's own reading or even intention.

What then constitutes strength for Bloom? In a word, the strong writer produces a strong misreading which is one with the ability to sustain and generate a multiplicity of further misreadings and will provoke others to 'swerve' creatively against the prevailing reading of the text. A weak misreading will in the end not survive over time because it is liable to be absorbed back into the precursor text. So, there have been many versions and paraphrases of the story of Oedipus, but for more than two thousand years these have all yielded to the power of Sophocles' text which remains central, Freud, for Bloom, providing the exception.

Bloom delights in elaborating complex models of the different moves that the strong misreader can make. To be successful, what must result is what he calls a 'transumption' of the precursor. The strong writer and his language tropes on his or her precursor in various ways, literalizing the figurative or reading the literal figuratively so as to co-opt a silence of the precursor. This may serve to mute the voice of the precursor, but the process may go further than that, so that by a combination of necromancy and ventriloquism, the strong writer may make it appear that the precursor is actually aping him. This is the basis of the apparently paradoxical claim that strong writers create their own precursors, which is borne out every time an eighteenth-century text, for instance, is described as 'Kafkaesque'. To keep to the example of Freud, how many nineteenth-century authors, for instance, Adolf Jensen, are now read, if at all, simply because Freud refers to them, whereas to contemporary readers it was Freud who was an unknown commentator on a well-known writer?

Why the Bible should interest Bloom is, I hope, clear from this brief account. No texts have stayed the course longer in Western literature. No texts have inspired, provoked, exasperated or nourished the Western literary tradition as have the biblical texts (though Bloom himself gives pride of place in the end to Shakespeare). Moreover, the Bible itself, of course, exhibits internally for Bloom all the tensions of transumption and canonization. The canonical texts of the Bible have won out over countless other texts that circulated in the ancient Near East, and indeed within the narrower circles of those who wrote and edited the canonical texts.

Bloom, since 1989 at least, has turned to the figure of J as the precursor of precursors, the most fearsome generator of misreadings, who stands sat the beginning of the whole tradition of Western literature and whose strength is shown precisely by the fact that any precursor texts or stories have been almost entirely obliterated by her (I use the pronoun Bloom chooses in *The Book of J*). Even works as strong as the Epic of Gilgamesh and the Enuma Elish succumb to her strength in misreading and re-reading their stories of creation, flood and family.

Of course, the status of J and the boundaries of any text that could be attributed to J are highly controversial topics. We misunderstand Bloom if we read him as another contributor to the endless elaboration of historico-critical accounts of the development of the Pentateuch. His characterization of J begins from the contemporary power of these texts to create what he quite happily calls a fiction of authorship. Bloom is not building a whole theory of influence on the shaky foundations of the Documentary Hypothesis, but is in his own right creatively misreading the biblical texts and the historico-critical (mis)readings as a prime example of the power of origination. He says boldly that his J is a fiction, but in the sense that each of us has our own Shakespeare, Tolstoy, Joyce, as a fiction — a partial picture generated out of texts.

He does adduce an argument for the existence of a textual complex attributable J in the book where he first conducts a sustained reading of J material, *Ruin the Sacred Truths*, by pointing out the omission of this material from the book of *Jubilees* (1989: 3). Although in later works he generally skirts any reification of J as an authorial presence, he sees the pointed suppression of these stories in *Jubilees*, which he describes as a weak, normative text, as a testimony to the threatening power of J's storytelling. What *Jubilees* cannot handle is the blasphemy of the God of J, the irreducible originality and boldness of her elliptical anthropomorphization.

His speculation that J is a woman is founded on three things: a desire to shock, and to annoy those critics who accuse him of misogyny; an acknowledgment of the strength of the women in J's stories (Sarah, Rachel) as opposed to the ambivalence of even the most heroic of the men (Abraham, Moses); but, above all, on her portrayal of Yahweh, whom he claims stands in the relation of a mother to a wayward child. Yahweh is the irony of mere maleness, Bloom says, and Yahweh's extraordinary behaviour including his tantrums, culminating in his attempt to murder Moses, are the ironic creation of the 'sly dark gaze' of J. J too, is, he argues, a great comic writer, after the mould of Kafka, for Bloom would claim it is through reading Kafka that we are able to appreciate the mordant irony, ellipsis and inconsequentiality which she represents. J is a virtuoso skater on the slippery surface of Hebrew utterance.

When, later, he specifically identifies J with Bathsheba it is, he admits, in the spirit of what he calls 'whole-hoggery'. On the back of this fundamental response to the strangeness and uncanniness of J's text, he builds a picture of the shrewd mother of Solomon, disillusioned by the disintegration of the empire under Rehoboam and inspired by her ultimate knowledge of the astonishing fullness of life in her husband David, who rewrites all the traditions of her adopted people with an ironic eye born of her dealings with her unfathomable spouse, who haunts her pages by his absence.

Bloom's 'Bathsheba/J' is an extravagant fiction, which Bloom himself is half seduced by, but what it grows from is a profound response to the originality of these texts. Bloom unfashionably stands against what he sees as the trend of what he calls the 'schools of resentment' — feminism and Marxism are particular bugbears of his — to denigrate or reappropriate these texts. He resists becoming part of what to him is a long and sorry history of normalization which begins with the figure he calls 'R', the great redactor of the Torah. He will not have the creative strangeness of such texts reduced to socio-economic categories. He wants to leave a space for the possibility of radical challenge to all the systems of social and economic control and oppression, a place for the uncanny, in the struggle of text with text. He also has no time for the co-opting of these canonical texts to what he sees as sectional interests, though he is not as blind as some make out to the normative weakness of white male academic readings. Bloom distances himself from what is commonly conceived of as postmodernism in its decentring of texts, but his insistence on the authorial is not as I read it a simple return to the modern. Bathsheba/ J is Bloom's way of personifying and so engaging with the seductive power of this text. I like to imagine my fictional Bloom — for such he is — reading the text with an appreciative gleam of the eye and occasional cries of 'That's my girl!'

He also takes great pleasure in representing himself as a solitary voice calling for the rediscovery of solitude, of the reader who reads in silence and alone, wrestling with great precursors, in order to expand her sense of herself — a plea directed against the easy bite-sized chunks of the postmodern stew. *The Western Canon*, in particular, is permeated with a sense of being a desperate final shot fired on behalf of the canon against the incoming tide of resentment, and against what Bloom, in his idiosyncratic version of a cyclical scheme of human history, calls the impending New Theocratic age. Now that Western culture has descended from the Aristocratic and Democratic ages to our present age of Chaos, Bloom fears a new orally based age of Theocracy where human values will be lost in a resurgence of rigid normalizing sanctioned by competing claims of divine competence. This, he would argue, is just the kind of resentfulness that in an earlier manifestation sought to obliterate the subvertive narrative energy of J in the tedious cycles of the book of *Jubilees*.

There is a sense, though, where even here Bloom is relying on a biblical tradition of prophecy of the inevitable. His canon, his book of books, is sent out as a challenge to a culture which may seek to abandon or ignore canon, or which may lapse into the weak reading he calls 'facticity', in which the figural world of the great creators is turned into historicity and dogma and where once again an appeal to 'literalism' will mask the claim to power of the resentful.

But what can we take from this to enhance our own reading of the Bible? Here are some questions from Bloom which give me pause for thought for my own work.

First, and most obviously, Bloom raises for me questions about the paradox of canonization in the way in which a seemingly normative process actually enshrines the bizarre and counter-cultural. So many of the biblical books — Ruth, Esther, Ecclesiastes, Song of Songs, the J material might serve as examples — do not seem to be typical works which conform to some accepted pattern of structure, style and content. Indeed, there are not many biblical books which do seem to fall into simple generic patterns, one of the problems of form criticism. Rather, more typically they combine, ironize and subvert forms, metaphors and themes. In what sense are any of the so-called prophetic books 'normal' examples of a genre? What are their precursors, or even their siblings? Where they do acknowledge, often covertly, their predecessors, it is usually to co-opt and re-read them. Misreading, not reading, is the order of the day in the process of the formation of the canon. For example, the Song of Songs is strongly misread as an allegorical text and so becomes acceptable as to the normative readings of the canonizers. The epilogues to Job or Ecclesiastes, whatever their origins, permit weak and normative readings of what are, on any other reading, deeply unsuitable books.

The canonization of such texts is perversely the permission for heresy because they are normalized into scripture by being misread. That normative scriptural reading is only one misreading among many. Once transmitted to the next generation of readers, the texts lie there in all their strangeness capable still of generating profoundly unsettling misreadings and re-readings. The power of these inescapable texts continues as commentators and creative writers alike wrestle with them.

Indeed, could the acknowledgment of this give rise to another reading of the process of canonization? Dare we imagine some post-exilic Harold Bloom or a bunch of his cronies, or a succession of them, compiling their lists of 'inescapable' books to be flung in the face of their own Chaotic age?

Bloom reminds us that it is the strangeness of texts that constitutes their claim to be re-read. It is the fact that some uncanny books demand and need to be constantly re-read and rewritten that determines their canonical status. So Bloom posits at one point that it is because Ecclesiastes is rewritten and retroped by Ecclesiasticus that the earlier highly contentious text rather than the later orthodox one is canonized within the Hebrew Bible. Ecclesiastes is the inescapable text; Ecclesiasticus merely offers one escape. This is of course by no means a historically responsible account of the canonical process, nor even quite fair to Ecclesiasticus, but it serves as a reminder that the process is more complex than we or those engaged in it may realize.

Canons are not simply political and normative constructions, though they are that and may be intended to be so by those who delineate them. Mercifully, in Bloom's account, they are self-deconstructing by definition because writers, not readers, finally make canons. What may be seen as an act of setting bounds to what may be real and therefore an implicit repression of the act of further writing, actually serves to generate more, and different writing. His sense of the competition of texts with texts and of texts with readers is a healthy corrective to what can lapse into a rather anodyne and cosy academic conversation, or to the passivity of certain so-called post-modern approaches where readings are simply juxtaposed. There is the smell of battle in the air in Bloom's writing and a sense, not of an ethics of reading, but the high and heady irresponsibility of those who seek not virtue but blessing. Bloom's J may be a sultry Holly-wood vixen, but even R was not a member of a Church of England Board of Social Responsibility either.

Bloom reminds responsible biblical scholars that they are the custodians of a set of highly irresponsible texts which portray God in the character of the jealous lover, warrior and trickster as well as judge and saviour. I admire and wish always to convey to my students the almost erotic charge in Bloom's wrestling. He gets joy from these texts — ebullience, abundance is something he rejoices in, and he can stimulate us to join battle with these texts with gusto.

As we have seen, Bloom tells us that it is a jungle out there. Even the carefully weeded lawns of a university college are the scene of titanic battles of survival between plant and plant, mole and worm, beetle and bird, cat and mouse. Bloom's message is that it is out of these wild texts that the cultivated fruits of our civilization come and we ignore them at our peril — and if in our ventures into some bosky glade we happen upon an elderly Jewish professor and the dark-eyed widow of both a Hittite warrior and an Israelite king locked in amo-rous dalliance, I hope our ethics will permit us to smile and gently pass by on our own pursuits.

6

MODERN GOSPELS OF JUDAS:
CANON AND BETRAYAL

In his *Against the Heretics*, written around 150 CE, Irenaeus of Lyons trawls through the increasingly bizarre varieties of Valentinian Gnosticism, eventually arriving at the real lunatic fringe, by his way of thinking:

> Still others say that Cain came from the Absolute Sovereignty above, and Esau, Korah, and the men of Sodom, along with every person of this sort, have the same origin. They were hated by the Creator because though attacked they suffered no harm, for Sophia took to herself what was her own in them. The traitor Judas was the only one of the apostles who possessed this knowledge. For this reason he brought about the mystery of the betrayal; through him all things on earth and in heaven were destroyed. They provide a work to this effect called the 'Gospel of Judas'. (*Adversus Haereses* 1.31.1; Grant 1997: 104-105)[1]

Here Irenaeus testifies to the existence of a work which apparently epitomized Gnostic resistance to the God of the Old Testament. It is a gospel attributed to the man who the canonical New Testament writers depict as the instrument of betrayal and who is vilified by subsequent Christian tradition as the epitome of human sinfulness and treachery. For its Gnostic readers, however, Judas was the champion of suppressed truth in a treacherous creation and the true bringer of salvation.

---

1.   Both Theoderet and Epiphanius also testify to the existence of this community, whom they call the 'Cainites', and of its gospel, but their dependence on Irenaeus is clear. The Swedish novelist Lars Gyllensten provides a fictional account of this community and their texts in *The Testament of Cain* (1967).

   Given that this Gnostic *Gospel of Judas* was lost long ago,[2] it might come as a surprise that a by no means exhaustive bibliographic search turned up a list of books which claim to contain the text of this lost gospel.[3] These are not simply novels which tell Judas's story or give his version of events, though a number of such works exist.[4]

2.   At the time of writing, various rumours were appearing on internet sites that a Coptic manuscript containing 62 pages of a *Gospel of Judas*, surmised to be the book that Irenaeus knew of, had been circulating for some time on the antiquities market and was now receiving scholarly attention. Rodolf Kasser of the University of Geneva is reportedly due to publish a scholarly paper on this manuscript in late 2005 (see, for instance, the Wikipedia entry on 'Gospel of Judas', <http://wikipedia.org/inki/Gospel_of_Judas>, accessed 2 August 2005.)

3.   The original version of this chapter was published before the useful survey of such material provided by Kim Paffenroth was available (Paffenroth 2002). Readers will find an interesting alternative discussion of Judas, but without the stress on the issues of canon which is my concern.

4.   These include, for example, Frank Yerby's *Judas, My Brother: The Story of the Thirteenth Disciple* (1969) which tells the gospel story through the eyes of Nathan, Jesus' brother-in law and double, and brother of Judas. It comes with an explicit 'health warning' to the devout reader and includes notes on the scholarly backing for various conjectures. Judas here is a cowardly cheat. Nathan's opinion of the gospel writers is uncompromising and often expressed. A typical outburst comes after the explanation that Judas did not stay around to kiss Jesus: '…your gospel writers were lunatics, surely, men who couldn't even manage to tell convincing lies, because their addled pates held no seat of memory' (1969: 384). Yerby's own views of the evangelists as expressed in the notes section are less intemperate but hardly less scathing. Similar in conception if not in style or content is Morley Callaghan's *A Time for Judas* (1983) which purports to be the reworking of a manuscript of Philo, a Cretan scribe working for Pilate. He befriends Judas and takes down his version of the events, in which Jesus chooses him to carry out the betrayal because of his fidelity, knowing that Judas will faithfully carry out this awful act where others would flinch (1983: 115-31). At the end of the book, Philo buries his account in the hope that 'the unbearable loneliness of Judas in the minds of all men on earth' (1983: 247) will be brought to an end when it is found and read. Taylor Caldwell and Jess Stearn's *I, Judas* (1977) is the autobiographical account of a rich young Pharisee who betrays Jesus on the understanding that all charges of treason would be dropped and to force his hand. William Rayner's *The Knifeman: The Last Journal of Judas Iscariot* (1969) offers the variant of a Judas who, having betrayed Jesus in the belief that this will inaugurate the Kingdom, does not immediately kill himself but is offered a new identity by the authorities which, in his disillusionment, he accepts. They spread the rumour of his death so that he can infiltrate the new Christian Church which has grown out of the rumours of Jesus' resurrection. Judas himself meets the risen Jesus and is converted, only to be told by a group of conspirators that Jesus had unknowingly been drugged on the cross and deludedly believes himself to have been resurrected. He is now proving a potential threat to the movement that has begun to grow and Judas is commissioned to kill him. When it comes to

These are books which purport to offer transcripts of an original gospel, some explicitly claiming to be the text referred to by Irenaeus.[5] It is the existence of these works which prompted the writing of this chapter. A brief survey of three of them may give a flavour of their variety.[6]

In the Polish novelist Henryk Panas's version of *The Gospel according to Judas* (1977 [1973]), a well-nigh centenarian Judas looks back and recounts with a dry, intelligent, sometimes pedantic, cynicism his version of the gospel events to an interested inquirer cast rather in the mould of Luke's Theophilus. Judas, and to that extent the author, shows a wide knowledge of contemporary Greek philosophy and of the various cults active at the time and is an educated foil to the intuitive and unlettered Jesus. Panas draws heavily on the Dead Sea Scrolls and uses the expectation there of two messianic figures, one priestly and one kingly, in his exploration of a pact between Jesus and Judas based round their common understanding of Isaianic prophecies. Judas, as a descendent of the High Priest Onias III, comes to understand himself to be the priestly messiah whereas Jesus is to take the role of the kingly messiah, the suffering servant destined to die, though the elderly Judas can only bewail his own youthful suggestibility. Panas manages to side-step the crucifixion by having Jesus disappear during a general riot in the temple. Judas offers several possibilities for his subsequent fate, but leaves the question unresolved. The book is a meditation on the human capacity for self-deception, something Judas acknowledges in his own history.

By contrast, the Irish writer Michael Dickinson's *The Lost Testament of Judas Iscariot* (1984) purports to be the text of an *apologia* addressed

---

the point, however, Judas kills his accomplice and allows Jesus to go unharmed, but is himself murdered by the agents of the Church.

5.   In this connection, see the intriguing discussion in Theodore Ziolkowski's *Fictional Transfigurations of Jesus* (1972) of the novelist Gerhardt Hauptmann's plans in the 1890s to write an *Evangelium Judae* in the light of his New Testament teacher's suggestion that the gospels give no evidence that Judas was an evil man (p. 107). Ziolkowski uses the term *evangelium judae* to designate a subset of what he calls 'fifth gospels' in Chapter 7 of his book (pp. 225-69), but in his usage it describes a group of novels where the narrator sees himself as a betrayer. His 'fifth gospels' are explicitly *not* purported reproductions of ancient gospel forms but tellings of a recognizable parody of the gospel story in modern terms.

6.   In addition to the three examples discussed in the text, G. Page's *Diary of Judas Iscariot* (1912) provides a rather homely and homiletic reading of the story. Other titles of which I am aware include M. Savelle's *The Gospel of Judas Iscariot* (1967); A.D. Baldwin's *The Gospel of Judas Iscariot* (1902); C. Schafer's *The Sanhedrin Papers Including the Gospel of Judas* (1973).

by Judas to Peter. Dickinson accounts for the betrayal in an interesting conflation of several familiar moves. Jesus himself asks Judas to hand him over, confident that he will be released when Pilate invites the people to nominate a prisoner, and Judas consents to undertake this task despite the public revilement to which he will be subject. However, when he meets Jesus and his followers in the garden, he gives the pre-arranged sign of the kiss not to Jesus but to his disciple Darius. This Darius is the rich young man whom Jesus sent away to sell all he possessed.

In Dickinson's version, Darius actually fulfils this command and then returns to become Jesus' follower. He also happens to bear a striking physical resemblance to Jesus and it is his suggestion that Judas should perform the switch. Darius is arrested and crucified. Judas, who had already arranged Lazarus's resurrection by the use of a drug, talks Jesus into taking advantage of the situation to stage his own resurrection. Jesus, while he consents, and insists that Judas make the marks of the nails in his hands, refuses to forgive Judas for his betrayal which consisted in *not* betraying him to the authorities. The last words of the book are scribbled by Judas as he waits inside the now empty tomb of Lazarus for Peter to come and read the confession, only to find that someone — Peter himself? — has rolled the stone back over the tomb mouth to seal him in.

Ernest Sutherland Bates's *The Gospel of Judas* (1929[7]) is particularly interesting. Bates is perhaps best known today as the editor of *The Bible Designed to be Read as Living Literature* (1936). He was both a biblical scholar and a professor of English and draws on these two areas of expertise to produce a gospel which, apart from a few rather well-turned pieces of irony, reads more convincingly as a text produced by a first-century Jew than most of its rivals in the genre. His Judas is an Essene who turns against Jehovah and the first part of the book consists of a counter-reading of the Hebrew Scriptures in which Satan explains Jehovah's origins as the most evil of the gods which men have created. Judas is drawn to Jesus' radical new message of universal wisdom, but in the desert Jehovah induces Jesus to preach weakness and spiritlessness despite Judas and Satan's best efforts. Judas plots to betray Jesus in order to make him realize that Jehovah will not lift a finger to save him and indeed tells Jesus that this is

---

7.   The book was first published in the United States in 1928 as *The Friend of Jesus* (New York: Simon & Schuster) but appeared a year later in England under Bates's original title. The implications of this apparent discomfort over the title in the United States are intriguing.

his intention. Jesus consents to Judas's plan in full confidence of Jehovah's loyalty. Judas has arranged with the priests that he can buy Jesus back for the same thirty pieces that he has been given to betray him but is betrayed in turn by the priests who have bribed the crowd to demand Jesus' crucifixion. At the end of the novel, Judas dies resignedly knowing that his death is no more or less meaningless than Jesus'.

What these very different texts share is a reading of Judas as at least as much the betrayed as the betrayer. He is betrayed by a Jesus who does not conform to his expectations and betrayed by the authorities who use him to further their own devious assault on Jesus. These betrayals are compounded by the malice or ignorance of the canonical gospel writers who misrepresent Judas's motives and actions in the interests of their particular theology. The gospel writers become villains of the piece, confirmed in their partisan reading by the verdict of the Church. Such readings appeal to, and feed on, the modern public appetite for rumours of conspiracy particularly in ecclesiastical circles. The scope of this can be seen in the publicity given to the accusations of concealment and dissembling that have grown up around the genuine discoveries of Dead Sea Scrolls and the Nag Hammadi documents. The present-day Church authorities are seen as allied with their predecessors, such as Irenaeus, in the preservation of an ideological structure by the suppression of truth.

This conspiracy theory itself provides material for novels, some directly engaged with the *Gospel of Judas*. Daniel Easterman's *The Judas Testament* (1994), Peter Van Greenaway's *Judas!* (1972)[8] and Cecil Lewis's *The Gospel according to Judas* (1989)[9] are all heady concoctions

8. Van Greenaway's novel contains extracts of the rediscovered gospel in which it appears that it was in fact Peter who alerted the authorities, driving Jesus to his death to fulfil the messianic prophecies, a conceit played out in the machinations of the Pope as Peter's successor to suppress the truth (1972: 72-80).

9. Lewis includes a translation of a supposed fragmentary gospel which seems to show that Judas agreed to take the 30 pieces of silver in order to learn of the priestly plot against Jesus. On the night of Gethsemane he tried to decoy the troops away from the garden until he gave Jesus away under torture, but was embraced by Jesus who knew this moment was foreordained. This is allied to the rather more unusual idea that an actual sharing of portions of Jesus' body took place at the Last Supper as the necessary preparation for the disciples to bring about the miracle of the resurrection. This version of the story is given in the context of the wider narrative of the journalist Jude Heddon who becomes involved in the discovery. At the beginning of the book he is found hanged, and we learn from his diaries that he has committed suicide, having succumbed to the temptation to sell the manuscript to the agents of the Church, thus betraying the true story once again (1989: 66-74).

of Vatican conspiracy, archaeological adventure and international crime built round the rediscovery of the manuscript of Judas's gospel and the reaction of the Church and the international criminal fraternity to this potential bombshell. These have been more recently joined by Simon Mawer's *The Gospel of Judas* (2005) where the life of the biblical expert and Catholic priest who is entrusted with deciphering the text mirrors the experience of betrayal, both in his illicit love affair in Fascist Italy and in his responsibility for the text.

In such books, the declaration and defence of a closed New Testament canon is often seen as the exercise of arbitrary power in defence of a self-regarding institution. Irenaeus could be arraigned as a prime instigator of this move. An express purpose in his writing *Against the Heretics* was to set bounds to the proliferation of gospels and speculative systems. The fact that his own writings survived while the Gnostic gospels were suppressed and lost is testimony to the power of the canon. He is one of the first to argue that four and only four gospels are to be accepted as authoritative. The defence he adduces for this conclusion is that there are only four zones of the world, four principal winds and four faces to the cherubim described in Revelations ch. 4. The causal link here is unclear to say the least, and the suspicion that similar justifications could be found for any chosen number must be strong.

For those who are irked by this seeming arbitrariness of the canon of scripture, Irenaeus's arguments seem all too typical. The case for what will count as valid evidence is decided before the trial, leaving the accused deprived of any possibility of defending himself. Judas's gospel is a victim of the process of canonization which enshrines those texts which cast him as the betrayer. Ironically, it is only through Irenaeus's attempt to discredit the *Gospel of Judas* that its existence is known to us. It is ousted just as Judas himself was expelled from the company of the disciples. Why was Judas marked out as the one who would have to bear this burden of guilt in the outworking of the drama of redemption? Is human destiny dependent on something as arbitrary as the choice of four rather than three or five for the number of gospels?

This question is behind the developing interest in the character of Judas and his rehabilitation in nineteenth- and twentieth-century literature. As Judas himself remarks in the Irish poet Brendan Keneally's prize-winning book-length poem *The Book of Judas*, 'All kinds of scribblers find me an absorbing theme' (1991: 372). In his major study of this resurgence, Jean Paillard (1995) traces it back to Klopstock's *Messias*. Thereafter, he explains, Judas's cause was taken up by De Quincey and D.F. Strauss and the radicals of the nineteenth century enlisted him as a fellow revolutionary. Later he became a Promethean hero in Nietzschean circles.

This interest in Judas, so Jean-Pierre Jossua (1995) contends in his review of Paillard's work, began before the World War II and continued after it, fuelled by a new empathy in European literature with the situation of Palestine as an occupied territory at the time of the gospel. This went along with a renewed sense of how the awful dilemmas of war lead people to agonizing choices or to discover that their actions are overtaken by the cruelty of events. The testimony of Dietrich Bonhoeffer in Nazi Germany bears this out: 'There is hardly one of us who has not known what it is to be betrayed. The figure of Judas, which we used to find so difficult to understand, is now fairly familiar to us' (1971: 11).

In the light of this, Judas the betrayer is re-read as Judas the misunderstood, or Judas the one who misunderstands. Rather than the demonic figure of the gospels driven by greed and envy, the new Judas is represented either as choosing himself to bear the blame for handing over Christ in order to serve the higher good his actions may enable, or else as the victim of misunderstanding. His story becomes a tragedy in which he is cast either as a Promethean figure defying the God who dupes Jesus or else as a hapless yet conscious Kafka-esque pawn of an incomprehensible doom.

It is as the power of the Church lifts, so Paillard argues, that Judas becomes a focus for anticanonical writing. To read the gospel story from Judas's point of view is the ultimate exercise in revision of the central canonical texts of Christianity. The furthest development of this is to be found in Jorge Luis Borges's short fiction, 'Three Versions of Judas', where he outlines the fictional career of the Swedish theologian Runeberg who argues that God did not just take on flesh in the incarnation but went to the extreme of becoming 'man to the point of infamy'. He chose to play out the vilest of all human destinies, that of Judas (Borges 1998: 163-67).

As Kierkegaard wrote in his *Journals*, 'One will get a deep insight into the state of Christianity in each age by seeing how it interprets Judas' (1970: 512). Those who feel that truth has been betrayed by the impositions of the Church and its definition of the canon adopt Judas as a figurehead and fictional spokesman. This is made explicit when Pierre Bourgeade, whose own *Mémoires de Judas* offers a complex multi-layered version of the story, writes, 'Isn't Judas modern man par excellence? Responsible for murder, he retains his nostalgia for the sacred.'[10] Bourgeade here finds modern humanity in a post-Nietzschean world where God is dead because human beings have murdered him, yet where the idea of the sacred remains as an impossible memory.

There is a note here which is well caught by Peggy Rosenthal: 'At the Nietszchean proclamation that God is dead...modernism doesn't celebrate; nor does it gloat cynically over the corpse as postmodernism will do. Modernism goes wistfully to the wake' (1998: xxxvii). Judas here comes to stand proxy for the modern reader on the boundary between the 'faithful' and 'faithless' reading of the text. There is a yearning for the religious vision which the text upholds and yet an anger that somehow the modern reader feels excluded from it, cast out from the company of those who can believe because the critical integrity which constitutes the modern identity is spurned by texts and institutions which rely on revelation and authority. This is epitomized in Frank Kermode's *The Genesis of Secrecy* (1979), his thought-provoking study of the poetics of Mark's gospel. It is, among other things, a masterly lament over his sense of exclusion from the canonical texts of the New Testament. The dedication of the book 'To Those Outside' makes the point explicitly.

Such ambivalence is also revealed in the fact that, in recreating this gospel, modern writers are not simply contradicting the New Testament. On the contrary, they are following a line which begins in the New Testament itself. Kermode argues this, suggesting that the character of Judas develops by narrative necessity from a plot-line which hangs on the act of betrayal. It all stems from Paul's account of the origin of the Eucharist in which the scene is set as occurring 'on the night when he [Jesus] was betrayed' (1 Cor. 11.23) with no mention of how or through whom this betrayal occurred. A narrative gap has been opened in the story which later writers are drawn to fill.

In Kermode's words, for the later gospel writers 'Betrayal becomes Judas' (1979: 85). On his understanding, the canonical writers wove together Old Testament material to fill out a character implied or even made necessary by the act of betrayal. Once posited, that character itself generates new narrative, which in turn generates new narrative gaps. Filling these gaps in different ways because of different theological and literary purposes, the canonical gospels and Acts diverge noticeably in their characterization of Judas, inscribing in the New Testament canon itself this process of the narrative development of character. To re-write Judas's story, then, is not to impose

10. The quotation appears on the back cover of *Mémoires de Judas* (1987).

alien notions on a fixed character but is faithful to these canonical and extra-canonical trajectories. The canonical Judas is a character in formation and a reflection of an evolving set of interpretations of the theme of betrayal in the gospel story. The continuing interest Judas arouses is derived in part from his use as a way of thinking through the process of the development and determination of the canon.

Such considerations bring out the intimate link between betrayal and canon. Kermode's phrase can be reversed: for the writers under discussion 'Judas is betrayal'. Judas allows the modernist resentment of the betrayal perpetrated by the Christian tradition to be expressed, the tradition that holds out a hope epitomized in the resurrection which it either fails to deliver or for which it demands too high a price. The contemporary gospels of Judas differ in their view of Jesus' resurrection, although most account for it either as delusion or deception, often engineered by Judas. In all of them, however, Judas is the one untouched by this resurrection, the one who the canonical New Testament writers see as doomed to death and as the awful example of eternal punishment. Judas is the despairing or defiant voice of those who see the proclamation of resurrection as a deceitful ploy or a cruel taunt in the face of human mortality. Judas becomes the suppressed, oppressed voice of 'modern man' in Bourgeade's sense, the voice of sceptical bewilderment and existential crisis, of the loss of hope in meaning which is silenced in the canonical texts but which now can speak in a secularized literature. It is the inscription of death in literature and in the canon which brings him into writing.

This relates to a parallel phenomenon in the modern literary treatment of Lazarus. Almost without exception in modern reworkings of this story, the case is made that Lazarus's restoration to life was a cruelty, condemning him to all the agonies of continued existence and the unique horror of a full awareness of what his second death will entail. The link between this Lazarus material and the deathliness of literature is made explicit by Blanchot in his essay, significantly entitled 'Literature and the Right to Death' (1995 [1949]: 300-44). What literature wants, he declares, is 'Lazarus in the tomb and not Lazarus brought back to daylight, the one who already smells bad and is Evil, Lazarus lost and not Lazarus brought back to life' (1995 [1949]: 327). Judas, then, the man without hope, the man for whom redemption is excluded, epitomizes this vision even more clearly. The work of the literary canon, it would seem, is to pile stones on Lazarus's tomb, to prevent disruption of the strategies of survival which are generated by and designed to mask the inexorability of death.

In exploring this link between the notions of canon, betrayal and death further, the work of Harold Bloom is illuminating. His controversial championing of the 'Western canon', most notably in his work of that title (1994), goes along with an increasing attachment to Gnosticism. Indeed, in his *Omens of Millennium* (1996) he makes much of the very Valentinian Gnostics whose work Irenaeus preserves by condemning. Bloom writes of the liberation that comes through the understanding of one's inner nature and its profound alienation from the realm of the created and the creator God. He says explicitly that, 'If gnosis makes us free, it can only be that it teaches us a resurrection that precedes death, even as the uncanonical gospel of Philip tells us of the Christ that "he first arose and then died"' (1996: 251). Bloom refers here to Oscar Cullman's distinction between immortality and resurrection, illustrating this with the contrast between Socratic and Christian views of death. Where Socrates hails death as a friend, secure in the knowledge of his soul's immortality, for Christ it is the last enemy. Christianity's vision of resurrection gains its force from its insistence on the need to undergo the real extinction of death. Resurrection is not survival.

For Bloom, the canon is precisely an 'instrument of survival', a phrase he quotes from Kermode. According to Bloom:

> A poem, novel or play acquires all of humanity's disorders, including the fear of mortality, which in the art of literature is transmuted in the quest to be canonical, to join communal or societal memory…the rhetoric of immortality is also a psychology of survival and a cosmology… All the Western Canon can bring one is the proper use of one's own solitude, that solitude whose final form is one's own confrontation with one's own mortality. (1994: 30)

In this view of the canon he is countered directly by Cynthia Ozick in her striking essay entitled 'Literature as Idol: Harold Bloom' (Ozick 1996: 137-59). She argues that Bloom's Gnosticism is idolatrous and in that sense anti-Jewish insofar as she defines Judaism negatively as the repudiation of idols, the legacy of Abraham in contrast to his idol-making father Terach. Ozick speaks for the voice of normative Judaism, which, she claims, eschews the modernist view and Bloom's agon of the belated. 'In Jewish thought there are no latecomers', she says (1996: 154); all generations stood together at Sinai and the Jewish liturgical experience is one of identity affirmed, not of identity wrested from a precursor. This is, she claims, the essence of the Second Commandment.

Yet the more true Ozick's assertion is for Judaism, the more belatedness becomes the Gentile's dilemma when confronted with Judaism. Western Christian culture is rooted in this sense of belatedness; its agonistic and often appalling relations to Judaism can well be described in terms of the revisionary ratios Bloom expounds in *The Anxiety of Influence* (1973). This reaction is what is epitomized in the figure of Judas through whom Western culture has worked out its anxiety over mortality, election and rejection. George Steiner in his typically baroque but pregnant essay 'The Two Suppers' (1996: 390-419), where he compares Plato's *Symposium* with John's account of the Last Supper, comments on the final phrase from the verse in the fourth gospel that ends the account of Judas going out on his fatal errand: 'And it was night' (Jn 13.30). 'Judas', Steiner writes, 'goes into a never-ending night of collective guilt. It is sober truth to say that his exit is the door to the Shoah… That utter darkness, that night within night, into which Judas is dispatched and commanded to perform "quickly", is already that of the death-ovens. Who, precisely, has betrayed whom?' (1996: 417). Hyam Maccoby has written passionately of the dark antisemitic shadow that the story of the traitor Judas, the archetypal Jew, has cast over Western culture in his *Judas Iscariot and the Myth of Jewish Evil* (1991). In his canonical manifestations, Judas the Jew, Judas who inscribes death, epitomizes the mystery of election and in particular its dark side of rejection. The responsibility for murder alluded to in Bourgeade's description of humanity today takes on an ominous concreteness in the conscience of the post-holocaust Gentile mind.

The irony is that when Gnosticism turns to Judas to repudiate election in the name of freedom and human dignity, it enshrines Judas, the rejected Jew, as the great opponent, not of Christ, but of Yahweh, the God of the Jews. Contemporary 'gospels of Judas' are a particularly pointed example of the use of biblical stories and the gospel characters in modern literature to rewrite resurrection as 'apophrades', to use the name which Bloom gives to the ultimate achievement of the strong writer. Bloom defines it as that power of revision whereby the successor can seem to be 'imitated by their ancestors'. It is, so he puts it,

> the triumph of having so stationed the precursor in one's own work that particular passages in his work seem not to be presages of one's own advent, but rather to be indebted to one's own achievement, and even (necessarily) to be lessened by one's greater splendor. The mighty dead return, but they return in our colors, and speaking in our voices, at least in part, at least in moments, moments that testify to our persistence, and not to their own. (1973: 141)

The gospels of Judas seek to allow us to have Christ return on our terms, and Judas, 'modern man par excellence', to have the final say. But this falls to nought in a cataclysmic sense if it turns out that what we display as the painted corpses of the carefully reanimated dead are in fact very much alive, and that by invoking them, we bind, or free, ourselves to operate on their terms.

As readers of any narrative, we have to acknowledge that we stand outside the story, unable to affect its unfolding, excluded both from the part of the hero and the role of villain. Here again, the arbitrariness of election conflicts with the Gnostic vision. In the light of this, the remaking of the tale becomes an assertion of freedom, or at least the conscious defiance of arbitrary exclusion despite the absence of hope that it can be rescinded, or else of an affirmation that the exclusion has no force because there is no real boundary to the tale.

There is a resentment here characteristic of neo-Gnosticism in Bloom's sense.[11] The neo-Gnostic vision is a repudiation of election and the sense of arbitrary exclusion of the belated. It finds its apotheosis in the resentment of the unchosen Gentile against the inexplicably chosen Jew. Gnosticism puts its stake on knowledge, which in principle is available to all. However, the consequence of this is not equality but elitism. Election and elitism are two categories often conflated but which are actually tangential to one another. It is that

---

11. The use here of the term 'resentment' recalls Nietzsche's account of *ressentiment* in *On the Genealogy of Morality*. In that text Nietzsche notoriously denounces the New Testament as the epitome of the vengeful, self-lacerating literature of the weak and the product of the *ressentiment* that constructs a general morality out of their petty injuries (see Nietzsche 1994: 201). In *Nietzsche's Case: Philosophy as/and Literature* (1993), Benth Magnus, Stanley Stewart and Jean-Pierre Mileur relate this concept to Susan Sontag's essay 'Against Interpretation'. They suggest that the limiting authoritative claim of interpretation, in the sense Sontag denounces, is the 'revenge of the reader' against a strong text (1993: 201). The New Testament, in literary terms, could be read as a revenge against the power of the Old Testament. In this sense, what is at stake in the present discussion is the strength of the canonical text. Which reading of Judas, the canonical one, or the Gnostic one, is the stronger reading, and which is the reading of resentment? One could construct an account (perhaps Kierkegaard provides material for one in *Sickness unto Death*) where the Nietzschean *Übermensch*, as an example of what Kierkegaard calls 'the despair that in despairs wills to be itself', is the one steeped in *ressentiment*, resentful of the spiritual strength of the saint and therefore decrying as weakness what he desires but cannot attain. In this present chapter, however, resentment is not simply a reaction against strength, but a reaction against betrayal. It does not arise simply from the brute facts of inequity and impotence, but from a sense of exclusion from a promised possibility of equality of power.

confusion which, far from solving the problem of election, actually builds resentment. Election becomes misconstrued by both the elect and the rejected as the possession of a secret, of a jealously guarded key. What more sure-fire source of resentment could there be? Bloom's *Western Canon* is at least as much a symptom of resentment as are any of the schools whom he berates in his own work. As with the novelists who speak for Judas, for Bloom the gospel writers become the great betrayers, the suppressers of the truth of Judas, which is ultimately the truth of death.

Yet Kermode's own analysis of the generation of character from act shows the limitations of this Gnostic approach. Any story carries its own life. Its characters are not consulted as to whether or not they wish to make a free decision to be included; they have no existence as characters outside the story but are generated by it. There is no 'strategy of survival' here, no gnosis which can give an infallible key to enable a character to join the story, and that in itself sets at defiance our instincts. Like children not picked for a team, readers who choose to do so may smoulder with resentment for those who are chosen or else declare that the game itself is meaningless.

The good news of the gospel according to Judas is that resurrection precedes death—but this gives death the last word. Literature then comes to being in the space between enlightenment and annihilation. The good news of canonical Christianity, however, is the prospect of death, a Jewish death what is more, as the final answer to that which cannot be evaded or postponed. A Christian literature writes out of death with hope in the ungraspable prospect of eternity.

Divine Spirit,

Make me attentive to the lap of the waves,
Make me attentive to the movements of the sky,
Make me attentive to the grasses that grow,
Make me attentive to the soul's every sigh.

Make me aware of the landscape that passes,
Make me aware of new scenes coming in,
Make me aware of each precious heartbeat,
Make me aware of the deep world within.

Make me alive to the eternal moment,
Make me alive to your Spirit Wind

7

READING LAMENTATIONS

Reading the book of Lamentations is an uncomfortable experience. Consider the following quotation from a modern Jewish woman writer as she wrestles with the experience of sitting through the reading of Lamentations in synagogue on the Ninth of Av:

> Whatever the Babylonians did to turn Jerusalem the city to rubble, it is the Jewish poet, I can't help feeling, who rips the bride Jerusalem's jeweled veil from her forehead, stripping her embroidered robes to flash us a glimpse of her genitals: 'ervatah' translated by the squeamish or modest translator as her nakedness. (Seidman 1994: 282)

Naomi Seidman's discomfort here leads her to an accusation which is at first startling but on reflection irrefutable. Whatever historical events underlie the trauma of destruction which give rise to the book of Lamentations, it is the poet of Lamentations who has chosen to centre the book round this strange, abhorrent metaphor of Zion as the raped woman, or, even more loadedly, the raped mother.[1] The text both bewails and yet dwells on the violation of the inner sanctuary, the most secret places, paradoxically exposing them to view in the ostensible act of expressing outrage. In this chapter, I shall examine the claim that this ambivalence between compassion for

---

1. For a powerful exploration of this metaphor and the complicity of male commentators with its rhetorical thrust, see Deryn Guest (1999). Her paper is grounded in the work of those feminist critics who have exposed the 'porno-prophetic' aspect of this text and others. My interest is to examine—not to exonerate—the sources of this set of metaphors in the reaction to trauma. In this regard, I treat the book as a unity, and refer here to the poet or writer of Lamentations as a shorthand for what may be a composite figure. Opinions on the origin of the various elements that make up the book and the history of its composition are varied, but at some point it reached its present canonical form and my concerns are with the internal dynamics and effects of this text. The latter part of this chapter raises I hope interesting questions over the wider topic of authorship and responsibility

Zion as a victim and yet justification of the punishment for her las-
civiousness — the same ambivalence as runs through Hosea, or the
story of the Levite's concubine in Judges 19 — is best explained if the
text is read as a symptom of melancholia and so of an ambivalence
which turns the anger of the survivor against the dead victim. The
implications of this for the responsibility of the author and indeed the
readers of the book can then be explored.

Melancholia is classically distinguished from mourning by Freud
(1991). As he uses the terms, mourning is the healthier process in that
it leads to an ending, whereas melancholia unhealthily persists,
leaving the melancholic trapped in an unresolved experience of abandonment which becomes turned in upon the self. Tod Linafelt,
however, in his reading of Lamentations (2000) makes an unorthodox
case for the benefits of melancholia rather than mourning.[2] Linafelt
contends that it is Freud's stern materialism which makes him insist
that what he calls 'reality' demands the acceptance that all 'libidinal
cathexis' — sometimes known as love — is withdrawn from the dead or
lost object. Linafelt argues that the unending nature of melancholia
holds out at least a species of hope for restoration of the beloved.

We could bolster Linafelt's argument by pointing out that on
Freud's own definition the very nature of Lamentations as a *text*
means that it inevitably represents only melancholia, not mourning.
Fixed in its written form, it endlessly repeats the same words to its
readers, frozen in the posture of abandonment. As text, it cannot
move to a point of new attachment. For mourning to reach its end, it
must move beyond the text. Linafelt himself traces the movement of
the Targumim on Lamentations and the liturgy of Tisha b'Av
towards a sense of the renewed relationship with God. These supple-
mentary texts allow a rhetoric and an ideology of survival both for
the community and the text.[3]

There is a dark edge to such strategies, however. A further insight
into the implications of what it means to see Lamentations as a text of
melancholia is given by Freud's later development of the idea in 'The
Ego and the Id' (1991) that melancholia can be represented as a revolt
against the loved one which becomes an ambivalence turned on the
self. Bereavement almost invariable evokes anger, but if I am angry at
the beloved who died, what a despicable person I am. In Lamentations, perhaps we see this in the self-chastisements of Zion. Self-

---

2.   This chapter owes a great deal to Tod Linafelt's generosity in sharing his
work in progress and to his readiness to enter into further discussion.
3.   See here Linafelt 1995.

reproach, however, is covert reproach of the other. The death is the cause of my anger and therefore it is the dead beloved who has reduced me to this state of self-abnegation.

This further analysis of melancholy may help to shed light on the particularly difficult use of maternal metaphors in the book of Lamentations. In 'The Ego and the Id' Freud interprets melancholia as evidence of the grip of the superego, which he describes as in this case a pure culture of the death instinct, on the unresisting ego. The superego, however, is also related profoundly to the internalized voice of the parent. This parental dimension is given a further refine-ment by Lawrence Rickels in his *Aberrations of Mourning* (1988). He draws on the work of the psychoanalyst Karl Abraham who claimed that a characteristic of melancholia is that it is the mother, not the father, who is invariably the prime site of identification and is the focus of what he calls the 'ambivalent cannibalistic impulse' which the melancholic gives way to.

The mother is thus the focus both of desire and frustration. More cryptically, Rickel also represents the mother as serving the interests of the dead by entrusting her mourning for a dead child to its sur-viving sibling. He speaks of the grieving mother as depositing the unmourned corpse of one of her children in the body of another little one who survives. The surviving child becomes, willy-nilly, the source of nourishment and life for the dead child, again a source of resentment and an odd sort of cannibalism — the dead child feeds off the living, but is also absorbed into the body of the living.

Bizarre as some of these claims may seem, there are intriguing fea-tures of the biblical treatment of these connections between food, death and womanhood which seem to bear them out, and which may be illumined by them. Alice Bach's chapter on 'Wine, Women and Death' in her *Women, Seduction and Betrayal in Biblical Narrative* (1997: 166-210) brings some of these points to the fore. She reminds us that the fall itself is a story of feeding, and motives of food and eating run through chs. 2 and 3 of Genesis. God's first prohibition is against eating, because wrong eating will cause death. Eve, at the serpent's instigation, looks at the fruit that is forbidden and adds a fatal word to God's own assessment of it. As part of creation, so Genesis 1 has told us, God has pronounced the tree as much as anything else 'good'. Eve now adjudges it 'good for food', following on perhaps from the slightly ambiguous implication of Gen. 2.9 where God makes every tree grow that is 'good for food'. Are the trees of life and the tree of the knowledge of good and evil additional to this list included or not? Either reading is supported by the syntax. As Bach points out, it is the woman who makes this judgment, and the man who seems to accept her in the role of the provider of food. That his punishment is related to food is thus fitting. The man, having eaten against God's will, will subsequently have to toil against a hostile environment to gain his food. The serpent, too, is condemned to eat dust.

The woman, however, is not cursed in relation to eating but with pains in childbirth. It is her crucial function of motherhood which is rendered a source of anguish and the target of divine wrath. This shadow over motherhood may lie behind the otherwise puzzling fact that in the patriarchal narratives, fertility itself often comes with penalties attached. It is said specifically of Leah that the Lord opened her womb 'because she was not loved' (Gen. 29.31). Hannah, whom Elkanah loved, bears no children, unlike her rival Peninnah (1 Sam. 1.2). As we have seen, Eve 'the mother of all living' is cursed by the pain of childbirth, and this is a theme repeated in subsequent narratives: the wife of Phinehas who dies in childbirth, calling her child Ichabod, 'no glory (1 Sam. 4.21); Rachel dying in childbirth calling the child Ben-oni, 'son of my sorrow' (Gen. 35.18); Rebekah crying out to know why she lives in the throes of the struggle between the children in her womb (Gen. 25.22).

Other biblical women besides Eve also bring death through food. Jael's offer of milk is implicated in the death of Sisera (Judg. 4), a story whose resonances with child-birth and nursing have been explored by several commentators, as is detailed by Exum (1995: 72-73). Rebekah's goat stew deceives Isaac into giving away his blessing, endangering both the firstborn's rights and exposing the vulnerability of authoritative male language to the wiles of women. Women bearing food can be a cause of temptation and danger. Tragic Tamar's gift of heart-cakes is an added incitement to the illicit desires of Amnon, which issue not just in his death but in the rebellion of Absalom.

Such a concern with the danger surrounding food is not an incidental feature of the biblical texts. The problems associated with distinguishing between forbidden and permitted food permeate the Mosaic legislation. Far from being an esoteric or trivial concern, they are brought to the heart of the issue of divine pleasure and divine disfavour. In this legislation, these categories are put in juxtaposition with an equally powerful concern with cleanness and uncleanness in sexual categories which again centres on women, on women's sexuality and the processes of procreation and childbirth.

This link itself is highly significant. Eating, sex, childbirth and nursing are brought together because each involves the breaching of the fundamental distinction between the exterior and the interior of the body. Levitical legislation has a reverence and horror for blood, and for its life-giving essence, semen. Much legislation surrounds the crisis which arises from the leaking of these life-giving fluids from their safe containment inside the body. Blood and semen out of the body are powerful sources of uncleanness. Equally, ingesting the blood of any animal is taboo. Conception, without which the whole edifice of social life collapses, astonishingly involves the emission of the life-giving semen into the body of the woman. This is followed by birth, the paradox of a new body moving from the forbidden interior of the woman out into the world, accompanied by blood and fluid. Suckling involves the transfer of fluid from the mother to the interior of the infant—the acceptable face of cannibalism. Hence motherhood itself carries with it uncleanness because it involves the breaching of boundaries.

A tangential but I think relevant text here is the strange but powerful prohibition in Exod. 23.19 against seething a kid in its mother's milk. Puzzling in itself, it has as is well known what may seem a disproportionate afterlife in Rabbinic legislation. Might this indicate that it articulates a deep anxiety which later generations constantly return to in an unceasing, because futile, effort to resolve its ambiguities? The image of the offspring cooked in the mother's nourishing fluid—its food become its death—epitomizes the breach of boundaries between the edible and the inedible, the maternal and the infantile, inside and outside the body and evokes a revulsion which must be guarded against in the elaborate provisions of the later laws separating milk and meat.

This attitude of revulsion directed at such breaches of the division between clean and unclean objects and acts is what Julia Kristeva terms 'abjection'. The particular characteristic of abjection, according to Kristeva, is that it is 'above all a revolt against an external menace from which one wants to free oneself, but of which one has the impression that it may menace us from the inside' (Guberman 1996: 118). The kid seethed in its mother milk is a paradigmatic case. It is assailed externally by the very fluid that internally forms its substance.

Such concern for the legislation of cleanness and uncleanness can, however, be read in reverse. In her *Powers of Horror* (1982), Kristeva explicitly traces the fundamental divisions represented by the categories of the clean and unclean in Levitical legislation to the need to distance oneself from the mother. She writes, 'The terms, impurity and defilement, that Leviticus heretofore had tied to food that did not conform to the taxonomy of sacred Law, are now attributed to the mother and to women in general' (1982: 100). For Kristeva, abjection is 'rooted in the combat that every human being carries on with the mother' (Guberman 1996: 118). This association is also explored by Dorothy Dinnerstein (1987) who sees a fundamental hostility to woman as mother stemming from the ambivalence over her role as first source of nourishment. The child feeds on the mother's body, but this means that the withdrawal of that nourishment, whether through the mother's failure to produce milk, or in the trauma of weaning, makes the mother the target for the first sense of rage and betrayal.

Does this give an insight as to why the writer of Lamentations not only harps on the pains of the mother and her degradation, but also lays before us the picture of the mother who not only fails to give suck but in the end devours her children? Such cannibal mothers appear specifically in Lam. 2.20 and 4.10 but this is again not an isolated occurrence. It is a motif which throughout the Hebrew Bible reappears to trouble the concept of motherhood. The ultimate sign of degradation and collapse for the culture of Israel, the possibility of mothers devouring their children is hinted at in Lev. 26.29 and made explicit as a curse in Deut. 28.53-57. Its fulfilment is predicted in Jer. 19.9 and also in Ezek. 5.10 and Zech. 11.9. 2 Kings 6.24-32 is the *locus classicus* where in a grim parody of Solomon's judgment, the king in Samaria is called on to judge between two women who have agreed to eat their sons when one reneges on her promise. The woman who eats her child strikes at the fundamental anxiety of paternity and patriarchy. If the woman to whom a man has entrusted his seed devours his children, what hope of survival has he?[4]

These considerations may help to explain some peculiar features of the text of Lamentations. One instance is the transition from a female to a male voice in Lamentations 3. Alan Mintz reads this as an acknowledgment that the female voice can achieve 'expressivity but not reflection' (1984: 32) within the code of the book. This may be an aspect of the matter, but there may also be here a transition between the voices of mother and son. The text cries out with the voice of the abandoned and resentful child, clinging to the constancy of the

---

4.   For an interesting reading of this episode in terms of its social critique, see Lasine 1991. The woman's perspective is opened up by Laurel Lanner (1999).

wrathful father, in its despair at and repudiation of the powerless and abandoning mother. The male survivor reassures himself of the continuing graciousness of God, but the paradox is that that constancy is to be proved by further destruction. The sure thing about God is that Edom too will feel his wrath and will know the misery that has been inflicted on Zion. Punishment is at least not abandonment. The sign of continuity, the thread of survival in the book is God's constancy in anger.

But again, whose existence is most threatened in Lamentations; whose survival is most in question? Zion survives, albeit as a raped and abandoned woman; the male voice of ch. 3 survives, imprisoned and abandoned though he is; the people of ch. 4 survive though they find the condition intolerable. Surely what is most at stake is whether God will survive, whether the people will follow their natural inclination to abandon the instrument of their torture. God's survival is asserted, but what is asserted is often what is most questionable. Zion's tormentor and the tormentor of the witness in ch. 3 is asserted as the principle of continuity, but it is a continuity of silence.

The final chapter of the book reiterates the pain and the burden, not of those who died, but of those who survived. They must now pay for the nourishment that they once received freely and carry the memory and the guilt of their forebears. In this chapter, too, we have a breakdown of the formal pattern of the book which with its pattern of chapters structured by acrostics is one of the most tightly constructed in the Bible. This formal restraint may be evidence of a weary rote of tired phrases, but it may also be the application of steel bands of formalism to uncontainable emotion.

The fact that it is the alphabet which gives the structure to the first four chapters of the book may also be suggestive. The order of the alphabet is both completely arbitrary and completely implacable. It may bespeak the iron necessity of a fate which unfolds as inevitably, as banally and unstoppably, as the recital of the alphabet, or it may be more analogous to the heroic imposition of structure by the prisoner in solitary confinement who forces himself to mark off rigorously the endless passing of indistinguishable days in order to preserve order, rationality and sanity. In this regard, Leonard Shlain's speculative and impressionistic account of the impact of the alphabet on the suppression of goddess worship in ancient Israel might find some warrant (Shlain 1998). His thesis is that the linear rationality of alphabetic is intimately tied to the rise of monotheism and to the repudiation of images. It is also coupled to the repression in ancient

Israel of women as cultic leaders.[5] It is at least suggestive that the
repudiation of Zion is contained in so explicitly alphabetic a text, and
that this structure is at its tightest in the third chapter which most
explicitly speaks in a male voice and looks to the male God.

In the light of these ambivalences, is the breakdown of this alphabetic acrostic in the final chapter of Lamentations a sign of collapse or
a liberation from the chains of capricious discipline? Either reading is
possible, it would seem. Yet the ghost of a structure remains in the
fact that this chapter also consists of twenty-two verses, though in no
discernible order. The reading of this as a final darkly satirical comment on the artificiality of all order and structure is more consonant
with the message of the final chapter. In it, the survivors bewail not
death but the conditions of their continued life. An odd petulance
sounds through the catalogue of their griefs, an ambivalence that
characterizes the survivor. For them, survival is the problem, not the
solution. The burden of survival is placed on them by the dead, and
their hope is the destructive power of God.

This is no celebration of the power of memory to overcome
disaster, but a protest at the burden of memory, the anger of the
surviving child who feels that his existence is only justified as a living
mausoleum, an epitaph to the now unburdened dead. In her study of
stories of trauma, Cathy Caruth points to what she characterizes as
the urgent question underlying all such narratives: 'Is the trauma the
encounter with death, or the ongoing experience of having survived
it?' She goes on to posit an oscillation in any attempt to relate the
story of a traumatic event between the 'crisis of death' and the cor-
relative 'crisis of life' or 'between the story of the unbearable nature
of an event and the story of the unbearable nature of its survival'
(1996: 7).

The unbearableness of surviving the destruction of Jerusalem leads
to a desire for punishment to be inflicted on those who conferred the
burden of survival. It is as if one should say, 'You deserve to die for
having inflicted on me the burden of memory and guilt I now bear
for surviving your death'. So the book would become, as Seidman
perhaps hints, the sentence of death passed on those who had
already died. The Jewish poet thus becomes the one who psychically,
if not literally, condemns the dead to their fate.

---

5. See particularly his discussion of the Hebrew tradition (1998: 72-119),
which, despite some very tendentious historical claims, raises explicitly the
question of the repudiation of female Zion (1998: 116-17), although without
mentioning Lamentations.

It is in this sense that we may approach an answer to the unsettling which Naomi Seidman raised of the responsibility of the Jewish poet for the despoliation of Jerusalem. We might almost rephrase this as the stark question, 'Did the writer of Lamentations destroy Jerusalem?' Of course not, in any direct historical sense, but the more important sense for the subsequent history of the text is not what happened, but how it was understood. The despoliation of Jerusalem is a historical fact, as well attested as any event in the ancient world. What matters however, is how it is construed. The writer of Lamentations sees it not as a military defeat, but as the rape and destruction of a city which bears the weight of the survivors' resentment of survival, a resentment, which, as we have seen, is shockingly, but not surprisingly, tied to the figure of the abandoning mother. The fate she suffers is one that she merits. In a horrid closed loop, the suffering of the child is laid at the door of the mother, and that suffering, caused by the destruction of the city, is read as the punishment *before the event* of the cause of the suffering.

The Lord's wrath, then, is not the cause of the suffering, and so resentment can be deflected from him. Rather, the city suffers the just punishment it deserves for the abandonment of its children, though that is a state brought about by the very events that befell it. Could we then go on to argue that by providing this model of survival through melancholia the poet makes it easier for the same destruction to be repeated? After all, what has been survived once may be survivable again. How far is the subsequent history of a people who survive incredibly through repeated destructions dependent on the development of a trope which can displace guilt backwards? What has the writer done in penning such a text?

An eerie light is cast on the question of the writer's responsibility by the Scottish writer Alistair Gray in his *Five Letters from an Eastern Empire* (1995). This short work very skilfully administers a series of shocks to its readers as one realizes that successive rugs, not to mention floorboards, are being stripped from under one's feet, leaving the reader teetering over an abyss, as the issue of historical responsibility for disaster is thrown open to question.

The book consists of a set of five letters and an epilogue. To fillet out its plot line is a travesty of a rich and allusive text but it is inevitable in this context. The letters are written by a young poet, named Bohu, to his parents. The setting is a mythical empire with elements of China, Japan and Egypt, not to mention Mervyn Peake's Gormenghast. The story that unfolds follows the novelty and excitement of Bohu's journey to the new capital of the empire and his induction as the imperial tragic poet. For our purposes, the first shock comes when Bohu is told that the great poem which he has looked forward to writing is to be a lament: a lament for the old capital, his beloved home town, which, so he is informed, has just been completely destroyed on the emperor's orders, together with all its inhabitants, including his parents. Bohu continues, nevertheless, to write letters to his dead parents and records the infinite but empty freedom the emperor has granted him by excusing him from all the petty restraints of the hugely elaborate court etiquette. He is free to write what he likes. In a typically bold manner, Gray supplies us with the text of Bohu's poem:

The Emperor's Injustice

Scattered buttons and silks, a broken kite in the mud,
A child's yellow clogs cracked by the horses' hooves.
A land weeps for the head city, lopped by sabre, cracked by hooves
The houses ash, the people meat for crows.

A week ago wind rustled dust in the empty market.
'Starve', said the moving dust. 'Beg. Rebel. Starve. Beg. Rebel.'
We do not do such things. We are peaceful people.
We have food for six more days, let us wait.
The emperor will accommodate us, underground.

It is sad to be unnecessary.
All the bright mothers, strong fathers, raffish aunts,
Lost sisters and brothers, all the rude servants
Are honoured guests of the emperor, underground. (1995: 49)

Motifs the reader has gleaned from Bohu's reminiscences of his childhood are woven into a lament where steely discipline turns mute acquiescence into an excoriating judgment on arbitrary tyranny.

Bohu's poem becomes an epitaph. In accordance with the custom of the empire, it will be written over his tomb, the tomb, where we learn, he has written it, sealed in with his servants as they all await death by asphyxiating herbs. It will literally be his epitaph, as well as that of his city, his parents and his lost childhood. He dies with no illusions that it will be read, however. Some gardener will paint it out, he feels, as its effect would too clearly be to provoke the people to rise against the emperor. He is content to have written the poem it was his destiny to write.

The sting in the tale comes with the appendix to the book, a short posthumous review of the poem by a figure Gray calls 'The Headmaster of Modern and Classical Literature', the chief censor and propagandist of the empire. He reports that the poem will serve the purposes of the empire perfectly, with just the deletion of one syllable from the title; the 'in-' from 'injustice'. As 'The *Justice* of the Emperor', it is to be distributed throughout the land and on that very day, the army will be ordered to destroy the old capital. 'Fieldmarshal Ko should take especial care', the report ends, 'that the poet's parents do not escape the general massacre, as a rumour to that effect will lessen the poignancy of the official biography which I will complete in the coming year'.

So we realize that Bohu's noble, serene and ultimately futile poem will become the instrument of the destruction it mourns. Under its revised title, it will quash the notion of rebellion as vain and shore up the power of the emperor and his circle by depicting his rule as an implacable natural force. The text will kill the parents whose memory it was designed to honour. Gray raises troubling questions about the function and consequences of the whole genre of lament and about the innocent, terrible effects of writing as it falls into the hands of those with axes of power to grind. In that sense, Bohu does posthumously become implicated in the destruction of the city which he mourns.

What, then, of the writer of Lamentations? Parallels and contrasts between Bohu's poem and the book of Lamentations crowd in upon us. In the end, Bohu's poem serves to propagate the rule of the emperor, who, we learn, is no more than a mummified puppet handed round the council of headmasters who use him as a ventriloquist's dummy. Analogously, Lamentations comes to be read as a text which ensures God's survival at the expense of Zion and her people. As is the case with the emperor's injustice, God's injustice is read as justice. Arbitrary disaster becomes punishment, inscrutable and ultimately unchallengeable.

Bohu's poem is permitted to survive as the emperor's vindication. As the protest he originally intended, it would have had no future. Linafelt (1995) argues persuasively that the book of Lamentations itself only survives into the canon because the nakedness of its appeal of the resentment, of the unanswered cry, has been softened in various ways in the subsequent tradition. At the simplest level of such rewriting, the second-last verse of the book is repeated after the final verse in liturgical reading. In another move, its desolation has been countered intertextually by referring to the comfort of Isaiah, which may indeed be directly responding to this material. Just as the one

syllable changed in the title of Bohu's poem changes its function
and assures it a new sort of survival, something similar has occurred
here. The stark implacability of the divine silence has been circum-
vented, the blow softened, the unspeakable brought into the realm of
language.

Linafelt, however, sees that this move from the starkness of Lamentation to the search for consolation ends with a renewed sense of
desolation in this century as writers affected by the Holocaust have
reclaimed the text. Where these contemporary writers differ from
their ancient counterparts is that they opt for abandonment almost as
a relief from the terrible image of a God who brings about destruction and punishment, resisting the awful picture of humanity as a
child clinging for comfort to the parent who is mercilessly beating
him. Lamentations brings us face to face with the core of human
ambivalence with its potentially hideous human and theological
consequences, an ambivalence that both reaches out and rejects, that
resents those whom it mourns, which shapes or knows a God in the
reflection of its own destructive caring by positing a human face of
God at the extreme of vulnerability.

In that sense, I argue that it is true to say that the writer of Lamentations does bring about the destruction of Zion, although whether
he can be charged with responsibility is a more complex question.
Through his work we read that destruction as the just result of the
divine wrath. It is that continuity of wrath which gives him the space
of consolation in the poem. The physical continuity of the city
becomes, at least in symbolic terms, subordinated to the continuity of
faithfulness in God. The unceasing lamentation for Jerusalem which
continues to this day is the price, and the occasion, for the continuity
of the surviving community. It is only because the destruction and
desecration of the city can be read as an inevitability and a proof of
divine faithfulness that the community can find a way of surviving
the subsequent, even more devastating desecrations under the
Romans and in subsequent generations. Whatever the intentions of
whoever was the Israelite Bohu who recorded his lament for the city,
the poet of Lamentations, the virtual author created through the
canonical text, destroys Zion so that the Lord may be seen to be faithful, and so that the community of the Father can outlast its mother's
ruin.

Read in this way, the book of Lamentations takes on what can only
be called a monstrous aspect. A similar perception leads Deryn Guest
to call for the excision of such texts as Lamentations from the

Scriptures (1999: 444-45). She softens this call by seeking to enter into dialogue with other readers who might react against her feminist critique. Taking up this challenge, I would make a plea for the text's retention on the same grounds that might lead many to exclude it.

Insofar as the Hebrew Bible is a source of revelation, it is a revelation of darkness as well as light, of the involvement of human — mostly, but not exclusively, male — fear, greed, insecurity and viciousness in all that speaks of the divine, and of the constant psychological process of the engendering of personifications on whom these emotions can be vented. The silent God of Lamentations, as much as the abused mother and the self-justifying son, are such personifications. Any attempt to come to grips with what it is to be human, and especially to be human in the face of the limit circumstances which attend the incursions of the ungovernable God with which the Hebrew Scriptures deals, must face these horrors squarely. One service among many that feminist critics have performed is to reveal the scandal of the divine, yet that scandal is a chastening reminder of the scandal of the human heart.

One writer who knew this human reality only too well is Dame Ivy Compton-Burnett, whose strange stilted novels at times echo Lamentations in their combination of formality and horror. She offers, however, a bleak but bracing insight which may serve as a postscript to this reading. Two of the characters in her novel *The Present and the Past*, Ursula and her brother Elton, are discussing the concept of disapproval. Elton avows he never feels it, concluding, '"I think people do such understandable things". "Yes", said Ursula; "I am often deeply ashamed of understanding them"' (1972b: 61). Reading Lamentations is in that sense deeply shaming and, in that very fact, potentially salutary.

8

The Rebellious Son:
Biblical Family Values

In his much-loved poem 'The Cotter's Saturday Night', Robert Burns writes of the poor but upright family which to him reveals the essence and backbone of the simple, honest peasant folk who constitute the glory of Scotland:

> The chearfu' supper done, wi' serious face
> They, round the ingle, form a circle wide;
> The sire turns o'er, wi' patriarchal grace,
> The big ha'-bible, ance his Father's pride. (Burns 1971: 119)

In this vignette, the little family has clustered reverently round to hear 'the priest-like Father read…the sacred page' (1971: 118). The scene that Burns chooses to demonstrate the unity of this ideal family is a gathering centred on reading the biblical text. 'From scenes like these', as Burns famously, or notoriously, asserts, 'old Scotia's grandeur springs' (1971: 120). It is from this archetypal moment, Burns implies, that the well-ordered world of the cotter is sustained. His own humble but honest toil, the canny housewifery of his beloved spouse and the obedience and respect for duty instilled in his children are rooted in the decent communal reading of the family Bible.

Nor should we overlook the fact that this Bible represents not just the focus of the family, but quite explicitly represents its continuity. This was the patriarch's own father's book, handed down from father to son and, although Burns does not say so, almost certainly the history of the family is inscribed within it. In careful copperplate, births, marriages and deaths within this little lineage would have been listed on the end papers of the book. It has become a record of the family's memory, a testament to genealogy. In this way, this humble family is aligned with the great dynasties of the text, the line that runs from Adam to Abraham, from Abraham to David, and from David to Christ – or at least to Joseph.

The poem also contains a somewhat arch glance towards the future of the cotter's family. The chaste but ardent passion of young Jenny who has been brought home by a young man is legitimated by the bashfulness and gravity of her swain. His reverent carriage and indeed his attendance at this family reading prove him to be of a different metal, so Burns avers, from the smooth dissembler who would ruin the maid and leave her parents distracted. The decent ordering of sexual relations that will ensure in generations to come the existence of a family worthy to receive in their turn the gift of the great Bible is thus assured. It is, Burns asserts, such families and such lives which will be as a 'wall of fire' around the nation.

What a comforting picture, what a model of stability to set before a world of marriage breakdown, divorce, child abuse, teenage anomie and sexual libertarianism — although the latter at least was perhaps more characteristic of the poet himself than this domestic idyll. And yet, one cannot help wondering what passages of the Bible were being read. For instance, was it, one wonders, the story of Lot's daughters seducing their father by getting him drunk (Gen. 19.30-38)? Or what about the story of the bold Tamar, praised in Genesis 38, who became ancestress to David by posing as a prostitute and seducing her father-in-law? How would the communal reading of such scandalous exploits accord with the world of the respectable family in the poem?

Perhaps it might be argued that such shenanigans are all that can be expected of the Old Testament, although Tamar makes her appearance in Matthew's version of Jesus' genealogy (Mt. 1.3) along with three other dubious women, Rahab, Ruth and the wife of Uriah, all of whom are associated with the defects of foreignness and extra-marital sexuality. If we do turn to the New Testament, matters hardly improve. Can we suppose that this pious father was reading Jesus' words as reported by Luke: 'If anyone comes to me and does not hate his own father and mother and wife and children and brothers and sisters...he cannot be my disciple' (Lk. 14.26)? Somehow one doubts it. But this brings us to the crucial question: What model of family is being presented in such teachings?

Of course, it could be said that to select such passages is a distortion simply to provide an easy point. The biblical tradition is, everyone knows, rooted in the family. From Adam and Eve, through the great rehearsals of genealogy, the stories of families form the bulk of its histories. 'Honour thy father and mother', instructs the fourth of the ten commandments (Exod. 20.12; Lev. 19.3; Deut. 5.16), cited approvingly in the New Testament by the writer of the letter to the

Ephesians (Eph. 6.2). What clearer endorsement of the family could we look for than that?

The biblical story begins with the creation of the human male–female couple, enjoined to be fruitful, and the recognition of Eve by Adam as his 'apt companion' is crowned by the following aetiological note: 'therefore a man leaves his father and his mother and cleaves to his wife, and they become one flesh' (Gen. 2.24). The family is established as a presupposition to the story.

Yet here already, at the founding of the first family, there is a source of contradiction: 'Honour your father and mother' — and leave them. The new family can only be formed by the breaking of the old. Notice that there is nothing said on the bond between parent and child in these texts. The first chapters of Genesis are no substitute for the likes of Dr Spock on child-rearing. Our modern and legitimate concern for the well-being of a child and the reciprocal affection of parents and children is not the focus of attention.

If we look a little deeper, indeed, we discover that, far from being celebrated by the text, the begetting and raising of children is presented to us more as a contingency plan, at times almost a necessary evil. In the face of death, which, once the fruit of the tree is eaten, both man and woman have to confront and deal with, the problem of survival becomes the text's key concern. Life now becomes an unending battle to stave off death. The family made up of man, woman and children is a structure of survival.[1]

The system of ideas which cluster around it in the Hebrew Scriptures is well expressed in the title of a paper by Herman Brichto: 'Kin, Cult, Land and Afterlife — A Biblical Complex' (1973). Brichto argues that the particular form of the family as an institution in the Hebrew traditions is characterized by the way it mediates all these aspects. So identity in the Hebrew Bible is established by lists of male ancestors, male because it was through the male seed that life was thought to be transmitted. Woman's contribution was to be the field in which the seed was planted; the necessary matrix for the continuation of life, but not its source.[2] A form of afterlife was also to be ensured by the future projection of this lineage, by supplying a line of

---

1.   This is almost explicit in the fourth commandment, which, as Eph. 6.2 reminds us, is the first commandment to be attached to a promise, a promise of long life and prosperity in the land or, in a word, of survival.

2.   For a discussion of the models of reproduction in the ancient world and their effect on the position of women and the understanding of human nature generally, see Stonehouse 1994 (in particular pp. 123-30).

legitimate male descendants who would 'remember one's name'. It is at least plausible that this concept of 'remembering the name' was for much of Israel's history linked to a cult of the ancestors where sacrifice and prayers were offered on behalf of ancestral spirits. The commandment to honour one's mother and father can be interpreted as reference to just such a cult. The duty to honour one's parents is not confined to their lifetime, and maintenance of this cult is necessary for the prosperity and survival of the community.[3]

Be that as it may, the link between the legitimate lineage and the prospect of survival or remembrance beyond death is clear. Yet this has profound consequences for the ordering of social relations. For men to ensure that their sons are their own descendants, they must put unassailable boundaries around the sexual activity of women. As the Latin legal tag has it, *mater certa est, pater incertissimus*: the mother is certain, the father is extremely uncertain. Only by draconian regulations can men allay the ever-present suspicion that their wives' children are not their own.

In this context of the necessity of maintaining the family line, it is thus possible to comprehend seemingly bizarre provisions such as the so-called 'levirate', the legislation for which is outlined in Deut. 25.5-10. A childless widow was entitled to expect to be married to her dead husband's brother in order to raise children who would keep up the remembrance of the dead man's name and maintain his legal claims to inheritance. Tamar in Genesis 38 is claiming her rights under this law and it is alluded to in the story of Ruth, where her kinsman has a prior claim on her over Boaz (Ruth 4.6). The sanction outlined in Deut. 25.9-10 against the one who fails in this duty is the fitting one that his family will be henceforth remembered as the 'house of him that had his sandal pulled off', a reference to the right of the outraged widow to pull off his sandal and spit in his face in front of the elders. By seeking to evade his responsibility to his brother's memory, the defaulter ensures that his own memory is one of disgrace.

The overriding concern to secure survival, both genetic and cultural, is made apparent. The topics of the relationship of such a model of social order to the development of patriarchy and the growth of the concepts of private property and inheritance are intriguing and highly relevant but beyond the scope of this chapter.[4] For our

3.   On this point, see Bloch-Smith 1992.
4.   The argument for a relationship between ancient Near Eastern culture and the development of patriarchal structures is set out forcibly in Gerda Lerner's *The*

purpose, the important thing to note is that such a system carries within it inevitable tensions. For women, it means that they have to surrender control of their sexuality to men. For men, it means that their hope of immortality and continuity depends on the fidelity of women. For fathers, it means that a son is both necessary for their survival, but also a constant reminder of death and a constant possible rival for the ownership and governance of the household. For a son, it means that his life and prospects depend on his father's largesse until his death. As a younger son, his prospects are blocked by both his father and his elder brothers. Ancient Israelite society, like many other societies ancient and modern, knew the necessity of finding ways of dealing with superfluous young men (in Biblical Hebrew the *ne'arim*) who drank, wenched and warred with no sense of economic responsibility because they were excluded from the property base and from the prospects of marriage within their society. We need not look far for modern parallels.

So the story of the family is bound to be one of ambivalences, of jealousies, rivalries and deaths. Cain kills his brother Abel and things proceed from there. The family becomes the arena of the breakdown of human relations precisely because it is the centre of expectations of nurture, of fulfilment, of life itself. At the core of this ambivalence is that fact that the family is designed to ensure survival not of the individual but of the line, the 'name'. It may then well happen that the family will sacrifice one of its members to the common good, or that individuals will come to feel that their own prospects of survival would be increased by the removal of rivals or the disruption of the family. The inherent instability of the family over time as one generation gives place to another also means that power inevitably shifts, alliances have to be reforged, claims have to be settled. Such negotiations are fraught with the possibility of failure.

So it is not surprising, whatever our initial expectations, to find that the Hebrew Scriptures are not only filled with tales of family conflict but that they also contain a series of counter-traditions which seek to repudiate the family, traditions in which the claims of father

Creation of Patriarchy (1986), especially Chapters 8 and 9. An intriguing discussion that develops on similar lines to the present one is to be found in D. Young's *Origins of the Sacred: The Ecstasies of Love and War* (1993: 74-112). Young gives an anthropological account of the evolution of love as a precarious mechanism for binding the male into the rearing of children. The precariousness of this may only too easily allow the eruption of anger and ultimately of murder into the family.

over son and son over father are denied or reformulated. A striking example is to be found in Ezekiel 20, one of the oddest chapters in a very puzzling book.

It contains a startling reversal of the injunction to honour one's parents. God says to his people, 'Do not walk in the statutes of your fathers; do not follow your fathers' abominations' (Ezek. 20.18). Even more shockingly, Ezekiel has God say, 'I gave them statutes that were not good and ordinances by which they could not have life' (Ezek. 20.25). Leaving aside the problems this remarkable verse may pose for our conception of God, such a command is a far cry from honouring one's parents and their traditions. This is permission to the new generation to make a new start, to forge their own traditions. Such a note of rebellion shows how near at times the Hebrew Scriptures get to advocating the overthrow of the reign of the father. The rebellion stops short, however, of open hostility.

On the other hand, the biblical reticence does not extend to the reciprocal aspect of the assault on the mutual responsibilities of the family: the possibility of filicide, of a father killing his child. That most disturbing yet influential of biblical stories, the binding of Isaac in Genesis 22, gains much of its awesome power from its exploration of the turning of a parent against a child, both in the story of the expulsion of Ishmael and the story of the sacrifice of Isaac.

The passage in Ezekiel to which we have already referred to continues with a chilling hint of something akin to this. After the Lord's amazing admission that he had given bad laws to Israel's fathers, he goes on to say, 'I have defiled them through these very gifts by making them offer by fire all their firstborn, that I might horrify them; I did it that they might know that I am the Lord' (Ezek. 20.26).

Debate has long raged over the existence of child sacrifice and the nature of the so-called 'cult of Molek' in Israel.[5] More often than not, the discussion seems to be animated by a concern to show that this practice could not have existed, rather than to investigate whether or not it did. There certainly is biblical and extra-biblical evidence to suggest that child sacrifice did occur, in the face of the obvious disapproval of the later editors of the biblical text who see this as the epitome of the corruption of the cults of Israel's neighbours. Whatever the truth of the matter, this passage in Ezekiel plainly claims not only that such a practice existed, but that it existed by Yahweh's decree.

5.   A useful survey of this debate, which itself concludes that such a cult was an accepted part of Israel's cult until the Deuteronomic reforms, is to be found in Heider 1985. See also Stavrakopoulou 2004.

Shocking as this may seem, it is not the only instance of a definite strand in the biblical traditions where parents turn against their children in contexts which are sanctioned rather than condemned by the text. It surfaces for instance, in Zechariah where the parents of a child who prophesies are enjoined to pierce him through (Zech. 13.3).

Most blatant, though, is the reference in Deut. 21.18-21. In this passage, provision is made for the parents of a 'stubborn and rebellious son', one who will not mend his ways even after chastisement, to bring their errant offspring before the elders at the gate of the city and denounce him as a glutton and a drunkard. This denunciation in itself is sufficient to require the men of the city to stone the boy to death. There is no mention of any judicial process. The death of the son is necessary to purge this evil from the midst of Israel. What a disturbing picture of the seeming destruction of the family! Parents turn on their own children and blot out their own chance of survival in the interests of the maintenance of the wider social conventions which are necessary to safeguard the survival of the people.

Not unnaturally, this passage seems to have caused considerable disquiet to later Rabbinic commentators who exercised their ingenuity to bring it into harmony with their concern to affirm family solidarity. It is discussed at length in *Tractate Sanhedrin* of both the Mishnah and Talmud.[6] The conditions which must be fulfilled before such a sentence can be passed become increasingly stringent both as to the nature of the offence and the circumstances of the parents. Indeed, the Jerusalem Talmud ultimately concludes that the law as it stands is so difficult to apply and seemingly illogical that its purpose can only be to remind us that God's laws are not predicated on human reason, while R. Simeon declares roundly in the Babylonian Talmud, '"A stubborn and rebellious son" — there never was and there never will be such'.[7] The passage exists only as an awful but ultimately unenforceable warning.

Or does it? I want to argue that the disturbing figure of the disobedient son and his wrathful parents is one which echoes through the biblical traditions. The book of Hosea, for one, takes the highest analogy and speaks of a God who is quite prepared to bring his beloved son Israel before the tribunal of history and to threaten him with utter destruction for his disobedience.[8] This is not the God who

---

6.   For a survey and commentary on this Rabbinic literature see Goldin 1952: 166-75.

7.   *Tractate Sanhedrin* 71a as translated by Danby 1919: 107.

8.   See Hos. 5.14; 13.4-16. The fact that these passages are counterbalanced by others in the book which speak of forgiveness and restoration is not strictly

is the shepherd of the much-loved Psalm 23, but a God who speaks of himself as a lion, a leopard, a she-bear without her cubs which will turn on the flock. God is revealed as the father who will, in extremis, do away with his stubborn and rebellious son.

And on the other side of the coin, what are we to make of a young man who, as we have already seen, says to his followers that unless they hate their father and mother they cannot follow him (Lk. 14.26),[9] who proclaims that he has come to set father against son, son against father, mother against daughter and so on (Lk. 12.53), and who repudiates his own relatives including his mother when they come to fetch him home with the words 'Who are my mother and brothers?', answering himself, 'Whoever does the will of God is my brother and sister and mother' (Mk 3.31-35)?[10] What could be a clearer case of the dishonouring of father and mother and of wilful disobedience?[11]

In such statements, Jesus, the unmarried, rootless teacher, is spokesman for a new world, one where the human ties of family are not the means to ensure survival but an obstacle to living the abundant life. What is promised in the Gospels is no mere continuity of the human comedy, but the utterly radical breaking down of the structures of human society and human personhood. His teaching in the New Testament is not predicated on survival but on resurrection which must call into question the nature of the family as a device for survival.

Clearly, then, it is no accident that when the Sadducees seek to entrap Jesus on the issue of resurrection, they cite the legislation on levirate marriage, that bizarre device to ensure survival (Mt. 12.18-27; Mt. 22.23-33; Lk. 20.27-38). This encounter shows starkly the incompatibility of the two world-views of survival and resurrection. The Sadducees ask Jesus to explain to whom a woman would be deemed to be married in the resurrection if she had been given as wife to

relevant to this argument. These destructive emotions and threats are not represented as idle bluster on God's part, whatever else may be said about them.

9.   See also the parallel in Mt. 10.37-38 which does not use the word 'hate' but rather speaks of the need to love Jesus more than mother and father. This is scandal enough.

10.   See also the parallels in Mt. 12.46-50 and Lk. 8.19-21.

11.   One could even argue that Luke's explicit note that Jesus was 'obedient' to his parents (Lk. 2.51) after his return from the escapade in the temple suggests that this charge of disobedience had already occurred to people. After all, he evades his parents and causes them to search anxiously for him, earning a rebuke from his mother. He then excuses himself by saying arguing that they should have know he had to be in his father's house. The ambiguity over who his father is, and therefore where he ought to be, is precisely the point.

seven brothers in succession. Matthew and Mark both record Jesus as explaining that no one marries or is given in marriage in the resurrection as they are like angels in heaven. Once the threat of death has been overcome, the need for procreation is at an end and the elaborate devices of the levirate become irrelevant. Luke, however, goes further in drawing a distinction not between the living and those in the resurrection but between the 'sons of this age' who marry and the unmarried state of those who are 'accounted worthy to attain to that age and the resurrection of the dead' (Lk. 20.34-35). This at least suggests that the unmarried state is a mark in this life of those who are destined for resurrection, not simply a consequence of the resurrected state.

This startling dismissal of marriage and the countervailing esteem given to the unmarried state has no parallel in the Hebrew Scriptures and is completely at odds with the positive duty to marriage that the Rabbinic tradition enjoins.[12] In this regard, Jesus would seem by his own celibacy to be setting at naught the requirement for the line to continue. The genealogies which introduce him in Matthew and Luke's Gospels are parodic subversions of the genealogical form. They never actually reach Jesus in whom the whole concept of the family line is brought to a close.

Even where, exceptionally, Jesus' teaching appears to buttress the institution of the family, other readings are possible. His repudiation of the Mosaic provision of divorce, by which he may seem to shore up the ideal of the family, has been seen by Jewish commentators as an attack on the continuity of the wider family, not a defence of it.[13]

12. The only place in which the Hebrew Scriptures allude to celibacy or at least abstinence as a virtue is in the context of the requirement for soldiers on active service to refrain from sexual activity. David pledges that his men have not touched a woman when he requests the bread from the altar at Nob (1 Sam. 21.4), and Uriah makes this custom the basis for his refusal to sleep with his wife Bathsheba when David recalls him from the front (2 Sam. 11.11). The otherwise anomalous celibacy of the Qumran community, if this was indeed their practice, can be related to their self-image as warriors prepared for the apocalyptic battle. There are suggestive pointers here to possible parallels in the practice of the early Church. The attitude of the Rabbinic tradition appears in passages such as this from the Talmud: 'The sages in the school of R. Ishmael taught: "Until a young man reaches the age of twenty, the Holy One sits and waits expectantly: 'When will this one take a wife?' But when a young man reaches the age of twenty and has still not wed. He says, 'May the bones of this one be blasted'"' (*b. Kid.* 29b-30a). The rabbis also drew on the story of Adam and Eve to show that man only achieves completeness as part of a couple (e.g. *b. Yeb.* 63a).

13. The relevant passages are Mk 2.10-12; Mt. 19.1-9; Lk. 16.18. The concession over the woman's adultery which appears in Mt. 19.9 may itself show a

In this view, it binds partners to sterile or incompatible unions which lead to an involution and destruction of the continuity of the lineage. There is in Jesus' ruling on divorce what we might call an 'Edenic impracticality'. The passage explicitly recalls the notion of man and woman becoming one flesh in Genesis. Marriage here becomes an expression of the ontological union of human partners, a metaphor for the union of Christ and his Church according to Paul, rather than a pragmatic accommodation to the imperatives of child-rearing.

Family, then, is reinterpreted as a matter of choice, not heredity. In the Gospel view, all the elements that Brichto saw as clustered round the concept of the family — kin, cult, land and afterlife — are subsumed in the radical action of God in resurrection. Jesus' call is to a resurrection which renders irrelevant all the human institutions designed to ensure survival. Such a call threatens profoundly all those whose understandable concern is to survive and to safeguard the continuance of their families and their culture.

It may not be a common move to draw a parallel in this regard between Jesus and the disobedient son of Deuteronomy, but it is there to be drawn. His fate, like that of the rebellious son, is to be put to death for his refusal to comply with the careful conventions of human society, so cunningly contrived to outwit the contingencies of death. Both threaten a radical unstructuring of human institution. Yet such a reading illumines the way in which the figure of Jesus in the Gospel narratives acts as a focus for the tensions inherent in the biblical model of the family. Jesus, the obedient son of God, slain by his heavenly father for the disobedience of others in some understandings of the atonement, is more obviously the one slain by the human wrath of those who see him as a blasphemous betrayer of the familial structure. He flouts his social responsibilities, disrupts the family life of his followers and places at the centre of his teaching the abominable claim that he is God's son rather than that of his human father.

But he is also identified by the tradition with the Father deserted and betrayed by those who had allied themselves to him as his spiritual children. In this tradition there is at once a convergence, a manifestation and a confrontation of the anxieties of anonymity, of abandonment, of the terror of forgetfulness which erupt through the stories of the biblical tradition. The filicidal tradition of the Hebrew

developing awareness of the difficulties of an absolute ban on divorce, and the fact that only the woman is mentioned clearly reflects the continuing assumption that men need to control women's sexuality, not the other way round.

Scriptures is both vindicated and transcended in this apotheosis
where Jesus becomes the triumphant victim of a human patriarchy
that cannot allow, because it cannot survive, his radicality. This
world where marriage and family are subordinated to the affiliative
family of the Church is also the one to be found in Paul's letters.

The fact is that it is hard to find any positive injunction to child-
bearing and child-rearing in the New Testament. It scarcely even
appears as an issue until the Pastoral Epistles. In 1 Timothy, child-
rearing is recommended, but only as a means of placing a check on
women's proclivity to sin. Women will be saved by childbirth. Young
widows, who otherwise will 'grow wanton against Christ' (1 Tim.
5.11), are to marry, bear children and to rule their households in
order that the enemy may have no excuse to revile the Church. These
and other provisions mark the accommodation of the later New
Testament writers to the inescapable fact that children are being born
into the Church, husbands are dying and life is continuing. It also
marks the re-emergence of the need to control women's sexuality, a
need which the radical teaching of Jesus elsewhere would make
irrelevant. Freed from the ties of property, family and sexuality, there
is a glimpse of a new equivalence between men and women which
soon succumbs to the realities of continued social existence.

The Church then takes it upon itself the task of ensuring survival,
but carries in its traditions a deep ambivalence about the role of
family, tradition and property. Such ambivalences over the dynamics
of the family are not to be explained as the product of some contemporary angst, some departure from biblical faithfulness, but are
right at the heart of the biblical tradition itself. Nor does this reflect
any simple polarization of New Testament radicalism versus the
conservatism of the Hebrew tradition. Both testaments know both
tendencies.

This encapsulates the problem in using the biblical tradition to
come to grips with the changing status of the family in contemporary
society. The biblical tradition offers no cure for the consequences of
our ambivalence to the family. Rather, it offers a range of partially
successful strategies of survival adopted, adapted and abandoned by
the various communities who have sought to live out their existence
under the consciousness of existence under the reign of the biblical
God.

The biblical tradition makes no coherent sense without this
overarching unity conferred by the enigmatic figure of its God. It is
not the purpose of this chapter to explore the theological problems
raised by such a claim. But without acknowledging this claim, there

is great danger in looking to the biblical tradition as a source of guidance in human affairs. The writer to the Ephesians is to be taken entirely seriously when he writes 'For this reason I bow my knees before the Father, from whom every family on earth is named' (Eph. 3.14-15). The biblical tradition of using the metaphors of family, of fatherhood and motherhood to express the relationship between God and the human sphere can only be taken on board if we are prepared to accept the notion that it is the human family, the human structure of relationships which is a metaphor for God's relationship to humankind, to Israel, to Jesus and to the Church.

The biblical picture is of a structure of human relationships which obliquely and imperfectly reflects the relationship of God with his Son, whether that son is Israel or Jesus. In contemporary society, this model of the ordering of human relationships has now been evacuated of the disturbing presence of God. The family itself—that poor, abstract, ramshackle, ambivalent concept—then becomes the basis for the right ordering of personal, sexual and social relationships. From the point of view of the biblical tradition, this is nothing more or less than idolatry: an idolatry of the idea of the family. Who can wonder, then, that when the going gets tough and problems arise, we fall into the age-old patterns of behaviour of the idolaters so mercilessly derided in the book of Isaiah? Staggering under the dead weight of the idols we hoped would ensure our survival, in the panic of flight we end up throwing these unwieldy burdens into the ditch. The structures by which we seek to ensure our collective survival can themselves become the chains that shackle us to intolerable situations. If the biblical traditions are viewed merely as ethical prescriptions to shore up such failing human structures, then it is little wonder that they too are cast aside as burdens rather than seen as a summons to new life.

What the biblical tradition can do for secular modernism is to hold before us these tensions and irreconcilabilities. It does not attempt to provide an easy integration of them. The communities which use the Bible are thus in a position to maintain continuity through discontinuity by activating different, even antithetical, aspects of the tradition because the tradition itself has accumulated through just such a process of readings, re-readings and misreadings. But this does entail the inevitability that the appeal to the biblical tradition to shore up our institutions brings with it not just the wood but the termites, to coin a phrase. We cannot appeal to one tradition as authoritative without having to accept other less amenable traditions as equally authoritative.

The radical critique of the family which is to be found in the Gospels and Paul is not reducible to any liberal agenda of social reform or any conservative politics of social control. The Bible, to borrow the title of R.P. Carroll's book, is a 'wolf in the sheepfold' (Carroll 1991). It is not a sheep dog. Those who do try to use it as such should realize the risk they run. It has taken centuries of domestication and cross-breeding to produce the structures of social morality whose collapse is now bewailed, structures which claim a dim ancestry in the biblical tradition but which have absorbed much of the ethos of the Greek and Roman traditions in the course of their evolution. When the wolf prowls, the sheep dogs bristle and howl, now the implacable enemies of their wild ancestors. So, too, the radical elements of the biblical tradition are often most threatening to those who are most inclined to appeal to the Bible as bolstering their vision of the Christian family. The biblical tradition is a wild, undomestic, unfamiliar one for us.

As such, it calls into question the idolatry of the family which may be one truly destructive force in contemporary society. It can remind us that the virtues of fidelity and self-giving nurture which the family embodies at its best are not somehow definitively consigned to one structure of human relationships. Such values are not best assured by making an idol of a particular social structure. Conversely, placing the family in this wider context of relationships paradoxically may strengthen it as an institution by showing its limitations. The pressure of human aspiration and of human sin does not have to be contained by this structure alone. It is not a failure of the family as such if it cracks under such a strain but of a society which has no sense of the transcendent which alone could bear that strain. The biblical tradition points to ways of living which are not dependent on the survival of this particular structure of survival. In this context, the family still, of course, has a role, but a contingent one. In this time of waiting, it provides the arena in which the virtues of patient communality can be practised.

9

FLESHING OUT THE TEXT:
RE-READING CIRCUMCISION

In his essay 'The Eyes of Language: The Abyss and the Volcano', Derrida (2002a: 191-227) reacts to an extraordinary letter found among Gershom Scholem's papers after his death.[1] It is addressed to Franz Rosenzweig, and dated 26 December 1926. In it, Scholem warns Rosenzweig of the dangers of the attempted secularization of Hebrew as the language of Israel. 'Hebrew is pregnant with catastrophes', he writes, and, earlier, 'This country is a volcano. It houses language.' The mistake is to imagine that the 'apocalyptic thorn' of the language has been pulled. 'Each word which is not newly created but taken from of [sic] the "good old" treasure is full to bursting.'
   Scholem continues,

> We do live inside this language, above an abyss, almost all of us with the certainty of the blind. But when our sight is restored, we or those who come after us, must we not fall to the bottom of this abyss? And no one knows whether the sacrifice of individuals who will be annihilated in this abyss will suffice to close it.

And further,

> After evoking the ancient names daily, we can no longer hold off their power. Called awake they will appear since we have evoked them with great violence… Those who called the Hebrew language back to life did not believe in the judgement that was thus conjured upon us.

This warning of the uncanny power of Hebrew, rooted in its inescapable but unrecognized connection to the symbolics of the biblical text, is startling, although the relevance or credibility of Scholem's underlying assumptions about language and its significance as yet another diagnosis of the endlessly ramifying complexities of Israeli

---

1.   A translation by Gil Andijar of Scholem's letter appears as an appendix in Derrida 2002a: 226-27. The quotations of Scholem above are taken from this.

politics is yet to be tested. It is certainly a highly idiosyncratic view. What struck me in reading his letter was the volcanic metaphor of the potentially catastrophic repressed violence of biblical language, and its foreboding that this repression in the word will have its conse-quences in real violence wreaked on real bodies. This repression is not confined to Hebrew, although Scholem's reaction is specifically so directed. All European languages rely on metaphors and vocabu-lary which draw their original power from the biblical text but which are now used indiscriminately and unwittingly in all sorts of contexts.

Let me now juxtapose this shattering text with another which also amazes me, for rather different reasons. 'Is there a relationship between the fact that every twenty-five seconds a male infant is circumcised and every fifteen seconds a man beats a woman?' asks Ronald Goldman MD in his book memorably entitled *Circumcision, The Hidden Trauma; How an American Cultural Practice Affects Infants and Ultimately Us All* (1997: 163). Circumcision is currently the subject of a fascinating and sometimes virulent debate centred mainly on the US, where the opponents of 'genital mutilation' and 'infant torture' marshal evidence to demonstrate the long-lasting traumatic effects of this procedure.[2] Goldman's book, sponsored by the Circumcision Resource Centre, Boston, is a good example of the genre. The topic brings into play a plethora of the discourses of the day: sexuality, masculinity, child violence and sexual abuse, human rights, torture, psychoanalysis, trauma, victimhood, body image, medical cover-up, medical authority, scientific discourse, conspiracy theory, cultural pressures and conformity, identity, Judaism and anti-Semitism, to name but a few. The biblical resonances are obvious, though the relationship of the contemporary debate to biblical discussions is an oblique one.

Goldman's argument is that circumcision, which its opponents insist is no minor operation, is not only the physical mutilation of an unconsenting infant, but the cause of a desensitizing of the male body which has lasting physiological consequences. The circumcised male is quite simply rendered less responsive to physical stimuli. What-ever the medical truth of this, we may note in passing that the ration-ale for the practice of circumcision offered by Moses Maimonides in

2.   For a relatively balanced historical approach to a highly polemical debate, see Gollaher 2000. Aspects of the internal debate in the American Jewish com-munity are discussed in Laurence A. Hoffman's *Covenant of Blood: Circumcision and Gender in Rabbinic Judaism* (1996), particularly in the final chapter (pp. 209-20).

The Guide for the Perplexed is that it serves 'to weaken the organ of generation as far as possible and thus cause man to be moderate' (1956: 378).[3]

Psychologically, Goldman argues, circumcision inflicts a traumatic betrayal on the infant, whose relationship of trust to the mother is terminally undermined. Goldman encapsulates his analysis in the following, somewhat ungainly, statement: '...the violent act of circumcision (what's done to children) may be an unrecognized perinatal factor that, in certain circumstances, increases the potential for adult violence (what they will do to society)' (1997: 171). Hence the link between the statistics of circumcision and male violence against women, he claims: desensitized and traumatized men wreak their vengeance for their affective crippling on the substitutes for the mother as betrayer. Adult male violence, particularly in the US, is exacerbated, at least, by the practice of circumcision.

The hypothesis, as Goldman presents it, would, I suspect, prove to be riddled with begged questions and unsupported statistics if further investigated. It is an extreme, but not unique, view, as the number of websites directed to 'circumcision survivors' testifies. What even such a speculative hypothesis bears witness to, however, is a complex of issues about body and text, wounded bodies and wounded texts, the repression in language and the repressed memory of physical and psychic trauma, focused on the phenomenon of circumcision. Circumcision is a recurrent theme in contemporary critical debate, most notably in the work of Derrida himself, but also in the writings of Julia Kristeva, where it becomes displaced into the symbolic realm as a way of talking about features intrinsic to language. In this way, circumcision also resonates with the concerns of Scholem's letter. Is there a link to be made between the violence potentially intrinsic in biblical language and the trauma of circumcision?

Some such connection is certainly suggested by the concept of a 'hermeneutics of circumcision' which surfaces in a transcribed conversation between three leading representatives of the school of Postmodern Jewish Philosophy — Steven Kepnes, Peter Ochs and Robert Gibbs — recorded in their jointly edited volume *Reasoning after Revelation* (1998). Kepnes introduces the idea that circumcision is 'an icon for the Jewish act of delimiting the logos' (1998: 37) in the context of a discussion of the distinctiveness of Jewish postmodernism in terms of

---

3. Interestingly, Maimonides treats circumcision in his discussion of the laws to do with marriage.

its strategies for countering logocentric reductionism. Gibbs takes the analogy on, but conflates circumcision and castration as strategies for humbling the phallogocentric ego, wondering if Origen's self-castration bespoke 'an excess logocentrism in his hermeneutics' (1998: 37).

Ochs takes Gibbs to task for this conflation and distinguishes between a castrating hermeneutic which attempts to sever the roots of logocentrism, which he regards as still a modernist strategy (given its logic of negation), and a hermeneutic of circumcision. 'For us...', he writes, 'circumcision, as opposed to castration, signifies a hermeneutic that preserves the text — or tradition or impulse — while delimiting its potential oppressiveness' (1998: 37).

This comment is taken up at some length by Elliot Wolfson in his 'Listening to Speak: A Response to Dialogues in Postmodern Jewish Philosophy' (Kepnes, Ochs and Gibbs 1998: 93-104), one of the several reflections by distinguished commentators on the dialogue between the three scholars which make up the latter part of the work. Wolfson refers to Ochs's 'incisive' (1998: 100) remark (pun intended?) but puts it in the wider context of a kabbalistic view of Torah as a concrete manifestation of God which is the product of an act of 'self-constriction' by the divine, something which Wolfson himself describes as an 'incarnational theology' of Torah (1998: 99). He takes issue with Ochs's rather sanguine characterization of circumcision as a release from oppression. Women and Gentiles might take a different view, he reminds him. That said, he continues as follows:

> There is no question, however, that the analogy that Ochs draws resonates deeply with the rabbinic tradition. Expanding on his comments, I would emphasize that circumcision as a trope for the hermeneutical process underscores the painfulness of reading, a painfulness that relates to the opening of the flesh that both marks and seals the covenant relationship between God and Israel. Divine writing and human reading share in the suffering of the text. (1998: 100)

Wolfson goes on to draw the analogy between the restriction of possible meaning that the reader has to accept in order to be faithful to the text and the self-restriction of the God who becomes concrete in Torah:

> The reader...must limit the range of possible meanings by learning how to decode the footprints that the author left behind in the text. In this sense, the hermeneutical process can be viewed as an emulation of the suffering of God that results in the constriction of the divine light into the form of the letters of the Torah. Reading, therefore, is a re-enactment of circumcision, an act of de-cision [his hyphenation], that brings the male Jew into a covenantal relationship with the God of Israel. (1998: 101)

This is a most intriguing discussion in our context, but note that Wolfson ends up with the male Jewish (religious) reader.[4] What of those readers whom the text excludes from the covenantal relationship, those whose circumcision is not being re-enacted, for whom the painful exercise of circumcised reading seems like oppression, precisely because they feel excluded from or indeed are unaware of the covenantal embrace of the text? Wolfson himself notes the potential oppressiveness of the kabbalistic concept of the homology between the 'covenant of the foreskin' and the 'covenant of the tongue' (1998: 100).[5]

This leads me to the following questions: Is Scholem's warning not related precisely to the fact that the language forged in a covenant predicated, in Wolfson's terms, on the painful self-limitation, or repression, of both God and the reader is now circulating with no consciousness of its underlying trauma? Or is Goldman not witness to a culture where circumcision is performed with no sense of covenant, desacralized and medicalized, where its trauma cannot be set against the gift of identity and the promise of restoration?

In this chapter I can do no more than trace some of these resonances and draw on some of the theoretical resources which Derrida and Kristeva offer in an attempt to illuminate how biblical metaphors and narrative dynamics pervade and problematize contemporary discussions of violence. There is nothing novel in claiming that biblical tropes underpin the violence of the contemporary world. Regina Schwartz in her insightful study *The Curse of Cain: The Violent Legacy of Monotheism* (1997) sees the principle of scarcity which underlies the dynamics of the biblical narratives as leading inevitability to a culture of violence. Monotheism and its ideology of one God, one land, one blessing, one chosen people: these pervasive ideas reinforce the conviction that survival depends on the domination or eradication of the other. Mark McEntire's *The Blood of Abel: The Violent Plot in the Hebrew Bible* (1999) reaches similar conclusions, pointing out how even the prophetic vision of peace is predicated on God's actions in

---

4. For a fascinating discussion of a hermeneutics of circumcision in a Christian context, see Annexe 3, 'La lettre et la circoncision', in François Martin's *Pour une théologie de la lettre: l'inspiration des Ecritures* (1996: 477-94). See also Michel de Certeau's fascinating correlation between circumcision as a conferral of meaning through removal and absence (of the foreskin) and the unpronounceable grapheme YHVH, which also creates meaning by acting as an 'absence' in the text (1975: 342).

5. Wolfson traces this concept to *Sefer Yetsirah* and cites a reference from the thirteenth-century Spanish kabbalist, Joseph Gikatilla.

destroying Zion's potential enemies. Yet what Scholem points to, and what Derrida and Kristeva explore, is an implication at another level which may suggest that a simplistic rejection of the biblical tradition and its ostensible message may be inadequate to come to terms with the insight it may bring to our understanding of the roots and reasons for human destructiveness.

We will return to Schwartz's theory later in our discussion but immediately I shall turn for help in understanding the relationship between language, violence and circumcision in the biblical text to Elaine Scarry's fruitful and still neglected reading of the biblical tradition in *The Body in Pain* (1985). Scarry finds the biblical rejection of visual signs of its god's presence striking in a cultural milieu where idols were universally accepted. The God of the Hebrew Bible is a voice, not a vision, invisible, unembodied and so constantly escaping the efforts of the human imagination to encompass him. This is made explicit in Deut. 4.12 where Moses reminds the people that on Horeb 'you heard the sound of words, but saw no form, there was only a voice' and from this argues for the ban on graven images (Deut. 4.16-31).

Human beings, in contrast to this God, are embodied, tied to the materiality, the vulnerability, changeability and ultimately the mortality of their bodies. How are voice and body to interact? The short answer, Scarry maintains, is by writing, by which she means the recording of the elusive voice in the transformation of the material world. God writes, literally, on the tablets of stone, but also, so Scarry claims, makes his mark on the world in his effect on human bodies. It is in the weapon and the wound that God is made known, through instruments which mark the changeable substance of the material world. The marks which are left are the evidence his unseen power and presence.

Just such an alteration is demanded of Abraham and his descendants as the sign of the covenant in Genesis 18. No verbal agreement, no written pledge is sufficient. Instead, Abraham's genitals are to be wounded, and his body bears an indelible mark as a permanent reminder to himself, and to those who see him naked, that he stands in relation to God. This mark is to be transmitted to all who bear the promise as his descendants. The continuity of the ungraspable God is etched into the flesh of the succeeding generations who bear the mark of circumcision. The mutability of the body is what enables it to become a record of memory, but also the bearer of a pledge for the future. The circumcised penis is a reminder of a past act of wounding, an act within the community, but also a promise: a promise that the bearer of the scar will be bound up in the destiny of the community and its otherwise unseen God.

This physical inscription of the presence of God by human wounding runs much wider than circumcision, of course. Jacob, wrestling with the angel, bears away both his blessing and a limp, a permanent wound. Others are blinded or blasted with leprosy as a sign of God's presence. The firstborn of Egypt are killed; Amalek is annihilated. Throughout the Hebrew Bible it is the wounding and scarring of human bodies that serves as the real earnest of God's presence with Israel. Either Israel or their enemies are smitten with plague or devastated by famine or war, and the promise that is awaited is a promise of more violence, either of punishment vented on the people, or the destruction of their enemies.

Confirmation that the wound's importance is as a sign of God's action comes from the fact that in the Hebrew Scriptures modification of the body by humans is frowned upon. Leviticus 19.27-28 is blunt: 'You shall not round off the hair on your temples or mar the edges of your beard. You shall not make any cuttings in your flesh on account of the dead, or tattoo any marks on you'; and Deut. 14.1 confirms this: 'You shall not cut yourselves or make any baldness on your head for the dead'. Of course, one only forbids what is a temptation, and wider cultural comparisons indicate that self-mutilation was a common counterpart of mourning. Ugaritic sources, which testify to a highly developed cult of the dead, bear this out and even the high God El gashes himself and 'ploughs his chest like a garden and harrows his back like a plain' in mourning for the dead Baal.[6]

---

6. See H.L. Ginsberg's translation of Ugaritic tablet V AB in the section on 'Poems about Baal and Anath' in Pritchard (1958: 110). There is evidence that such practices were not unknown in Israel itself. Jeremiah 41.5 describes the aftermath of the murder of the governor Gedaliah by Ishmael son of Nethaniah: 'The day after Gedaliah's assassination, before anyone knew about it, eighty men who had shaved off their beards, torn their clothes and cut themselves came from Shechem, Shiloh and Samaria, bringing grain offerings and incense with them to the house of the Lord'. No-one seems to disapprove of their actions or their appearance in the temple. Seventy of them are indeed killed in their turn by Ishmael but this seems to be more for their political opinions than for their mourning practices. In Jer. 16.6 the writer seems to take it for granted that people gash themselves and shave their head for the dead, in a context where the whole point is the suspension of what are implicitly normal mourning practices, and this is borne out in similar passages in Ezek. 7.18 and Mic. 1.16. These practices may not simply have been mourning rituals, however. The prophets of Baal gash themselves with knives in their vain attempt to compete with Elijah on Mt Carmel in 1 Kgs 22. The connection of self-wounding with prophecy in Israel as

This at least suggests that the legal material of the Torah is countering a set of accepted cultural practices which it seeks to redefine as abuse. It seems jealous to reserve the power of modifying the human body to God alone. Deuteronomy 32.9 could not put this more starkly: 'See now that I, I am he [or: I am the one]: and there is no other God beside me: I shall kill and I have brought to life; I have wounded [or smashed] and I shall heal [or repair] and there is no one to save you from my hand'. Wounding is God's business. It is also significant that, as clearly as Hebrew grammar can convey it, the point is made that what God has already done is to wound; it is healing which is held out as the uncompleted act of the future. Wounding and healing, death and the bringing of life are for God's hands.

Circumcision is the exception that proves the rule, in that the modification of the human body by human action is explicitly enjoined. God's presence is not directly visible, but his action in the world is readable from wounded bodies. However, this licit action itself serves to repress through the biblical text a complex of cultural practices related to wounding and violence. Circumcision becomes the permissible remnant of a now forbidden and denied cultural impulse. In its biblical form it is a trope which severs Israel from a widespread cultural and religious set of signifiers in its ancient Near Eastern context which depend on the wounding of the body.

Circumcision carries a particular significance because it intersects not only with the wound, but with procreation and with the marking out of gender. There are pragmatic aspects to this: there are not so many possibilities of marking the male body indelibly and in a gender specific way, yet without inflicting major physical disability. Israel is by no means unique in its practice of circumcision either within the global context of anthropology or indeed among its ancient Near Eastern neighbours. Herodotus credits the Egyptians with the invention of circumcision and indeed Freud argues that it was introduced by the Egyptian Moses not as a mark of distinction, but as a mark of respectability.

However, in most other cultures where it is practised, it is a rite associated with puberty, performed by older men on the boys of the

---

well as in Baalide circles is hinted at in the odd passage in Zech. 13.6 where the prophet, now ashamed of his calling, will have to answer the question, 'What are these wounds on your body?' Other bodily marks—perhaps what Leviticus condemns as 'tattooing'—are also referred to in passing. Isaiah 44.5, for instance, describes without condemnation one who writes on his hand *l^eyhwh*, 'belonging to Yahweh'.

tribe. Where Israel is unusual is in the fact that the rite is performed on infants. One traditional line of justification for this depends on an association with the story of the Akedah which is often interpreted as a prohibition of another widely attested practice in the ancient Near East, the sacrifice of children. This too is a practice which biblical texts seem to acknowledge in Israel, even as something that at one time was construed as a divine requirement (Ezek. 20.25-26) but which the explicit rhetoric of the text condemns fiercely. Once again, in biblical thought, what is forbidden, the killing of children, becomes a divine prerogative — Egypt's firstborn, the unnamed child of Bathsheba and David, the children of Babylon in Psalm 137 all attest to a possibility of the displaced action of God. If circumcision substitutes for the practice of child sacrifice, it also acts as a metonymic reminder of it. Each male child is put to the knife. Circumcision becomes the acceptable sign of a troubling discourse in this case of the violence of fathers against their sons which otherwise is excluded from the text.

Julia Kristeva in her *New Maladies of the Soul* (1995) offers a further insight into the exceptional nature of biblical circumcision. She points out that the purity of the cult explicitly demands the exclusion of anything deformed or wounded, including a specific prohibition of men with damaged genitals. The body must bear no trace of its debt to nature: it must be clean and proper in order to be fully symbolic. In order to confirm that, it should endure no gash other than that of circumcision, equivalent to sexual separation and/or separation from the mother. Any other mark would be the sign of belonging to the impure, the non-separate, the non-symbolic, the non-holy.

Circumcision here, to coin a pseudo-Lacanianism, is 'the wound which is not one'. Its function, Kristeva explains, is, like food taboos, to mark separation without the need for sacrifice:

> ...what the male is separated from, the other that circumcision carves out on his very sex, is the other sex, impure, defiled. By repeating the natural scar of the umbilical cord at the location of sex, by duplicating and thus displacing through ritual the pre-eminent separation, which is that from the mother, Judaism seems to insist in symbolic fashion — the very opposite of what is 'natural' — that the identity of the speaking being (with his God) is based on the separation of the son from the mother. (1995: 100)

In Kristeva's reading, this dynamic reflects the pain yet possibility of the development of the human subject, which entails the abjection of the maternal as the price for access to the paternal gift of the word. Here we come closer to a connection between circumcision and language.

What she does not mention, however, is what might seem the counter-argument represented by Howard Eilberg-Schwartz and others[7] that circumcision represents a feminization of the Jewish male, which chimes with the anger expressed by some American men who regard themselves as 'circumcision survivors' and resent what they experience as a theft of some aspect of their masculinity. Circumcision may be a displacement of the navel according to Kristeva, but it is more commonly read as a displacement of castration. There are Jewish commentators who see it precisely as a form of assurance to the boy that the undeniable aggression of the father, which Freud sees as manifest in the child's fear of castration, can be acknowledged, but will proceed no further.[8]

However, what Kristeva may point to, and what Goldman suggests, is that performed before the child has entered into the linguistic community, on an eight-day-old child, the trauma is experienced in a preverbal context where only the maternal is real. The trauma of this displaced wound is displaced onto the mother. The cut of castration and the severing of the umbilical cord are conflated. Hence Kristeva's insistence in *Powers of Horror* that the dynamic of biblical legislation expresses an abjection of the maternal. The centrality of circumcision, to the exclusion of any other modification of the body, is of a piece with this insight.

Paradoxically, this central function of circumcision is borne out by Paul's apparent rejection of it in the New Testament. In Phil. 3.2 he turns on what he calls 'these impure dogs', against these 'workers of evil, against those who make incision in their own bodies' (a periphrasis which masks the rather crude pun replacing *paratomes*, 'circumcisers', with *katatomes*, 'choppers'). Why is Paul so hard on the advocates of circumcision, when in the next few verses he is prepared to declare his own circumcision as at least a potential matter for boasting?

---

7. See, e.g., Chapter 6, 'Unmanning Israel', in Eilberg-Schwartz's *God's Phallus and Other Problems for Men and Monotheism* (1994: 137-62), and a recurrent theme in the work of Daniel Boyarin.

8. Hoffman (1996: 2) cites a quotation from an article in the *New York Times* 'About Men' column by Joshua J. Hammerman, a conservative rabbi, who celebrates for each father 'this experience, even vicariously, of inflicting upon his child a ritualized blow so intense as to make him shake and recoil, yet so controlled that no damage is done, to signify that this will be the worst the child will ever know from his father's hand' ('About Men: Birth Rite', *New York Times Magazine* [13 March 1994], p. 28).

The answer may be because we are once again in a world where the believer's body is the visible site of divine action, the manifestation of an invisible agency. His objection is in direct line with the disapproval manifest in Leviticus and Deuteronomy of human alterations to the body. It is God's business to alter bodies, not ours. It is not circumcision which is the problem, but those who presume to circumcise.

In Phil. 3.21 this divine prerogative is explicit. Paul tells us that we await a saviour 'who will change the fashion of this humbled body of ours, making it conformable to the body which is his in his glorified state, and who will accomplish this by exerting the very power which he has to make all things subject to himself'. What has altered is that this appropriation of the right to alter human bodies by God has now been made absolute so that even the once licit wounding of the circumcision has become a trespass on the divine prerogative of altering the human body.

The marks that matter now are the apostolic signs of suffering.[9] This is made abundantly clear at the end of the letter to Galatians, where the issue of circumcision is particularly to the fore. Paul sums up his position in the final verses: 'As for circumcision or the want of it, they count for nothing. What counts is that there is a new *ktisis*.'[10] Paul clinches this with an assertion of the basis for his claim to authority, which is also his evidence for being himself a new creature: 'From this time onward let there be nobody who will be a cause of trouble for me; for I bear the marks of Jesus imprinted on my very body' (Gal. 6.17). Paul's body is now the sign of God. But,

---

9.   Writing to the Philippians, Paul hopes for 'sufficient courage so that now as always Christ will be exalted in my body, whether by life or death' (Phil. 1.20). The Philippians are privileged to join Paul in this witness by suffering: 'For it has been granted to you on behalf of Christ not only to believe in him, but also to suffer for him, since you are going through the same struggle you saw I had, and now hear that I still have' (Phil. 1.29-30). These final clauses are the important point. The Philippians may not have seen Christ, but they have seen Paul, and Paul's struggles. As they read his letter they are now hearing the narrative of his continuing sufferings. Their share in these sufferings, he has told them, is exactly the sign that paradoxically they, who seem to be in such trouble, will be saved, while their enemies, who no doubt are congratulating themselves on their superior strength, are actually confronted with the sign of their destruction. Once again we are in the world where destruction is intrinsic to the manifestation of God in the world — the only question is who will be for the chop.

10.   *Ktisis* here could mean either an 'act of creation' or a 'creature'; cf. 2 Cor. 5.17.

paradoxically again, these shared marks, on Paul's own body, include the sign of circumcision.[11]

Yet does this not leave modern Christian readers in a recurrent dilemma? What evidence do we have now here of the state of Paul's body? Somewhere in Rome, we may believe, that body is buried awaiting the resurrection Paul so confidently expected, but no longer bearing those marks which Jesus has laid on it. In this connection, it is surely significant that the final book of the New Testament, and one of the last to be adopted into the canon, the Revelation of St John, reverts to an apocalyptic picture of kingdom of God which is accompanied by the most comprehensive slaughter and drastic modification of the bodies of the enemies of the kingdom to be found in the biblical corpus. In the absence of the body of God or his disciples, the heaped bodies of his dead enemies become the sign to be awaited.

What the modern reader does have, however, which neither biblical Israel nor the early Church had in its present form, is the Bible. The wound, God's writing on the mutable flesh of humanity, can be inscribed in written text. In this regard, we come close once more to the account of the Torah that Wolfson offered as a text which 'arises from God's own suffering' related to the 'opening of the flesh that both marks and seals the covenantal relationship between God and Israel. Divine writing and human reading share in the suffering of the text' (Kepnes, Ochs and Gibbs [eds.] 1998: 100).

In a remarkable passage in *Moses and Monotheism*, Freud indicates how the biblical text can act as the bearer of the wound:

11.	Space does not permit an adequate treatment of the complex issues around Jesus' circumcision in Christian thought. Suffice it to say that the Feast of the Circumcision celebrates a proleptic wounding of Christ's body as a foretaste of the crucifixion. The fact that this Feast has been redesignated in recent years as the Feast of the Holy Family could open up a whole new layer of discussion of the repression and return of the maternal. For further discussion, see Leo Steinberg's groundbreaking work *The Sexuality of Christ in Renaissance Art and in Modern Oblivion* (1996), especially pp. 50-71. Steinberg tackles the question of the lack of the physical evidence of circumcision in Renaissance depiction of Jewish biblical figures, including Christ, in the context of his claim that there is a consistent trope of *ostentatio genitalium*, the positive exhibition of Christ's genitals as a testimony to the incarnation. Steinberg sums up the artists' dilemma as follows: 'The honorific seal of a compact between man and God was manifestly a shameful scar. Between these conflicting positions the gulf was unbridgeable — deeper than the theological issue, wide as the divergence between, say, Hellenic sculptor and biblical prophet. Where the twain finally meet in Christianity they collide in a culture shock never quite overcome' (1996: 158). That shock, it could be said, is what still resonates in the debates we are outlining.

The text, however, as we possess it today will tell us enough about its own vicissitudes. Two mutually opposed treatments have left their traces on it. On the one hand it has been subjected to revisions which have falsified it in the sense of their secret aims, have mutilated [N.B.] and amplified it and have changed it into its reverse; on the other hand, a solicitous piety has presided over it and has sought to preserve everything as it was, no matter whether it was consistent or contradicted itself. Thus almost everywhere noticeable gaps, disturbing repetitions, and obvious contradictions have come about — indications which reveal things to us which it was not intended to communicate. (Freud 1985: 283)

Critics and readers have, since antiquity, been aware of the seams and scars in the text, the pieces that seem to have dropped out, or become misplaced or disfigured, the duplications and the graftings, the distortions and disjunctions. The biblical text itself bears wounds, more or less healed. Higher criticism, like much medicine, in the interest of healing the patient has dissected it, stripping off layers, hacking off or transplanting bits and pieces, rather as if Dr Frankenstein took up employment as a plastic surgeon. The biblical text has been stripped and separated into layers, shown to be myopic in its view of women and of the cultures of Palestine. This process has proceeded apace throughout the last few decades, but to critical eyes it appears innocuous compared to the wholesale pillaging of the corpus of the Hebrew Scriptures by Paul and other early Christian writers, who pull the brightest threads out of the textile of the Hebrew Scriptures to weave them into their own books, dismembering it in order to rebuild its story, an activity blithely continued by its dissection into lectionaries and reading, and the search for sermon texts, dragged out of context.

All texts, Frederick Jameson has argued, involve effort in production, an effort which can only be justified if they offer some promise of resolution to the tensions of the community for whom they are produced. The pain of the exile, the destruction, the anxiety over the continuity of Israel and the promise, the pain of the withdrawal of the physical presence of Jesus, give rise to the texts of scriptures. That pain is expressed as wounding, notably in a book such as Lamentations, where the hope of the people is placed in the wounding Father, at the expense of the battered and sexually brutalized mother Zion. A wound, a scar is a memory of contact, which at times stands duty for the longed-for caress.

The processes of fracture, rupture and fragmentation, so characteristic of so-called postmodernity, are not likely to cease, and media manipulation of the text will disseminate and dismember it with accelerating ease. Yet the text itself encodes and displays its own fracture and rupture. The Bible is pulled apart by the tensions it seeks to embody — hope and dread, life and death, inclusion and exclusion, choice and responsibility, promise and betrayal. It is a text in tension, the product of anguish and loss — the loss of the temple, the loss of the land, the loss of the body of Jesus. It is a battered survivor of a text, which bears the anguish and the guilt that are a survivor's lot. The Bible as sign is a sign of the rupture that leads to the wound as sign. It also bears witness, in the trace of the scar, to the agony of healing.

But can we finally close the loop and argue that the Bible is not simply a wounded but a circumcised text, and that it is as a result of this that it encodes a violence which Scholem detects? Here we can return to Derrida, who explores the concept of the circumcised word in his essay 'Shibboleth' (Hartman and Budick [eds.] 1986: 307-48). In this he follows Paul Celan in a semantic sidestep which seems to arise in response to a line of Maria Tsvetayeva quoted in the original Russian by Celan as the epigraph of a poem in his *Die Niemandsrose*: 'All poets are Jews', writes Tsvetayeva or, more accurately, 'All poets are Yids'.

Derrida takes this line as a pretext to develop the idea of circumcision as a diagnostic of poetic language. The original story of the use of the word 'shibboleth' to single out and kill the fugitive Ephraimites (Judg. 12.5-6) brings the linguistic and the physical together — after all, Derrida reminds us, it is a physical incapacity to pronounce the word that dooms the Ephraimites, something that can be related to the odd expression Moses uses of his own problems with articulation in Exod. 6.12 and 6.30, when he claims to be of 'uncircumcised lips'. A physical incapacity brought to light by the failure to speak a word leads to death.

Derrida meditates on the idea as follows:

> ...the circumcised word, the word turned Shibboleth, at once both secret and readable, mark of membership and of exclusion, the shared wound of division [*blessure de partage*], reminds us also of what I will call the double edge of every Shibboleth. The mark of an alliance, it is also an index of exclusion, of discrimination, indeed of extermination. One may, thanks to the Shibboleth, recognize and be recognized by one's own, for better and for worse, for the sake of partaking [*partage*] and the ring of alliance on the one hand, but also, on the other hand, for the purpose of denying the other, of denying him passage or life. One may also, because of the Shibboleth and exactly to the extent that one may make use of it, see it turned against oneself: then it is the

circumcised who are proscribed or held at the border, excluded from
the community, put to death, or reduced to ashes merely on the sight
of, or in the name of, the *Wundgelesenes*. (1986: 340)[12]

Paul, or more accurately later readings of Paul, it could be argued,
turns the 'shibboleth' of circumcision against Israel—what once
marked out the chosen people now marks out those who are rejected.
Scholem's warning is also directed to those who may find themselves
on the wrong side of a divide they have mistakenly seen as a safeguard. Hebrew as a mark of a secular nationality may not lead to
security but insecurity, he seems to imply, and the displacement of
the sacred may lead to the rise of religious fanaticisms within and
beyond the community marked by language. Something has been cut
away from the language, some level of resonance hidden from the
conscious life of the community.

This may be particularly true of Hebrew, though I feel in no place
to comment further on that, but is it confined to Hebrew? Are not all
European languages at least imbued not only with their own sacredness, but with a sacredness that comes from their being summoned
into writing by the biblical word? Is there a volcano waiting to erupt
in the inarticulacy of our spiritual vocabularies, an energy of violence
which can, as is only too possible, seize on the biblical text itself and
use it as a weapon?

Reading the literature of those who liken the circumcision of
American men to a new holocaust exposes one to the inarticulate
rage at what is perceived as an irreparable injury and assault by some
circumcised men. This, one cannot help feeling, has become the focus
for some other, much wider sense of frustration which simmers below
language because the secularized language, which is all so many of
us have to express ourselves in, cannot speak deep enough. An aspect
of this may be ascribed to the fact that this rage stems from a pre-
linguistic trauma, but Derrida points to another issue in his constant
insistence in 'Shibboleth' on the uniqueness and unrepeatability of
circumcision. It can only happen once. Each man has only one foreskin to be removed. There is both a particular irreparability implicit
in this, but also no possibility of retribution. The trauma of circumcision cannot be overcome by the *lex talionis*, a foreskin for a foreskin,
when the circumcised father, or, if Kristeva is to be believed, the

---

12. *Wundgelesenes* is the final word of Celan's poem *Dein vom Wachen*, a
typical neologism which might be translated the 'wound-read'—in the present
context, a pregnant term.

mother who has no penis, is seen as the perpetrator. Where is the pain to go?

In an unpublished paper on 'Forgiveness and Resentment: Kierkegaard, Levinas and Weil',[13] Patrick Sheil discusses the dynamics of revenge and points out that it can never rest at the level of 'tit for tat', of strict reciprocity. If I respond to your attack with an equal display of force, this still leaves the most important disparity between us untouched. Your attack was an unprovoked assault on an innocent victim; mine is a justified retaliation against a guilty party. We may sustain equal physical injury, but you will not suffer the sense of outrage and betrayal that I suffered. In order to even up the score, I have to go further by assaulting your innocence and provoking you to outrage, which then begins a new cycle as you now feel the victim of an unjustifiable or even unforgivable attack.

History all too chillingly bears witness to the accuracy of this analysis. The discussion which followed the presentation of Shiel's paper turned, interestingly, to Psalm 137. Its notorious blessing on those who dash the children of Babylon against a rock is a prime example of the escalation of revenge which results from the fact that the initial condition before the offence can never be restored. Babylon's innocence must be assailed, its people must experience outrage, and how better than through an assault on its innocent: its children. Further biblical examples could be multiplied.

As Sheil put it, the characteristic word of revenge is 'more'. It is here that an assumption of plenitude, as Schwartz seems to advocate, can lead to violence — the plenitude of the vendetta, where there are always more victims, and more ingenious atrocities, to assail the innocence of the offender. The *lex talionis*, the 'eye for an eye', is where the principle of scarcity can step in to limit the spiral of revenge. 'One for one' is its watchword. The law steps in to cut off the excess that revenge demands. Yet the excess must be discharged somehow.

The answer in the Hebrew Scriptures is to displace it onto the divine: ' "Vengeance is mine", saith the Lord, "I will repay" '. Human wounding, and the wounding of the innocent, as we have seen, is God's business. So he demands the life of David's newborn son in recompense for Uriah's life (2 Sam. 12) or the firstborn of Egypt for the lives of the Hebrew children slain at Pharaoh's orders (Exod. 11.4-8).

---

13. The paper was delivered at a one-day conference of the Søren Kierkegaard Society of the United Kingdom on 'Kierkegaard and Modern European Thought', 11 May 2002, University of Essex, and is cited with gratitude for the author's permission and useful further discussion.

God, we might say, is the name for the non-reciprocal, for the excess which can injure innocence, or in terms which are drawn from a recent essay of Derrida's, the name of 'sovereign cruelty'.[14]

Part of the anger felt by the survivors of circumcision is precisely the sense that their innocence has been outraged and that helpless children have been made to suffer this irreparable damage. The helplessness is, as Philo made explicit, part of the point.[15] Who would consent to circumcision, even as the sign of the covenant, as an adult? American medical circumcision is thus, rather as Scholem warned about the Hebrew of his day, a sign without significance, one which has been cut adrift from the ritual context in which it found meaning. Its meaning is now given in medical terms, insofar as any justification is sought at all. The most common reason given by parents who are asked why they chose to have circumcision performed is that they did not want their son to have to endure the mockery of others in the locker room. It is a norm because it is a norm. Its effects, then, cannot be incorporated in a collective narrative of identity so that the loss and pain it inflicts can be seen to have a compensation. There is nowhere for the search for recompense to go.

This same sense of a void where there should be a point of discharge for human frustration fear and pain is to be found in an essay by another great Jewish, indeed Israeli, writer, Haim Bialik. In his 'Revealment and Concealment in Language', written in 1915, Bialik discusses the constant renewal of words necessary because words are a talisman against the human fear of nothingness, but eventually themselves become tainted by the nothingness they exist to conceal.

14. In her recent collection of Derrida's writings entitled *Without Alibi* (Derrida 2002b) Peggy Kamuf includes a text entitled 'Psychoanalysis Searches the States of Its Soul: The Impossible Beyond of a Sovereign Cruelty' (pp. 238-80). In this paper, Derrida argues that cruelty has to be distinguished from violence in that it is the infliction of suffering for its own sake. He argues that sovereignty and cruelty are co-implicated, but also that there is a beyond of cruelty which is also beyond all drives and principles—part of his ongoing concern with the Kantian notion of radical evil. This 'beyond' is another instance of the excess of revenge. Although Derrida does not take this line, the point where cruelty and sovereignty both coincide at their absolute point is in the divine. On another tack, which Derrida does follow, it finds a resting point in the state's arrogation to itself of the death penalty. Derrida is particularly disturbed by the place of the death penalty in US society. There is a whole nexus of issues here which could be explored in a parallel study.

15. Gollaher (2000: 13) cites Philo's justification for infant circumcision as follows: 'It is very much better and more far-sighted of us to prescribe circumcision for infants, for perhaps one who is full-grown would hesitate through fear to carry out this ordinance of his own free will'.

As he puts it, '...the word or system has been worn out by being manipulated and used, is no longer able to conceal and hide adequately, and can, of course, no longer divert mankind momentarily. Man, gazing for a moment through the open crack, finding to his terror that awesome void before him again, hurries to close the crack for a time — with a new word' (Bialik 2000: 22).

Bialik's vision of the abyss beyond language is the negative image of Scholem's, but the effect and the danger is the same. In this context is Derrida's much overused phrase, 'Il n'y a pas hors texte' a comfort or a terror — or symptom? Or — and here I admit that the metaphor takes on a heady uncanniness that I cannot yet quite grasp — rather than itself representing the wounded phallus, is the Bible the excised and disregarded foreskin of our phallic culture? Is it the text, the parchment, severed from the unseen phallus of the invisible God? In a post-Christian, post-Jewish, world, do we collectively live out the trauma of an unrecognized circumcision?

Eilberg-Schwartz (1994: 208-209) points out what he calls the 'irony' that though circumcision marks the covenant, Rabbinic Judaism defined it as a sign that is to be hidden when praying to God. In the biblical text, priests are not to run the risk of exposing their nakedness at the altar, and in later Judaism, it is forbidden to recite the Shema naked. There is a paradox in a sign that is to be hidden and a paradox too, that, simplistically, if a man is identified as a Jew, that gives anyone who meets him a knowledge of an intimate detail of his anatomy that would otherwise only be revealed in intimate or carefully circumscribed social circumstances. Circumcision is a site of trauma and concealment, and the circumcised text is also one which conceals the trauma of its identity and gives voice to the concealed traumas of its circumcised producers.

Something of what I am grasping towards is to be found at the end of Kristeva's remarkable chapter 'Lire la Bible' in *Les nouvelles maladies de l'âme* (1993), which I cite here in French as the published translation does not quite catch the double edge in her writing. Kristeva encourages us to read the Bible again: 'Relisons, une fois de plus, la Bible. Pour l'interpréter certes, mais aussi pour y laisser se découper, se couper, nos propres fantasmes, nos délires interprétatifs' (1993: 189). We can translate the passage as follows: 'Let us, one more time, read the Bible. To interpret it, certainly, but also to let it cut out, cut for itself, our own fantasies, our interpretative deliriums [but note the allusion to *lire* itself in this word]': alternatively '...to let our own fantasies, our interpretative deliriums, cut themselves out, cut themselves, from it'.

Here the pivotal metaphor is of cutting but it is ambiguous in its reference. Does the Bible cut us or do we cut it? Earlier, Kristeva has described the Bible as 'a text which plunges its word into the side of my loss, but in order to allow me, in speaking of it, to face up to it in the knowledge of its cause' (1993: 179 [my translation]). For Kristeva, reading the Bible can act as a prophylactic against violence: 'Never in any way better than in the Bible does one observe this transformation of sacrifice into language, this superseding or displacement of mur- der into the system of meanings' (1993: 180 [my translation]). That system of meaning includes its own fracturedness, its own status as a text of survival, its witness through its wounding to the suffering of its readers and the suffering of its God.[16] Precisely because it attests textually to the trauma of circumcision, the irreparable assault on the innocent that severs from the mother in the name of the father, it offers the best hope of insight into the displaced fury of those who are circumcised physically or linguistically. The Bible, Kristeva insists, constitutes us as its readers as inhabitants of a borderland where our fragility and our solidity are confounded.

But by the same token, the Bible may always offer — or threaten — the possibility of reversal, of the transformation of language into sacrifice if its system of meanings is unravelled. The shibboleth cuts two ways. The offer of circumcision, as Dinah's rapist — or was he her lover? — and his people found out in Genesis 34, may not be an offer of identity, protection and community, but the foretaste of a fatal wounding and a fatal exclusion. As David Halperin reminds us in another context:

> We cannot suppose that the contents of the communal unconscious are necessarily bright and kindly. The contrary is far more likely to be true. There is much there that is dreadful and monstrous, which we nonetheless ignore at our peril. Access to these dark and terrible realms, however indirect, may be a necessary part of what religion means for us. A religious teacher or text that can grant us such access has the potential for doing us great service, as well as enormous injury. (Halperin 1993: 223-24)

16. See here Elliot R. Wolfson's essay 'Divine Suffering and the Hermeneu- tics of Reading: Philosophical Reflections on Lurianic Mythology' (Gibbs and Wolfson [eds.] 2002: 101-62) where Wolfson cites a remarkable passage on 'textual circumcision' from Marc-Alain Ouaknin's *Mysteries of the Kabbalah* (2000) in which Ouaknin explains reading in terms of a process of cuts that the reader must make in the text: 'It is a circumcision of the text, but also the circumcision of God revealing Himself as text' (Gibbs and Wolfson [eds.] 2002: 137; citing Ouaknin 2000: 321).

Access itself, however, may demand that injury as its price. Whether it is the loss is a foreskin, or loss of the union with the maternal that the move to language entails, the Bible both demands and mourns it. How we react to such loss, and where we displace the resentment that it can engender, is fundamental to our reaction to the scandal and the violence of the biblical text.

10

WHAT THE BIBLE CAN DO TO A CHILD:
THE METRICAL PSALMS AND *THE GAMMAGE CUP*

Is the Bible a children's book? I suspect that for most biblical critics, at least, the answer would be a rather puzzled 'Of course not'. The suggestion that the Bible was written for children seems unlikely and, in any case, the concept of children's literature applied to ancient Israel is surely an anachronism. Yet for as long as I can remember I have been exposed to the Bible. For me, and for many of my generation in Scotland, the Bible was part of our childhood reading, as it has been for generations of children in Western, particularly Protestant, cultures. I am not thinking here of the Bible rewritten for children, the subject, for instance, of Ruth Bottigheimer's excellent study (1996). It is the Bible undiluted to which we were exposed.

For this child, at any rate, the Bible was a part of my earliest reading. Immediately this suggests a number of further questions. How did this early encounter affect the way I now read the Bible? How, indeed, did it fit into my wider experience of reading? If Graham Greene is correct when he writes, 'Perhaps it is only in childhood that books have any deep influence on our lives' (1999: 13), this is an important issue. As a voracious reader from an early age, to trawl through the whole range of intertextuality which such self-searching might bring out would be fascinating, but would go well beyond the scope of this chapter. Luckily, I recently made the rather unexpected rediscovery of another beloved book from my childhood: Carol Kendall's enchanting but neglected fantasy *The Gammage Cup* (1990 [first published 1959]), which I first read under its British title of *The Minnipins*. Re-reading it, I rediscovered scenes I had long half-remembered which, I think, affected, or at least confirmed, my attitude to texts and still have repercussions in my approach to biblical reading. Juxtaposing these two memorable texts of my childhood has thrown light on what the implications of reading the Bible as a children's book might be. This in turn raises the question of what we mean by 'children's literature' and suggests some intriguing questions about the interactions of personal histories and cultural norms in reading.

The Metrical Psalms

As a preliminary sortie into these questions, in what follow I shall attempt to explore the question of the effect of childhood reading of the Bible by reflecting on my own reading experience. I was brought up as a moderately Presbyterian child in the Edinburgh of the 1960s. For an evocation what that meant, one need only turn to Muriel Spark's *The Prime of Miss Jean Brodie*. When I asked myself what my earliest memories of the Bible were, I had a sudden flash of fuzzy-felt pictures of Abraham and a camel which derive from my Sunday School from the age of three. I suspect many children could recall similar impressions. What struck me as more distinctive, and particularly Scottish, was that an established part of my education from the age of six or seven was to learn by heart metrical psalms and paraphrases. These were culled from the Scottish Psalter of 1650, still printed in the back of Bibles sold in Scotland.[1] These strange transpositions of Hebrew poetry into rhymes and rhythms related to ballad metres, sung to foursquare but often ruggedly powerful melodies, are deeply imbedded in the cultural memory of any Scot of my age or older.

I was surprised what returned almost effortlessly to mind. Especial resonances came from a quaintly powerful setting of Psalm 24 often used to introduce communion services:

> Ye gates, lift up your heads and sing!
> Ye doors that last for aye
> Be lifted up, that so the King
> Of Glory enter may.

---

1.   For an enjoyable history of the Scottish Psalter, recording its derivation from the Anglo-Genevan Psalter of 1561 through various revisions until the form still current was reached in 1650, see Patrick 1949. The Paraphrases, versifications of passages of both the Old and New Testaments, were published by a Committee of the General Assembly in 1781 in response to a long-standing demand for an expansion of the scope of worship to include more specifically Christian material, although many of the passages chosen came from the Old Testament. Both psalms and paraphrases were included entire in the Revised Church Hymnary of 1928 on which I was brought up.

I always loved that. The tune was stirring, but the words have stuck because even then I felt their fascination. The personification of the doors singing and lifting up their heads has a curious excitement, as does the implied power of apostrophe in that weird word 'Ye'. The strange enjambment of the verse and the annoyance that it is only at the end that one realizes that 'aye' is to rhyme with 'may' and not with 'sky' also make it memorable. What rang most clearly in my memory, however, was the little shiver caused by that 'that so' and the inordinate delay of the innocuous auxiliary verb. Language was being twisted under constraints which could ride roughshod over conventions of grammar in the interest of some conceived higher purpose. The tortured syntax exposed some of the sinews of English in a startling way.

Other well-known lines from Psalm 121 which I learned then reinforce this point.

> I to the hills will lift mine eyes
> From whence doth come mine aid.

A great part of the charm of this was the shifted word order, the quaint euphony of 'mine eyes', and the licensed ungrammaticality of 'from whence'.

Far from these crabbed contrivances dampening my enthusiasm for poetry, I was even then intrigued that compression and distortion may lead to unexpected juxtapositions and unlikely meanings. For a good Presbyterian child, this was God's Word, after all, and he had a right to do what he liked with grammar. He could play with words in other ways too:

> All people that on earth do dwell,
> Sing to the Lord with cheerful voice.
> Him serve with mirth, his praise forth tell,
> Come ye before him and rejoice.

Undeniably, this version of Psalm 100 has a plain and sturdy grandeur. Again, though, syntax goes by the board, but the inspired oddity of the word 'mirth' in the third line also stuck in my mind. There is the assonance of its first letter with the last letter of 'Him', emphatically but unidiomatically dragged to the start of the line, and the hidden rhyme with 'earth' in the first line. The word itself was an unfamiliar one, but I knew its connotations of rather uncontrolled laughter. It seemed rather surprising, but also a relief, that that would serve the Lord.

What learning the metrical psalms taught me was that the rules of language could be played with and that there could be a visceral delight in the incomprehensible. I was thus intrigued to come across a quote from Willa Cather which also touches on this effect of biblical reading.[2] In an essay on Thomas Mann's *Joseph and his Brothers* she writes, 'The effect of the King James translation of the Bible upon English prose has been repeated down through the generations, leaving its mark on the minds of all children who had any but the most sluggish emotional natures' (1936: 102). In her novel *My Ántonia* she gives an example of how this emotional effect extends to the oddities of the text when she records the deep impression made on her character Jim by his grandfather's reading from the psalms. What particularly catches the young man's imagination is not the sense of the text, but his grandfather's intonation of that eminently incomprehensible word 'selah': 'I had no idea what the word meant: perhaps he had not. But as he uttered it, it became oracular, the most sacred of words' (1954: 13).

The Bible was full of this resonant incomprehensibility. 'Hallelujah' and 'Amen' are the most prominent members of this class of biblical words which, to a child, had no meaning but their sound and their texture on the tongue. Biblical names had the same quality — Jehoshaphat and Jehoiakim, Bildad the Shuhite, who, as all children knew, is the shortest man in the Bible, and those wonderful and mysterious lists in Chronicles. Not just the names of people either but of peoples, lands and cities: Ramoth Gilead, Ur of the Chaldees, the Wilderness of Zin.[3]

For a Scottish schoolchild, the strangeness of the language of the psalms had a further resonance with other things we had to learn: the Scottish ballads and the poems of Burns. Here too were the same characteristics of a constrained verse form and a queer syntax, with a fine seasoning of unfamiliar and sometimes bizarre, yet musical words. *The Ballad of Sir Patrick Spens* was one we learnt by heart:

---

2.   I owe this hint to Judith Dusinberre's discussion of Cather in *Alice to the Lighthouse* (1999).

3.   That this relish of the mystique of such names and such words is not just a private quirk is borne out in Lin Carter's afterword to the Pan edition of some of Lord Dunsany's fantastic tales, *Beyond the Fields We Know* (Carter 1972). Carter draws attention to the fact that not only Dunsany's prose style but the names of his invented cities and characters were profoundly influenced by the Bible. Carter sees this as the beginning of a rich tradition of 'Hebraic' names still evident in fantasy writing, mediated through H.P. Lovecraft.

The king sat in Dunfermline toun
Drinking the blude-red wine.
'O whaur will I get a skeely skipper
Tae sail this ship o' mine?'

For a modern urban Scots child, much of this was a foreign language. What a lovely word 'skeely' is—so much more crafty that mere 'skilful'—and how much redder 'blude' is than 'blood'. The Psalms supplied such words too; what on earth was a 'tabernacle'—yet didn't it trip off the tongue?

Another resonance was with the work of Lewis Carroll. Set in a ballad metre and filled with marvellous words was a poem like 'Jabberwocky':

'Twas brillig, and the slithy toves
Did gyre and gimble in the wabe;
All mimsy were the borogoves,
And the mome raths outgrabe.

We will have occasion to discuss the wider importance of Carroll's work later, but this poem brings echoes not only of linguistic play, where half-recognizable but wholly mysterious words stand in perfectly proper sentences, but also evokes the mysterious bestiary of fantasy: toves, borogoves, raths, bandersnatches and the Jabberwock itself, 'with eyes of flame'. Something of that also come through the Psalms and chimed with my devouring of fantasy literature:

Praise God from earth below,
Ye dragons and ye deeps:
Fire, hail, clouds, winds, and snow,
Which in command he keeps.
Praise ye his name,
Hills great and small,
Trees low and tall;
Beasts wild and tame.

There in the Psalms themselves were those potent denizens of imagination's realm: dragons—and what is more, dragons of the deep!

That the metrical psalms have had a significant wider influence on subsequent literature has been carefully demonstrated by Coburn Freer. He argues persuasively for their importance to sixteenth- and seventeenth-century poets, especially George Herbert, and traces the influence further to such poets as Watts and Cowper and, in a later generation, Browning and Hardy. Auden is the modern poet he cites as 'voracious and perverse enough' (1972: 15) to use the metrical psalms, quoting in support of this Naomi Michison's testimony that

Auden was fascinated by their inversions. Lines by Auden, indeed, sum up as well as any the phenomenon we are pursuing:

> Blessed be all metrical rules that forbid automatic responses,
> Force us to have second thoughts, free from the fetters of self.[4]

Freer in his study goes on to suggest that the influence of the metrical psalms was twofold:

> ...first, a flagrant crudity of technique that could highlight extremely sophisticated statements. More importantly it permitted the speaker to comment on the manner in which he treated his subject, while in the very process of treating it. (1972: 48)

He goes on to explain what he means by this last sentence, arguing that the religious poets of the time drew on the example of the metrical psalms in making their stumbles part of their message; 'as one finds one's self by losing one's self, so the poem may complete itself by what may at first seem to be a loss of control' (1972: 49).

All in all, we reach the odd conclusion that much of the signifi-cance of the metrical psalms lies in the fact not that they are master-pieces, but that they are badly written. Freer quite baldly asserts, 'most metrical psalms are, quite frankly, miserable verse' (1972: 6). Donald Davie in the introduction to his anthology *The Psalms in English* agrees, and indeed finds some comfort in the universal opin-ion of every generation of critics that the versification of the so-called 'Old Version' of the metrical psalms produced by Sternhold and Hopkins in 1551 is 'wretched' (1996: xlvii). For Davie, this is impor-tant as it gives some support to the idea that there is a lowest com-mon standard by which poetry can be judged on technical and stylistic grounds, without considerations of class, gender or socio-politics.

Freer, on a similar track, goes on to an interesting discussion of what makes bad verse bad. He refers to the classic treatment of inep-titude in Demetrius's *On Style*, where badness is seen to be a viola-tion of decorum. Freer suggests that there may be a kind of verse which violates even more basic conventions of lexicon, syntax and rhythm, of which the metrical psalms are his key example.

What is at work in such cases is not so much a refusal of conven-tion, but a reversal of priorities. The greatest bad verse writer of all time, according to many critics, is the nineteenth-century Scots weaver William McGonagall, who can achieve a sublime banality

---

4.   Quoted as the epigraph to Brodsky.

and naive absurdity, but who nevertheless, though rhythm may creak, sense reel and sentiment ooze, always achieves some sort of a rhyme at the end of his lines.[5] This convention overrides all others in his work. It is the application at all costs of the severe metrical constraints of the Scottish Psalter which not only permits but demands the tortuous dismemberment of syntax, the juxtapositions of register and the oddity of its vocabulary. Bad poets, of course, are the ones who display to the reader, despite themselves, the artifices of their craft which good poets conceal.

The relevance of this to the child as reader is hinted at in a passage from Freud's *Jokes and their Relation to the Unconscious* on children's acquisition of language:

> During the period in which a child is learning how to handle the vocabulary of his mother-tongue, it gives him obvious pleasure to 'experiment with it in play', to use Groos's words. And he puts words together without regard to the condition that they should make sense, in order to obtain from them the pleasurable effect of rhythm or rhyme. Little by little he is forbidden this enjoyment, till all that remains permitted to him are significant combinations of words. But when he is older attempts still emerge at disregarding the restriction that have been learnt on the use of words. (1976: 174)

Freud sees the beginning of jokes in the struggle between the child's play with language and the critical censorship, external and soon internalized, that rejects what is meaningless or absurd. Jokes serve to undercut that distinction by finding situations where such inhibitions are subverted (1976: 177-78). Imaginative activity is rebellion, so Freud says.

Freud goes on to declare, somewhat surprisingly, that 'children are without a feeling for the comic' (1976: 288). What he means, it turns out, is that children actually know what they are laughing at. Freud argues that adults laugh at someone falling over because it is somehow 'comic' whereas children laugh from *Schadenfreude*. Indeed, he goes so far as to wonder if the comic should be regarded as 'the lost laughter of childhood' and to make the child the explanatory middle ground for the study of laughter. When an adult finds another adult funny, Freud suggests, the underlying comparison is 'That is how he does it — I do it in another way — he does it as I used to do it as a child'.

---

5.   The influence of the metrical psalms on McGonagall might be worth further investigation. Interested readers can find some of McGonagall's *Poetic Gems* on the website of the William Topaz McGonagall Appreciation Society at <http://www. taynet.co.uk/users/mcgon>.

The relevance of this discussion is that children can see in the work of 'bad' poets an adult failure in the same struggles they have with the conventions of language. The fact that this is an adult who struggles, and who struggles in the name of a text which is also the source of authority and convention adds to the fun, and reinforces the hope that language will always provide an escape and a means of subversion.

The link with the child is explicit in another way as well. Almost as soon as they appeared, there were calls for the revision of the 'childish' ineptitude of the metrication of the psalms, a move which gathered momentum as the passing of time increased their quaintness. On the other hand, Patrick quotes a remarkable passage by the eminent Scots Professor William Robertson Smith, a great influence on Freud, where he argued against one such revision as follows:

> As the Old Testament Church [*sic*] left for our guidance a perfect model of a *childlike* [my emphasis] faith and devotion…it is essential that this model should be kept in all its simplicity. Every artificial touch, every trace of modern taste must be avoided… A translation of the psalms for devotional use must be, above all things, simple, even naïve. This great requisite our Scottish version has fully realised and to have done so is a merit that outweighs a hundred faults. (Patrick 1949: 226)[6]

Robertson Smith turns the argument on its head by explicitly claiming that the psalms are in essence childlike and that this, together with the rough simplicity of the Scottish psalms which reflects it, is a virtue. This argument is part of a widespread view in nineteenth-century liberal circles of the Old Testament as representing in some aspects a childlike religion which in the Christian revelation reaches a new maturity.

A whole book could be written on the effects of this metaphor both on the view of Judaism and its implications for intellectual attitudes to the 'simple folk' who filled the pews of Scottish Churches. My point here is rather different, however. The childlikeness, rather than childishness, of these metrical psalms is to be found not so much in their naïveté as in the scope they give, often unwittingly, for a sense of linguistic play which deconstructs their claim to plainness, simplicity and directness of communication. The earnest effort to make language conform to simple verse for simple folk intended to instil a sober regard to the plain sense of scripture paradoxically ends up as

---

6.   Patrick cites this quote as from an Address in Aberdeen Free Church College, published in the *Presbyterian Psalmodist* for 1872: 105.

the gateway to a sense of language as a field of fantasy and imaginative construction.

As bad poetry, to use that term, they give us the spectacle of a claim to authority or propriety stuttering through a lack of ability to control language. If language evades this authoritative control, what does this say about the reach of the authority's power? There is a subversive delight in watching language wriggle out of the grasp of those who seek to use it as a tool to limit the imagination. Equally, however, there is a childlike wonder in the possibilities of language that open up, and deeper sense that there may be truths which are too much for language at its most eloquent.

Embedded in my childish experience, and in our cultural and linguistic memories, are texts which struggle against the constraint of language. These lumbering but potent Gullivers are tied down by versifying Lilliputians, and strain at the bonds of grammar, syntax and vocabulary, claiming the authority of a truth which is barely articulated or articulable.

The Gammage Cup

It is at this point that I want to turn for further illustrations of this point to a book which opened up this possibility to me in childhood, and which, looking back, I realize had a powerful influence on the way I now read the biblical text: Carol Kendall's *The Gammage Cup*. It concerns the doings of a race of small people (the Minnipins) who, so their legends have it, fled from their enemies, the Mushrooms, through a river tunnel into a hidden valley and were miraculously saved by the flooding of the tunnel they had climbed up. For several hundred years, they have lived peacefully in this impregnable refuge, protected by the river and by unscaleable mountains on every side. A harmonious way of life has evolved, much of it based on the increasingly hazy lore of Gammage, the mythical leader of their escape. The resonances with the biblical story of exodus to the promised land hardly need pointing out.

In Slipper-on-the-Water, the village where the main story takes place, however, there are distinctive features of the culture based on the discoveries of the one Minnipin who has ever left the valley and returned: Fooley the Magnificent. Having flown over the mountains and back in a balloon, he brought with him treasures from the outside world, now carefully preserved in the town museum. Unfortunately, his landing was a rough one which not only destroyed the balloon, and so any chance of reusing it, but also knocked the labels

off the objects. Fooley himself, so legend has it, was knocked unconscious in the crash and thereafter could remember nothing of what
happened to him outside.

So the Minnipins are confronted with these mysterious artefacts,
and the equally mysterious names that somehow attach to them. Sign
and referent have literally come apart in this momentous event. How
will they disambiguate them? Well, by dint of comparison with what
is familiar. There are two drawings in the basket, for instance. One
shows a large house with a tree in the garden, and the other shows a
strange pattern of vertical and horizontal lines which connect pictures of decorated shields. Fooley's detached labels include 'The
Painting' and 'The Family Tree'. This is an easy one to resolve. The
tree is so prominent in the drawing of the house, that there can be
little doubt that this is 'The Family Tree' — and what a pleasant idea!
From that time on, every house in Slipper-on-the-Water had a tree
outside it, the family tree of those who lived there. That meant that
the design of lines and shields must be 'The Painting'. So that's how
paintings are done in the outside world! Ever after, the official
painters of the village rang variations on the themes of shields and
lines. Only the children, and the maverick woman known as Curly
Green, painted things supposed to look like the real world, which the
official painters sneered at as 'daubs'.

The passage that most intrigued me, however, was one where
three characters give their interpretations of 'The Poem' (Kendall
1990: 47-53). This is a mysterious, and revered, verse which Fooley
brought back from over the mountains. It runs as follows:

> Mary had a little lamb,
> Its fleece was white as snow;
> And everywhere that Mary went
> The lamb was sure to go.
>
> It followed her to school one day —
> It was against the rule;
> It made the children laugh and play
> To see a lamb in school.

After Fooley's return, this text becomes the model for all subsequent officially recognized poems. They must begin 'someone had a
little something' and carry on in that vein. The passage where this
poem is interpreted is one in which Wm., the official poet, is writing
a welcome poem for the return of the village mayor. Wm.'s name
tells us that he belongs to the leading family of Slipper-on-the-Water,
the Periods. These are the descendants of Fooley and have adopted

the distinguished practice of naming their children from a list found in Fooley's balloon of words that no one could decipher, but all of which ended in a full stop or period: Etc., Geo., Eng., for instance. The Periods are the jealous guardians of Fooley's heritage and are imposing an increasingly intrusive uniformity on the other villagers.

Muggles, the timid but mildly eccentric Minnipin who looks after the museum, begins the discussion by asking Wm. if his new poem will be sad. Asked why she expects so, she replies by revealing that 'The Poem' had always seemed sad to her. Not knowing what a 'lamb' is, she imagines it to be a white mouse, perhaps taking a cue from its littleness. Neither does she know what a 'school' may be. She deduces from the fact that the children only begin to laugh and play once the lamb and Mary have arrived at school that the children were ill, as otherwise they would be playing anyway. 'School' then must be some kind of hospital. The implication is that Mary herself must be ill to be going to school 'and altogether it is a sad sort of poem isn't it?' (Kendall 1990: 48).

Muggles's reading reflects the problems of deduction which faces any reader confronted with a text which comes from an unfamiliar culture with unfamiliar terms, not least the biblical reader. The reader cannot help noticing, however, that her predilection is to examine the emotional situation implicit in the poem and then try to build a scenario around that emotional truth which she thinks she has seen. As in many rabbinic interpretations of problematic passages, she seizes on a transition in the text. Why does it make the point that the children *began* to laugh and play? This turns the reader's attention to the question of what they were doing before. Muggles takes it as natural that children would be playing, perhaps reflecting her own genial nature, now clouded by the increasing conventionality of the village.

Wm.'s reaction as the official voice is scathing. For Muggles even to suggest that the poem is sad is a slur on the central text of Minnipin culture. Instead, he interprets the word 'lamb' as 'friend'. The poem is a cautionary tale about the friend turning up at a village meeting, which he was too young to attend in any case, in a garish white cloak instead of the standard Minnipin green one, and the children's laughter was ridicule at the spectacle he was making of himself. Muggles herself is wearing her rather daring orange sash and the other nonconformists of the village stand out by their predilection for bright colours. Wm., as a Period and therefore a member of the establishment, turns the poem into a didactic tale which preaches conformity.

His reading in turn is countered by Walter the Earl, the heir of an ancient family, and the eccentric reader of ancient documents in his family's keeping. These form a countertext to 'The Poem', but only he can decipher them. He leans on this superior knowledge to undermine Wm.'s conventional reading. 'School', he argues from his study of the older language, means a shoal of fish. So far so good. Having postulated fishing as the semantic field of the poem, he interprets the unfamiliar word 'lamb' as a derivative of 'lamprey'. This parasite is attached to Mary, herself a fish, and therefore follows her. The children are laughing at this unfamiliar sight. Walter then turns this interpretation against Wm., declaring that the children are foolish to laugh at what was a threat to their food-supply. He ends up by roundly declaring that the poem itself is ridiculous.

Wm. is routed for the moment, and Walter takes the chance to explain to Muggles, who is both delighted and scandalized by his behaviour, that the ancient scrolls show that, far from losing his memory in the crash of his balloon, Fooley was indeed a fool, even before his flight. No brave adventurer, he had been carried off by accident.

I can still remember how entertaining I found these re-readings of the story as an eight-year old. Returning to the book, I am now more able to appreciate the subtlety with which Kendall tailors the interpretations to the characters' perceptions, personality and social location. Part of the joke for the reader is that all the interpretations are 'wrong', and not only childish readers can feel a certain smugness at being smarter than the characters in a story.

This helps Kendall to reveal the political aspect of interpretation. Wm.'s reading is a blatant claim to authority. He declines to explain his reasoning, unlike Muggles who ponders aloud as she interprets. He dismisses her reading as 'utter nonsense', while he uses expression such as 'obviously' and 'that's clear enough' in lieu of explanation for his own interpretations.

To such claims of transparency and authority Walter opposes his expert knowledge. Walter's scholarship, however, proves to be just as misleading as Wm.'s claim to authority from the reader's point of view — a salutary lesson for all academic readers of the Bible. Kendall does leave it open for the reader to wonder how seriously Walter is dealing with the text, and how far his interpretation is simply a device to discomfit Wm. His stern diatribe against the poem is, we are told, interrupted by a surreptitious wink to Muggles.

The parallels to biblical reading are almost too obvious to need stating. The Bible comes to us from 'over the mountains', so to speak,

and we are in little better position than the Minnipins to give defini-
tive meaning to the practices and beliefs of the ancient culture which
gave rise to it. The official poet's wrestling to cram all meaning into
the form of 'Mary had a little lamb' is not so far removed from the
valiant efforts of those who turned the psalms into ballad metre.
Kendall's book is also full of just the kind of joy over the play of
language to which we have referred.

Her book is also a plea for the acceptance of diversity and uncon-
ventionality. In a later interview, Carol Kendall talks about the origin
of her sense of the stifling influence of conformity:

> A few years ago, at least twenty years after *The Gammage Cup* was
> published, I was asked what first influenced my feeling about confor-
> mity, and I gave the matter some heavy thought. A long-forgotten
> story gradually took shape in my mind, one from the old *Child Life*
> magazine I subscribed to when I was perhaps nine years old. It was
> about a costume party, and went something like this: 'Everybody' was
> having costume birthday parties that year—it was the very latest
> fad—and the mothers met in protest to plan an end to their children's
> copy-catism. When the day of the party finally came and the children
> began to arrive at the birthday house, they found that their secret
> costumes were exactly like all the other secret costumes. They were a
> party of sheep.
>   The real beginning in my interest in conformity surely lies in that
> story, its author unknown to me. I had forgotten it over the years, but
> the memory was there all the time, safely stowed in my head. (May
> and Straub 1981: 250)

Kendall's childhood reading thus has a deep influence on her later
writing. The fact that sheep appear both in 'The Poem' and in the
story she later recalls may not be accidental.

For my part, reading as a child influenced by Kendall's book, the
metrical psalms became a entrée into the subversive possibilities of
interpretation. They confirmed for me the self-destructive effect of
convention, which in its attempts to squeeze diversity into uniformity is almost bound to heighten the sense of difference and lead to the
rupture of the supposed unity. As a child who would rather be a solitary reader than take part in the conventional activities of my peers,
this is a message which confirmed me in my sense of difference. It
also confirmed me in my suspicion of those who claimed to know the
meaning of texts.

I remember even as a child rejecting the kind of literalizing reading
of the parables, for instance, which my good Sunday-school teachers
gave me. I still vividly recall my indignation at being told that the
incident where Christ walked on the water was easily explained if

one realized that the Sea of Galilee was prone to very shallow sandbanks which the water barely covered. Christ simply walked out on one of these. Quite apart from the fact that the people who he supposedly took in by this act were professional fishermen, which stuck me even then as an unlikely scenario, somebody somewhere was being taken for a fool. Either Christ thought the disciples were fools, or the evangelist thought his readers were fools, or my pious teacher thought I was a fool.

Even then I suspected that this convenient piece of hydrography might owe more to the need for an explanation than to any real characteristic of the Sea of Galilee. To have this shabby trick peddled to me as a way of saving the authority of the biblical text was intensely irritating. I knew even then that stories did not work like this, and that the suspension of disbelief they called for was not to be equated with simple credulity or a shameful sort of willed ignorance. The story gave a glimpse of another world, or, more accurately, a transfigured version of the world we live in. My acceptance or rejection of it was not concerned with plausibility, but with believability. Whatever happened, something in the text was being traduced. Just that sense of play, of wonder, of the ability to turn a text so that its facets sparkled in the light of its imagined world, was missing.

The American writer Annie Dillard records her own similar experience as follows:

> The Bible's was an unlikely movie-set world alongside our world. Light-shot and translucent in the pallid Sunday-School watercolors on the walls, stormy and opaque in the dense and staggering texts they read us placidly, sweet-mouthed and earnest, week after week, this world interleaved our waking world like dream.
> …What arcana! Why did they spread this scandalous document before our eyes? If they had read it, I thought, they would have hid it. They didn't recognize the vivid danger that we would, through repeated exposure, catch a case of its wild opposition to their world. (1988: 134)

The Bible as a Children's Book

To this day, then, I think my interpretation of the Bible is coloured by my encounter with it as a children's book among children's books. In this regard, it is quite striking how little attention is paid to the Bible in historical surveys of children's reading.

One notable exception to the general neglect of the Bible in this regard is John Goldthwaite's *The Natural History of Make-Believe*. In this idiosyncratic reading of the tradition, he traces children's books in the West back to the book of Proverbs. He holds little brief for Proverbs as a book children ever read with pleasure: 'It is no leap to imagine Israel's young elite having to commit these sayings to memory and loathing everyone of them... Here the eternal father stands, scandalized before the hormonal stupor of the eternal adolescent' (1996: 5). Yet Goldthwaite sees the proverb, the 'annoyingly stable truth', as the necessary substrate for the world of make-believe.

His ideal of children's fiction is *Pinocchio*, which he reads as a fairly faithful modern reworking of the book of Proverbs. The errant son rebels against the father and meets the chastisement of Lady Wisdom in the person of the Blue-Haired Fairy, often in situations and terms which can be closely paralleled from the biblical text.

On the other hand, Goldthwaite is particularly scathing about the book which many other writers regard as the real turning point in literature for children, Lewis Carroll's *Alice's Adventures in Wonderland*. This he sees as an appalling betrayal by Carroll of his duty as a clergyman to instruct children. In the name of innocent play, he professes to abdicate the obligation to teach his readers. Yet, Goldthwaite argues, every book teaches, and what *Alice* teaches is a specious and irresponsible relativism. Not content with God's world, Carroll invents his own. Not content with language as a medium to convey truth, he displays its arbitrariness.

Intriguingly similar points are made about *Alice*, though with an entirely different conclusion, by Juliet Dusinberre. In her *Alice to the Lighthouse* (1999) she convincingly argues that *Alice* is an essential precursor to Virginia Woolf's fiction, liberating the (female) child to make autonomous judgments on her world against the spurious authority of tradition and patriarchy. What was a vice in Goldthwaite's opinion is a virtue in Dusinberre's, as the breakdown of language allows a creative escape from the dead hand of the father and his proverbs.

Goldthwaite and Dusinberre represent in this regard versions of the two sides of a fundamental debate which can be traced through the history of children's literature. John Rowe Townsend, for instance, structures the early chapters of his *Written for Children* (1995) around this. The division is standardly made between books of instruction, which are predicated on a view of the child as a defective being which needed instruction to overcome the effects of innate sin, and books of entertainment, which see the child as in some senses innocent of the adult world, and if anything needing protection from its corruption. Locke's *Thoughts on Education* of 1693 are often cited as a prime influence in the gradual move towards the second attitude and hence to the production of a specific genre of literature designed for children. In Locke's view, entertainment might draw the child into learning willingly, rather than having knowledge beaten into him.

Though this is a relatively common view of the case, Karín Lesnik-Oberstein (1994) makes it clear that the debate can be carried back almost two centuries further in her discussion of the roles of Luther and Comenius in the reform of education. Luther championed the setting up of schools for all children, where their instruction might be enticing and attractive, not to say seductive, as much a source of pleasure as playing with a ball. Yet Luther was clear that these schools exist to train readers of the Bible. Under the guise of entertainment, instruction is taking place.

Lesnik-Oberstein reminds us of the darker side to this. This play itself is under the controlling power of God. On the one hand, Luther lays the Bible open to the manifold interpretations of the individual. On the other, he invokes the Spirit, and his own function as commentator, to rein in that meaning, while decrying the claims of the pope or anyone else to limit the freedom of the reader. Lesnik-Oberstein explicitly draws parallels between Luther and the modern-day critic of children's literature. She sees a similar dynamic at hand where freedom of the actual child reader becomes subsumed in the concept of the child promoted by the critic, or indeed the educationalist.

In this, she acknowledges her debt to a seminal book by Jacqueline Rose: *The Case of Peter Pan: On the Impossibility of Children's Literature* (1984). In this work, Rose points out that almost without exception what is called children's literature is written by adults, reviewed and appraised by adults and the bulk of it bought by adults. There is a long tradition of praising those writers who are thought to be able to recollect their childhood, but even they are writing for some virtual construction, the 'child reader'. All implied or virtual readers are fictions, in that sense, but there is a particularly noticeable gap between the producer and the consumer, the adult author and the child reader, in children's literature.

Rose characterizes children's literature as follows: 'There is, in one sense, no body of literature which rests so openly on an acknowledged difference, a rupture almost, between writer and addressee' (1984: 4). She argues that the child in children's literature is always the creation of adult desire and is about adult investment and adult notions of what the child ought to be. In this sense children's literature is a literature of seduction, drawing the child into the world of the book away from its own reality towards an adult fantasy. All literature is based on the seduction of the reader, it is true, but Rose here again emphasizes the asymmetry between author and intended reader. 'Children's fiction sets up the child as an outsider to its own process and then aims, unashamedly, to take the child *in*' (1984: 2). Though Rose does not make much of this herself, there is a telling ambiguity in the final phrase 'taking the child in' — *in*cluding the child, or *de*luding it? How far is the subversive voice of children's literature a deceptive or seductive freedom offered by a complicit adult?

What strikes me is that, taken on its own, Rose's statement about the distance between author and reader could surely be as well — or better — applied to the Bible's relation to its readers, especially when it is understood as scripture. What literature is more concerned to make the point both of the distance between its divine author and its human readers, and indeed to emphasize the nature of the rupture between them? Furthermore, what literature is more concerned with the seduction of these readers, with the enactment of the divine desire for the human?

Carrying this point further, Lesnik-Overstein uses Rose's work to explore the parallels between the father–son relationship between God and humans and the relationship between the child reader and adult author. Here we may introduce a comment from Gabriel Josipovici's *The Book of God* (1998). The Bible is unique, he says, in that 'it is the only book in our culture where the child's relation to books is perpetuated into adulthood' (1998: 8). Josipovici is explicitly thinking here of the fact that the Bible is still read aloud to us, but his remark has wider resonances. As he says later, '…the one relation between fathers and children which towers above all others is the relation of God to man, and in particular to Israel' (1998: 145). Reading Judg. 10.11-16, he extends the analogy: 'What we have here…is exactly what we might expect of a conversation between a loving father and an ever-naughty but charming child' (1998: 145).

Both Lesnik-Overstein and Josipovici remind us that the Bible constructs its readers as children and explicitly calls them the 'children of Israel' or the 'children of God'. In that important sense, the Bible quite literally presents itself as a book for children. The question then is whether it is a book of instruction, or of entertainment, or a book which itself deconstructs that opposition. Is it a book of paternalistic conformity, as Lesnik-Overstein and Rose would warn, and Goldthwaite would applaud, or is it a subversive spur to the risks of creative play?

Against Goldthwaite, I simply bring my own experience as a child who found in the Bible elements which have much in common with a poem like Carroll's 'Jabberwocky'. The 'irresponsible' attitude to language that Goldthwaite decries in Carroll seems to me traceable to the biblical tradition itself as transmitted to me. Goldthwaite appears to underestimate the element of play in the Bible itself. It is far from a simple book of instruction, and insofar as it does contain instructional elements it displays an awareness of all the tensions over convention to which we have alluded. In both the Old and New Testaments, the instructions it offers are often direct counters to the conventions of human society.

In any case, insofar as it is a book about law and custom, it is a book about law resisted and broken, and at times overturned. Ezekiel, for one, is clear that the conventions of previous generations are not to be followed, and goes so far as to say that God gave bad law. Moreover, where the reading of law is enjoined, it is enjoined as a delight, not as a sober exercise in self-improvement. Meditation on the Torah is not a grim reading through an instruction manual, but a source of joy and the Rabbinic tradition outdoes any other in the playful use of puns, assonance and seeming inconsequence in its revelling in the texture of the text.

In the New Testament, Jesus' use of puns and of jokes against the authorities seems to have more in common with the subversive strand of children's literature, where the forces of convention, the responsible adults who bear the tradition, are incapable of fathoming the secret which can bring down their structures of authority.

One verse which may best sum up the anomalies we have explored is to be found in the very book which Goldthwaite, quite convincingly, holds up as the paradigm example of children's literature as he understands it. It is Prov. 8.30. In this chapter of Proverbs we have Wisdom herself, a figure of imagination, redescribing creation. A whole dimension is added to the plain account of Genesis. She seems guilty of the same act of literary revision which Goldthwaite found so reprehensible in Carroll.

In 8.30 what we learn is that day-by-day her business is not to teach but to rejoice, or play, before the Lord. Rather than performing the role of a celestial school-mistress, she is described as a *sha'ashu'im*, just the kind of playful reduplicative word which strikes us in nonsense rhyme, and one which commentators still boggle over: 'darling'? — 'plaything'? — 'playmate' — even 'little child'? In addition, she tells us that in her daily and perpetual play 'my delight was with humankind', itself an enigmatic phrase in the Hebrew. We can read out of it that it was her delight to play with humankind, or that she took pleasure in humanity, or with a slight wresting of the syntax, that humankind was the object of her desire.

Right at the heart of Proverbs, then, we find the enigmatic invitation to play which, in this dark world, must always hold its dangers as well as its delights. The seductive adult can turn into the child abuser, the smiling child in the playground can turn out to be a bully. The playfulness of language can indeed mean that it may treacherously slip and betray us. But all the instruction in the world will not substitute for the interchange of delight and fear, of dangers courted, sometimes overlooked, which make up the true learning of childhood, dangers and delights for which the imaginative world of the children's book, the Bible included, can offer both entry and escape.

11

THE BIBLE AS WOLF:
TRACKING A CARROLLIAN METAPHOR

Wolf in the Sheepfold is the British title of the book by Robert Carroll which in the United States appeared as *The Bible as a Problem for Christianity*.[1] Carroll himself referred to the work in his introduction to the second edition as just plain *Wolf*. Throughout it, Carroll evokes the metaphorical resonances of the wolf and its wildness in his resistance to what he calls the 'domestication' of the Bible, a charge that is common among more radical biblical scholars. What *Wolf* calls for is a reintroduction of the wolfish Bible and wolfish reading into the tame flocks of the Church and the Academy. The Bible as wolf; the biblical scholar as wolf; what are the implications of such metaphors? In this chapter, I want to delve into these questions as a way of reflecting on Carroll's work and its significance for those who come after him.

Of course, as a contemporary scholar the first place I turned to was the internet. Enter 'Bible' and 'wolf' on a search engine and you may well come across 'Watchful the Wolf'. He is small, cuddly and stuffed with beans, one of the Bible Verse Babies™ available from <http://www.bibleverse.com>. Like his colleagues, he comes complete with his own Bible verse to reflect on: 'But you be watchful in all things, enduring afflictions' (2 Tim. 4.5) and a suitably homiletic description:

---

1.   The book was first published in 1991 by SPCK, London, as *Wolf in the Sheepfold: The Bible as a Problem for Christianity*, and simultaneously by Trinity Press International, Philadelphia, as *The Bible as a Problem for Christianity*. The second edition was published in 1997 by SCM Press, London, as *Wolf in the Sheepfold: The Bible as Problematic for Theology*. In the acknowledgments for the new edition, Carroll records his gratitude that the subtitle of the new edition restores his original intention (p. x). In the light of his own reflections on the effects of marketing decisions on biblical reception, this is an interesting comment! Throughout this chapter, references are to the second edition.

> Watchful, our baby wolf, is always looking out for food as well as danger. We too must keep our focus on Jesus, and see, even with trials, that we will someday be with Him in paradise.

Going one better than his secular Beanie Baby rivals, Watchful does not have a simple birthday, but a born-again day. As one of the testimonials helpfully listed on the website says, 'In today's world with all the evils on the internet, this is a God-send'.

Robert Carroll's likely response to this would, I fear, be unprintable. However, Watchful certainly seemed to me a God-send, almost too apt an example of the domestication of both the wolf and the Bible Carroll so opposed. It is easy enough to see how what Watchful represents pulls the teeth, so to speak, of the wolf as animal and symbol and also of the biblical canon. Both are marketed as a commodity which will comfort children, reassure adults, and make money for enterprising Christian businessmen. Carroll's own work on the Bible as commodity (Carroll 1998) has pioneering importance in elucidating some of the social and economic factors which shape our cultural reception of the Bible.

Yet is the call for the 'authentic' wolf—or text—wild and with teeth, any less socially determined? It may reflect the aesthetics of the romantic or even gothic imagination rather than dealing with the reality of the interaction between animal and human, text and reader, in the complexity of twenty-first-century global society. Is it true to the wolf, or to the Bible?

To answer these questions, I shall explore the way in which the image of the wolf still acts as a vehicle for mediating social and cultural conflicts in contemporary discourse and then to reflect on the parallels in the operation of the Bible as culturally significant text. The justification for this approach can be found in Lévi-Strauss's well-known aphorism: 'Animals are good to think [with]' (1969: 162). Wolves seem to have been particularly good to think social structures with. Like humans, they are a predatory pack species with elaborate social structures and complex family relationships. They function as the 'other', to use that much overworked term, but in an ambivalent way. They are both the potentially lethal enemy and rival and also the representatives of a parallel, and perhaps purer, social order and mode of harmonious existence in the world. The wolf, so near and yet so far from the human, has lent itself to the cultural consideration of the boundaries between human and animal and to the breaking of such boundaries. We need only think of the prevalence of middle terms between human and wolf available to story-tellers and theorists alike: the dog, the tame wolf in human's pack; the wide-spread myths of the werewolf, the man transformed to wolf; and the wolf-child, the human infant reared in a loving alternative family.[2]

Rather than explore these issues in detail, I want to combine two routes into the exploration of the resonance of the wolf as metaphor and the light this may shed on the cultural status of the Bible. First, the use and significance of the wolf in children's literature is a particularly pertinent index to the associations which it calls up and the cultural space it occupies. Secondly, instructive parallels to arguments over the status of the Bible can be found in the impassioned debates over the reintroduction of the wolf into its former range both in the United States and in Europe, including the Scottish Highlands. These political and practical debates are themselves witness to the range of mythologies which have condensed around the wolf, often with little justification in biological and historical fact and more to do the metaphorical expression of hidden anxieties in individuals and communities.

This point is borne out by Mary Midgley who speculates in her essay 'The Problem of Living with Wildness' (2001) that the turn to agriculture led to a change in the attitude of mingled fear and respect that humans accorded to animals. The domesticated beasts came to be despised as commodities, while their potential predators came to be regarded as enemies. She argues that human vices were projected onto these animals, in particular in northern Europe onto the wolf, which was seen as cruel, sly and cowardly. This meant that people not only felt justified in killing the predators who were often depicted as malignly antisocial, but were able symbolically to kill the vices that disrupt communal life. 'Killing the personification makes them feel that they have actually killed the vice. They are symbolically destroying their own wildness' (2001: 182).

The picture looks a little different if you are not the farmer, however. Here is the final paragraph of a children's novel, *The Last Wolf of Ireland* by Elona Malterre, which is the story of Devin, a young boy who with his friends secretly rears the last wolf in Ireland.

---

2.   David White's *Myths of the Dog-Man* (1991) is a fascinating exploration of the way in which the dog and the dog-man have been used culturally to deal with alien cultures while Staley (1995: esp. 147-99) offer a remarkable Christian theological reflection on the relationship of dog and human. Baring-Gould (1995 [1865]), though elderly, remains the classic treatment of werewolves along with the learned but bizarre work of Summers (1933). Newton (2002) discusses sensitively the issue of wolf children.

> The earth between Devin's feet shook with the fury of the storm, and the wind began to howl like a wild thing. Devin saw that the wolf's yellow eyes were closed, and in the wind he seemed to hear the terrible howl of all the wolves that had been killed in Ireland. Their cries seemed to rise with the wind, and the rain began to fall, and it seemed to Devin that nature was weeping — for the last wolf of Ireland was dead. (1990: 127)

Here the extermination of the wolf takes on quite a different resonance. In a paper for the journal *Irish Geography* on the fate of the Irish wolf, Kieran Hickey (2000) sees its extermination as a direct result of British rule. He tells us that there is evidence of a clear difference in attitude between the British settlers, who wanted to reproduce the English countryside in their demesnes and thus viewed the wolf as vermin to be exterminated, and the Irish population, who certainly feared the wolf but did not seek its eradication. Hickey demonstrates that the native Irish and the wolves were equated by the settlers as twin threats to the settled order of civilized society which had to be removed. A similar equation of Native American peoples with the wolf can be seen in the settlement of the American West, with even more drastic consequences.

In the Scottish tradition, the role of sheep and wolf can in some aspects approach reversal. In a parallel children's story, Michael Morpurgo's *The Last Wolf*, this time set in Scotland, the last wolf of the title is befriended by a young orphan who is living wild as a survivor of the battle of Culloden, which in Scottish history epitomizes the crushing of Gaelic civilization. Explaining his choice of subject matter, Morpurgo writes in an author's note, 'Wolves were hunted down and wiped out, in much the same way, I thought, as the rebels who fought for Bonnie Prince Charlie against the redcoats' (2002: 91). As Robbie, the hero of the book, says, 'Wolf and rebel, we were inseparably bound together by the very nature of our common plight' (2002: 42).

In this spirit, and echoing earlier Gaelic poets,[3] the contemporary Glasgow writer Edwin Morgan calls for the return of the wolf to the Highlands:

3. The great, and illiterate, Gaelic poet Duncan ban Macintyre (1724–1812), for instance, begins his 'Oran nam Balgairean' ('Song to the Foxes') with the lines

The foxes have my benison
because of their sheep hunting,

Are these the sheep of brindled face
that caused dispeace through all the world;

Bring back the wolf!
He's not long gone, you know.
He went out when sheep came in.
Sheep cleared men and women.
Now let wolves clear sheep. (1997: 23)

A key myth in the formation of Scottish national identity is the Highland Clearances which followed Culloden, when thousands of Highland villagers were evicted from their lands and sent into forced emigration to make room for the great estates to stock sheep. Morgan, somewhat wryly, adapts this trope to the context of the new tourist Highlands where the stern wilderness is re-branded as a winter playground with the resort town of Aviemore at its centre:

A little wildness please,
A little howling to be heard from the chalets,
A circling of yellow eyes at Aviemore. (1997: 23)

The point is that in this context sheep are the symbol of oppression and dispossession. It is the wolves that are the liberating force of rebellion and revenge.

To Carroll, an Irishman in his own words 'in exile' in Scotland, with the long memories of both heritages, it is not surprising that the wolf in the sheepfold becomes a positive symbol of resistance and of the establishment of identity. The Bible as wolf in this sense is a text that resists the totalizing pressures of theologians and of religious communities and, taken seriously, turns back on them, giving voice to the oppressed and the ignored.

But the wolf remains an ambivalent symbol. Even in Morpurgo's book, the epithet can be applied to both sides in the conflict: the captain of the ship who rescues Robbie speaks of the British Redcoats, not the rebels, as the wolves. Robbie and the wolf, called Charlie after Bonnie Prince Charlie, make their way to Vermont, where Charlie reverts to the wild while Robbie builds a house and a new family.

Though the book ends there, the story could have an ironic continuation. Historically, many of the Scots driven across the seas became in turn part of the colonial society that drove out and exterminated both Native Americans and the American wolf. Their new settled identity makes an enemy of the native inhabitants who, like the Native Irish, had developed a more symbiotic relationship to the

The land to be laid waste to us
and the rent to become dearer? (Macleod 1952: 347).

wolf. The history of European expansion can show many such stories where the biblical rhetoric of the exodus and conquest means that a wolfish ferocity of conquest and plunder could be justified.

The Scottish ramifications of the story of the wolf do not end there, however. It was another emigrant Scot, John Muir, who was the prime mover in the American national parks movement and the rediscovery of wilderness. In the wake of his pioneering work, the wolf has developed another symbolic status as the epitome of wild nature, of something lost under the blear and smear of drab civilization. The surprisingly large contemporary literature of wolf books, wolf pictures and wolf preservation societies is evidence of this. The doyen of wolf writers, Barry Lopez, puts it this way:

> When, from the prison of our cities, we look out to wilderness, when we reach intellectually for such abstractions as the privilege of leading a life free from nonsensical conventions, or one without guilt or subterfuge — in short — a life of integrity — I think we can turn to wolves. We do sense in them courage, stamina, and a straightforwardness of living; we do sense that they are somehow correct in the universe and we are somehow still at odds with it. (1995: 249)

This positive sense of otherness often goes along with a sense of the wolf as the representative, not of wanton destruction, but of an alternative order, older and sounder than contemporary human society, a lost possibility for the human. Resonances can be found here too with readings of the Bible which see it as the indispensable voice of otherness, of a divine challenge and alternative to human social order and cultural convention.

But the danger here is what we may call an aesthetic approach to wildness, the approach that provides the funding for the ever increasing tourist trade in Antartica, for instance. Wilderness becomes an adjunct of the civic lifestyle, something that can provide a titillating glimpse into another and excitingly dangerous world, while all the time satellite phones and the other protections of the technological society act as an assurance that the teeth of the wilderness will never really bite. Wilderness then becomes something to be played with imaginatively but which has no actual impact on the possibilities of the observer's life. Such an urban nostalgia for the wolf as the epitome of the wild, free and untamed can clash with the realities of life in a rural economy. The reintroduction of wolves to areas where they have been driven out is politically, ecologically and ethically much debated. Farmers and hunters are often vehemently opposed to such reintroductions.

Nicholas Evans uses these tensions as they are worked out in a small Montana community that is faced with wolf reintroductions for the backdrop to his second novel *The Loop* (1998). The novel plays on the fact that the programme of reintroduction is not only opposed in its own right, but because it is seen as a prime example of federal government interference. What represents freedom for one group is seen as restriction by others who, in their view, cannot allow senti-mentality to undo generations of hard struggle to tame the wilder-ness.

The nostalgia for the wolfish Bible may be of the same order. Looking back at the record of religious wars and social repression sanctified in the name of the Bible, it is understandable that it should be either rejected or tamed by communities who seek to maintain their own survival.

In any case, there is a paradox in the idea of recreating wildness. Throughout almost all of its present range, the continued survival of the wolf depends on human benevolence. In Evans's novel, the wolf biologist finds her traps for the wolves in order to collar them are being sprung, not by a hostile rancher, but by the young man who has befriended her. Evans gives us his inner justification for this act as follows:

> It wasn't that he thought she meant to harm the wolves. Far from it. But once she got collars on them, they wouldn't be free. They could be found and got rid of whenever anyone chose. It was weird these biologist people didn't get it. But then maybe in the end they were just like everyone else, unable to stand other creatures being truly wild and forever trying to tame and shackle them. (1998: 206)

The question arises whether, in these days of wildlife management and satellite tracking, any wolf can be truly wild. Analogously, what might we be doing as biblical scholars who flatter ourselves that we are the wild end of the discipline? Is our nostalgia for the power and wildness of the Bible merely an aesthetic fantasy, good to play with, but one that does not threaten our livelihoods or our flocks, so to speak? How wild is our Bible? How wild are we? What place, for instance, would the wild Bible have in the life of a university? Even to be able to raise these questions demands the taming structure of academic convention and discipline. Reintroducing the Bible to post-modern culture may evoke many of the same tensions and compro-mises that the reintroduction of the wolf demands.

This brings me to the second strand of these considerations. Both the children's books that I cited above ally the child and the wolf in a quest to create and maintain an identity in the face of an imperialist and colonialist power. That is certainly not the only function that wolves play in children's fiction, however. Marina Warner's *No Go the Bogeyman* (1998)[4] is a fascinating treasure trove of information and reflection on the topic of the human and the animal and the importance of children's literature in understanding some of these tensions. She discusses in particular the role of the wolf in children's tales and nursery rhymes, seeing its prevalence there as a consequence of the actual danger of encountering wolves in times of famine in former times. Yet, as we have seen, there may be more to the usefulness of the wolf to the storyteller than simply its historic menace.

The very first of Ovid's *Metamorphoses*, Warner herself reminds us, is that of the tyrant Lycaon who served up human flesh to Zeus in a test of the god's powers. His punishment is to be turned into a wolf. He has broken a fundamental taboo, the demarcation between (inedible) human flesh and (edible) meat. In turn, by divine power the demarcation line between human and animal is broken, and the wolf, or the wolf-man, is the bridging figure.

The most famous story-wolf of all, the one in Little Red Riding Hood, is the wolf in Grannie's clothing, the predator in the guise of the carer. This story in its many conflicting versions has been the subject of much analysis.[5] Feminist and Marxist critics have seen it as a tale of repression. The bad girl who strays from the path, seduced by the dangerous wolf, is punished and has to be rescued and restored to socially acceptable bounds. We can see here the way in which the shepherd, if you like, can use the wolf to keep the flock in line. The threat of the hostile other excuses, or indeed requires, the submission of the sheep to their masters.

More subtle are the psychoanalytic readings which have taught us to see this wolf as the dark side of love and sexuality. Bruno Bettelheim, for instance, in his highly influential treatment of fairy stories *The Uses of Enchantment*, sees the eating of Red Riding Hood by the wolf in the following terms, which we may feel run the risk of falling into self-parody:

> Little Red Cap [he uses this name, drawn from the Grimm brothers' version], having been projected into inner darkness (the darkness inside the wolf), becomes ready and appreciative of a new light, a

---

4.   Her earlier volume *From the Beast to the Blonde* (1994) also offers intriguing insights in this area.

5.   Zipes (1993) and Tatar (1999) offer a wide variety of versions and critical commentary. For a delightful exercise in the perhaps unlikely genre of German theological whimsy, see Pesch 2000.

> better understanding of the emotional experiences she has to master, and those others which she has to avoid because they are as yet beyond her. Through stories such as 'Little Red Cap' the child begins to understand—at least on a preconscious level—that only those experiences which overwhelm us arouse in us corresponding inner feeling with which we cannot deal. Once we have mastered those, we need not fear any longer the encounter with the wolf. (1978: 181)

Warner for her part argues that such psychoanalytic approaches have made the monstrous a projection of the child and something that is ultimately to be accepted, even embraced rather than countered. In her view, this fails to take seriously both the specificity of stories, in that they can be reduced to aspects of one psychoanalytic metanarrative, but is also in danger of being a defensive projection of adults. The monstrousness that is thought to peek out from children is a sign of burgeoning sexual appetites, or in a Freudian sense, a matter of acknowledged and then mastered desire. What this psychoanalytic paradigm tells us is that we are no longer able to conceive of ourselves as separate from the animal. We carry the animal within us. We, but especially children, are 'hairy on the inside'.

This striking phrase is from Angela Carter's 'The Company of Wolves', her extraordinary retelling of Little Red Riding Hood. 'She knew the worst wolves are hairy on the inside', Carter writes (1996: 218). But Carter's point is not a simple identification of the animal and the human. She explicitly says it is the most dangerous wolves that are hairy on the inside, not us. To twist her words and argue that we are all 'hairy on the inside' blinds us to the real dangers that beset us as adults and particularly as children and lead us to deny the reality of the human as well. Denying the difference between human and animal, man and wolf, undermines the sense of human identity, and perhaps more accurately, is a symptom of a prevalent despair over the human.

It is precisely this despair which emerges in Julia Kristeva's allegorical novel *The Old Man and the Wolves* (1994), a book that centres on the murder of the Old Man who is convinced that his city is being taken over by wolves in human shape.[6] The narrator reflects:

> ...there can be no doubt, either for the believer or the poet: faced with the power of any divinity...human beings are helpless and, in their helplessness, change shape. And their transformation produces a story, and time strikes out henceforward in whatever direction is

---

6.   A rather different work, but one which uses material from a cognate realm of metaphor to express its own sense of unease at the human condition, is Herman Hesse's *Steppenwolf* (1965).

required of it. But we belong to a different world: One shape is replaced by another, every image blots out its neighbour and man degenerates into beast through sensational tales... (1994: 182)

And she asks rhetorically 'What metamorphoses can there be if the frontier [between good and evil] no longer exists?' (1994: 181).

In his book *Lost Icons*, Rowan Williams draws on Walker Percy's amusing, illuminating and exasperating work *Lost in the Cosmos* (1983) to point out that the desire to be one with the animal may betoken an all-pervasive loneliness in the postmodern self (Williams 2000: 169-73). It is a commonplace that a series of revolutions, linked in short hand to the names of Copernicus, Darwin and Freud, have displaced humanity from its unique place in the universe. Humans are now animals among the animals. And yet, the capacity for self-reflection and for language seems to make a breach, as Lopez pointed out above. Human beings seem uniquely at odds with the universe.

At the same time, the social revolutions of the last few decades, driven by a quest for autonomy and expanded possibilities of choice risk, engendering a solipsism which is fundamentally isolated. In the terms of the quotation from Kristeva, humanity has set its face against its helplessness, against the accidents of birth and death. Where everything is possible, where the metamorphoses of cosmetic surgery and the promise of genetic modification make identities fluid and the subject of choice rather than chance, the ubiquity of change makes transformation either impossible or meaningless. In a way that the Kierkegaard of *The Sickness unto Death* would recognize, this despair may lead either to a despairing denial of real difference, or a defiant yet still despairing embrace of isolation. Oddly and incoherently, it seems to be quite possible for the despairing to combine both reactions.

Though neither Williams not Percy make this explicit, we can in fact trace here another contradictory thread of sympathy between wolf and human. The loneliness of the wolf and his howl is an evocative trope though in actual fact wolves are intensely social beings.[7] The fascination with the fate of the 'last wolf' and the endangered lives of the scattered surviving packs speaks to that sense of beleaguerment. The end of the preface to the second edition of *Wolf* carries

---

7. Charles Bergman, for instance, writes, 'The howl of the wolf speaks of regions in nature, and in ourselves, that we can never tame, never control. But we can learn to live with it. Occasionally, even if only for a few minutes, we can hear that demonic music in their howls, feel the ecstasy of those haunting echoes' (1997: 119).

something of the same atmosphere. 'I write to contribute to a solidarity of the lonely', Carroll states (1997: xv), and the final words of the preface are a quotation from the Scottish poet James Thomson's unrelieved charter for pessimism, *The City of Dreadful Night*. The poet evokes as his audience a lonely fellow wanderer who says to himself:

> I suffer mute and lonely, yet another
> Uplifts his voice to let me know a brother
> Travels the same wild paths though out of sight. (1997: xv)

In the trackless wastes of the dark city, we catch an echo of the lone wolf's call. Carroll seems to take on the character of the voice not crying in the wilderness, but crying from the depths of the encircling city, from the cage, the cry of the 'university administrator with a little light academic work thrown in', his self-description in his unpublished presidential address to the Society for Old Testament Study in 1999.

Ted Hughes's poem 'Wolfwatching' gives a bleak, but important, warning here. The poem contrasts two wolves in a zoo cage in London, the old, white-haired wolf who has been ground down by the fact of his captivity and the young wolf, not yet reduced to the same state, but already carrying the ominous symptoms of such defeat:

> His eyes
> Keep telling him all this is real
> And that he is a wolf — of all things
> To be in the middle of London, of all
> Futile, hopeless things. (1989: 14)

In her discussions of the poem, Ann Skea reads this in the context of the 'wolf-masks' which she sees as a constant feature of Hughes's poetic persona, with Hughes casting himself as the old wolf who subsides 'in a trembling of wolf-pelt he no longer knows how to live up to' (1998: 13).

One of Robert Carroll's great gifts was his often unsung and unappreciated care and support for those younger scholars who he felt recognized the power of the texts they were studying. Only the cubs know the care that the old wolf puts into their nurture. Part of that care may be that the old wolf's life and death take their meaning as warning as well as example. There are cages aplenty for the academic wolf, and indeed, the academy may enjoy a visit to the zoo once in a while, but has it a place for the wolf unbound? In an academic culture increasingly bound to market forces, the gradual crushing of

the spirit and imagination by the all-too-real fact of the great surrounding city is a constant danger.

But this sombre note is not the last word. In Skea's reading of
Hughes's poem, the verse itself belies the characterization. Its lines
are not simply a 'few tottering steps' belying old poetic habits but a
powerful statement in which 'Hughes's abilities to evoke the wolf-
energies, old and young, is demonstrably as strong as ever' (1998: 9).
The same is true of *Wolf*, the final paragraph of which is a powerful
and characteristic evocation of the excitement open to the bold
biblical reader: 'If you want neatness, close the book and turn to
theology. But if you can tolerate contradiction and contrariety and
can handle hyperbolic drive and chaotic manipulation of metaphor
then the Bible will burn your mind' (Carroll 1997: 147).

Biblical scholarship with a burnt mind—now there is a thought to
conjure with. Do we dare that, dare to get close enough to the text for
its heat to sear us, for the wolf to devour us? Why, indeed, would we
wish to? If it is not unreal romanticism, is it simple irresponsibility to
seek to tap the 'wolf-energies' of a text which can be implicated in
more death and destruction than almost any other?

Unlikely as it may seem, there writer who most helps me here is
Hélène Cixous. Listen to her on the wolf:[8]

---

8.   This rather strange but powerful line of thought in Cixous's work has
convoluted roots. It emerges in *Rootprints* during a conversation between Cixous
and Mireille Calle-Gruber when the latter asks Cixous to retell Marina
Tsvetaeva's story of the wolf who loves the lamb he does not eat (1994: 107).
Cixous explains that this relates to Tsvetaeva's essay 'My Pushkin' (see Tsvetaeva 1980: 319-62). In it Tsvetaeva recounts the spell Pushkin fell under, which
she as a six year old also succumbed to—the spell which leads to love for the
father's murderer. Pushkin, she says, fell under the spell of the character of
Pugachev, the ruthless Cossack pretender to the tsardom who is a key figure in
Pushkin's historical novel *The Captain's Daughter*, which he wrote after complet-
ing his *History of the Revolt of Pugachev*. Tsvetaeva also wrote a later essay entitled
'Pushkin and Pugachev' (see 1980: 372-403). In it she comments on Pugachev's
surprising acceptance of the young hero of *The Captain's Daughter*, Grinev. She
wonders why that is and answers herself 'The pull on his heart. The black
creature who had come to love a nice white one. The wolf—isn't there a folk tale
like that?—who had come to love a lamb. This man loved a lamb that he did not
devour, maybe just because he did *not* devour it, the way we, villains and non-
villains, often get attached to a person because of our own good deed' (1980:
376-77). She argues that Pugachev's attachment to Grinev is based on the impossibility that Grinev should serve him. It is this passage which forms the basis of
Cixous's discussion.

The wolf says to the child: I'm going to eat you up. Nothing tickles the child more. That's the mystery: why does the idea that you're going to eat me up fill me with such pleasure and such terror? It's to get this pleasure that you need the wolf. The wolf is the truth of love, its cruelty, its fangs, its claws, our aptitude for ferocity. Love is when you suddenly wake up as a cannibal, and not just any old cannibal, or else wake up destined for devourment.

But happiness is when a real wolf suddenly refrains from eating us. The lamb's burst of laughter comes when it's about to be devoured, and then at the last second is not eaten. Hallelujah comes to mind. To have almost been eaten yet not to have been eaten: that is the triumph of life. But we've got to have the two instants, just before the teeth and just after, you've got to hear the jaws coming down on nothing for there to be jubilation. Even the wolf is surprised. (1999: 94)

Cixous sees the lamb's love for the wolf as derived from a sense of being the exception — we are the one who is not-devoured, 'the wolf's chosen one' (1999: 93), or, as her conversation partner Mireille Calle-Gruber puts it in *Rootprints*, 'a lamb-that-is-not-eaten-but-that-could-be' (1994: 108). The wolf's love for the lamb, on the other hand, demands the sacrifice of the wolf's very definition as the one who eats the lamb. Cixous talks of the loneliness of the wolf, 'the infinite solitude of the wolf, invisible and unrecognized except by itself' (1999: 98). But the wolf is not 'delupinized', to use Cixous's term. The whole dynamic depends on the fact that the wolf could and would eat us — only it does not. In *Rootprints*, she goes on to explain 'We are all wolves in love… To not want to devour the other is not a mark of love, but a mark of disinterest' (1994: 111).

We can put the same issue from the lamb's point of view: it is a sad thing when no one thinks us even good enough to eat. Marina Warner points out how the stories of wolves gain a hold over the childish audience by playing on the fascination and fear of the notion of being devoured, being good enough to eat, of becoming meat rather than flesh. Angela Carter recalled the way in which her maternal grandmother told her the story of Little Red Riding Hood: 'At the conclusion, when the wolf jumps on Little Red Riding Hood and gobbles her up, my grandmother used to pretend to eat me, which made me squeak and gibber with excited pleasure' (cited in Tatar, 1999: 9). Being good enough to eat is to know the affirmation and danger of being desirable. If we know we are edible, we know we have worth, that we are desired.

How does this relate to the issue of the Bible as wolf? It seems to me to have intriguing resemblances to the relationship between the Yahweh of the Hebrew Scriptures and Israel. Jack Miles in his

God: A Biography asks 'What is it that makes God godlike?' and answers his own question as follows:

> God maintains his peculiar power as a literary character because in him—around and through whatever fusion of ancient Semitic deities he represents, that which is most radically unanswerably terrifying in human existence is endowed with voice and inattention as well as with caprice and silence. (1995: 327)[9]

This is a God of peril, often spoken of in metaphors derived from the great predatory beasts, who from time to time threatens his own flock with destruction. No one need doubt that the God who destroys Israel's neighbours and enemies is also capable of devouring Israel. The Jewish poet Edmond Jabès in a characteristic aphorism observes 'We are the prey of various scriptures' (1996: 77). Yet Yahweh makes an exception, though a rather strange exception, of the beloved remnant of his people. He is the lonely God inextricably tied to the beloved Israel who demands the sacrifice of meat, and even of human flesh in the form of the foreskin, or of the firstborn and yet who protects the lamb, even, in the New Testament, offering himself as the sacrificial lamb.

Does this allow us to think that the fascination of the Bible may be the terrifying thrill for the reader of the possibility of being the chosen, of being the lamb loved by the wolf? Cixous, in her allusive way, explains why we need the real wolf, the dangerous wolf, the wolf that could eat us but does not, not just the possibility of a wolf—or the wolf as Beanie Baby. We need to know we are good enough to eat. To do this, we need to know that there is one who could and would like to eat us. Insofar as the Bible testifies to the reality of the wolf, of a God who could devour us yet does not, it becomes indispensable for the worth of the human.

The great reconciling vision of Isaiah comes irresistibly to mind here. 'The wolf shall dwell with the lamb', reads Isa. 11.6, and the next verse holds out the promise of a common meal between predators and prey, where one is not the meal of the other:

> The cow and the bear shall feed,
> their young shall lie down together;
> and the lion shall eat straw like the ox. (11.7)

---

9. Miles's subsequent study, *Christ: A Crisis in the Life of God* (2001), contains a highly suggestive exploration of the biblical metaphor of the Lamb. His take on this is rather different from Cixous's line here, but there are intriguing cross-links.

The lamb takes a risk here, but so to does the wolf. The wolf risks either being delupinized, of losing his essential nature as predator, or of succumbing to the temptation of his love for the lamb as meat, not as flesh. Both risk their identities, but love does not depend on the loss of identity, on the merging or metamorphosis of wolf into lamb. On the contrary, it is only because the devouring gaze of the wolf and the alluring flesh of the lamb hold steady in each other's presence that the miracle of love is possible.

In his own way, Robert Carroll bore witness that that tension could not be elided for the sake of neat theology or comfortable social structures. 'I could have written better and I could have written more', he says in the preface to *Wolf*, 'but I have written what I have written. I stand by it' (1997: xiv). We wish he had written more, we wish we could write as well, but whether we agree with him or not — and there was nothing he liked better than a good argument — we can be grateful for his stand, which was not without personal cost. He leaves us his conviction that witnessing to the reality and vital importance of the wolf, of that in the Bible which can 'burn the mind', was something essential to the human spirit, and something to take a stand for.

BIBLIOGRAPHY

Aiken, Susan H.
  1990   *Isak Dinesen and the Engendering of Narrative* (Chicago: University of Chicago Press).
Ardener, Shirley (ed.)
  1975   *Perceiving Women* (London: Malaby Press).
  1978   *Defining Females: The Nature of Women in Society* (London: Croom Helm).
Bach, Alice
  1997   *Women, Seduction and Betrayal in Biblical Narrative* (Cambridge: Cambridge University Press).
Baldwin, Aaron Dwight
  1902   *The Gospel of Judas Iscariot* (Chicago: Jamieson-Higgins).
Baring-Gould, Sabine
  1995   *The Book of Werewolves* (London: Senate [first published 1865]).
Barth, Karl
  1957   *Church Dogmatics*, II/2 (ed. G.W. Bromiley and T.F. Torrance; trans. T.H.L. Parker *et al.*; Edinburgh: T. & T. Clark).
  1961   *Church Dogmatics*, IV/3 (ed. G.W. Bromiley and T.F. Torrance; trans. T.H.L. Parker *et al.*; Edinburgh: T. & T. Clark).
Bates, Ernest Sutherland
  1929   *The Gospel of Judas* (London: William Heinemann).
  1936   *The Bible Designed to be Read as Living Literature* (New York: Simon & Schuster).
Bauman, Zygmunt
  1992   *Mortality, Immortality and Other Life Strategies* (Cambridge: Polity Press).
Bergman, Charles
  1997   'Hunger Makes the Wolf', in Robert Busch (ed.), *Wolf Songs: The Classic Collection of Writing about Wolves* (San Francisco: Sierra Club Books): 113-20.
Bertung, Birgit
  1984   'Har Søren Kierkegaard foregrebet Karen Blixens og Suzanne Broggers kvindesyn?', *Kierkegaardiana* 13: 72-83.
Bettelheim, Bruno
  1978   *The Uses of Enchantment: The Meaning and Importance of Fairy Tales* (Peregrine Books; London: Penguin Books).
  1979   *Surviving and Other Essays* (London: Thames & Hudson).

Bialik, Haim N.
    2000   *Revealment and Concealment: Five Essays* (Jerusalem: Ibis Editions).
The Bible and Culture Collective
    1995   *The Postmodern Bible* (New Haven: Yale University Press).
Blanchot, Maurice
    1995   *The Work of Fire* (trans. C. Mandell; Stanford, CA: Stanford University Press [French original 1949]).
Bloch-Smith, Elizabeth
    1992   *Judahite Burial Practices and Beliefs about the Dead* (*Journal for the Study of the Old Testament*, Supplement Series, 123; Sheffield, JSOT Press).
Bloom, Harold
    1973   *The Anxiety of Influence: A Theory of Poetry* (New York: Oxford University Press).
    1975   *A Map of Misreading* (New York: Oxford University Press).
    1989   *'Ruin the Sacred Truths': Poetry and Belief from the Bible to the Present* (Charles Eliot Norton Lectures 1987–88; Cambridge, MA: Harvard University Press).
    1994   *The Western Canon: The Books and Schools of the Ages* (New York: Harcourt Brace & Co.).
    1996   *Omens of Millennium: The Gnosis of Angels, Dreams and Resurrection* (London: Fourth Estate).
Bloom, Harold, and David Rosenberg
    1991   *The Book of J* (trans. David Rosenberg; interpreted Harold Bloom; London: Faber).
Bold, Alan
    1986   *Muriel Spark* (London: Methuen).
Bonhoeffer, Dietrich
    1971   *Letters and Papers from Prison* (ed. E. Bethge; London: SCM Press, enlarged edn).
Borges, Jorge Luis
    1998   *Collected Fictions* (trans. A. Hurley; London: Allen Lane/The Penguin Press).
Bottigheimer, Ruth
    1996   *The Bible for Children: From the Age of Gutenberg to the Present* (New York: Yale University Press).
Bourgeade, Pierre
    1987   *Mémoires de Judas* (Paris: Gallimard).
Brichto, Herman
    1973   'Kin, Cult, Land and Afterlife—A Biblical Complex', *Hebrew Union College Annual* 44: 1-54.
Brodsky, Joseph
    1997   *On Grief and Reason: Essays* (London: Penguin Books).
Budde, Karl
    1876   *Beiträge zur Kritik des Buches Hiob* (Bonn: A. Marcus).
Burke, Carl
    1966   *God is for Real, Man* (New York: YMCA).
Burns, Robert
    1971   *Poems and Songs* (ed. James Kinsley; Oxford: Oxford University Press).

Caldwell, Taylor, and Jess Stearn
    1977   *I, Judas* (New York: Atheneum).
Callaghan, Morley
    1983   *A Time for Judas* (Toronto: Macmillan).
Cameron, Deborah
    1992   *Feminism and Linguistic Theory* (Basingstoke: Macmillan).
Carroll, Robert P.
    1976   'Postscript to Job', *The Modern Churchman* 19: 161-66.
    1991   *Wolf in the Sheepfold: The Bible as a Problem for Christianity* (London: SPCK).
    1997   *Wolf in the Sheepfold: The Bible as Problematic for Christianity* (London: SCM Press, 2nd edn).
    1998   'Lower Case Bibles: Commodity Culture and the Bible', in J. Cheryl Exum and Stephen D. Moore (eds.), *Biblical Studies/Cultural Studies: The Third Sheffield Colloquium* (*Journal for the Study of the Old Testament*, Supplement Series, 266; Sheffield: Sheffield Academic Press): 46-69.
Carroll, Robert P., and Stephen Prickett (eds.)
    1997   *The Bible: Authorized King James Version with Apocrypha* (Oxford: Oxford University Press).
Carter, Angela
    1996   'The Company of Wolves', in *idem, Burning Your Boats: Collected Short Stories* (London: Vintage): 212-20.
Carter, Lin
    1972   'Afterword: The Naming of Names: Notes on Lord Dunsany's Influence on Modern Fantasy Writers', in Lord Dunsany, *Beyond the Fields We Know* (ed. Lin Carter; London: Pan/Ballantine): 290-99.
Caruth, Cathy
    1996   *Unclaimed Experience: Trauma, Narrative and History* (Baltimore: The Johns Hopkins University Press).
Cather, Willa
    1936   *Not Under Forty* (New York: Alfred A. Knopf).
    1954   *My Ántonia* (Boston, MA: Houghton Mifflin).
Certeau, Michel de
    1975   *The Writing of History* (trans. T. Conley; New York: Columbia University Press.
Cixous, Hélène
    1999   'Love of the Wolf', in *Stigmata: Escaping Texts* (trans. Keith Cohen; New York: Routledge): 84-99.
Cixous, Hélène, and Mireille Calle-Gruber
    1994   *Hélène Cixous, Rootprints: Memory and Life Writing* (trans. Eric Prenowitz; New York: Routledge).
Clines, David J.A.
    1990   'Deconstructing the Book of Job', in Martin Warner (ed.), *The Bible as Rhetoric: Studies in Biblical Persuasion and Credibility* (Warwick Studies in Philosophy and Literature; London: Routledge): 65-80.
    1995   'Varieties of Indeterminacy', *Semeia* 71: 17-27.
    1997   *The Bible and the Modern World* (The Biblical Seminar, 51; Sheffield: Sheffield Academic Press).

Coats, George W.
  1981   'The Curse of God's Blessing: *Gen* 12.1–4a in the Structure and
          Theology of the Yahwist', in J. Jeremias and L. Pertt (eds.), *Die
          Botschaft und die Boten Festschrift für Hans Walter Wolff zum 70.
          Geburtstag* (Neukirchen–Vluyn: Neukirchener Verlag): 31-41.
Compton-Burnett, Ivy
  1972a   *Daughters and Sons* (London: Victor Gollancz).
  1972b   *The Present and the Past* (London: Penguin Books).
Craigie, Peter
  1983   *Psalms 1–50* (Word Biblical Commentary, 19; Waco, TX: Word
          Books).
Danby, Herbert
  1919   *Tractate Sanhedrin, Mishnah and Tosefta: The Judicial Procedure of the
          Jews as Codified Towards the End of the 2nd Century A.D.* (London:
          SPCK).
Davie, Donald
  1996   *The Psalms in English* (London: Penguin Books).
Dawkins, Richard
  1976   *The Selfish Gene* (Oxford: Oxford University Press).
  1982   *The Extended Phenotype* (Oxford: Oxford University Press).
  1989   *The Selfish Gene* (Oxford: Oxford University Press, rev. edn).
  1993   'Viruses of the Mind', in B. Dahlbom (ed.), *Dennett and his Critics:
          Demystifying Mind* (Cambridge, MA: Basil Blackwell).
  1995   *River out of Eden: A Darwinian View of Life* (London: Weidenfeld &
          Nicolson).
Delitszch, Friedrich
  1869   *Biblical Commentary on the Book of Job* II (trans. F. Bolton; Edinburgh:
          T. & T. Clark).
Dennett, Daniel C.
  1991   *Consciousness Explained* (London: Allen Lane).
  1995   *Darwin's Dangerous Idea* (London Allen Lane).
Derrida, Jacques
  2002a   *Acts of Religion* (ed. G. Andijar; London: Routledge).
  2002b   *Without Alibi* (trans. Peggy Kamuf; Stanford, CA: Stanford
          University Press).
Dickinson, Michael
  1994   *The Lost Testament of Judas Iscariot* (Dingle: Brandon).
Dillard, Annie
  1988   *An American Childhood* (New York: HarperPerennial).
Dinesen, Isak (Karen Blixen)
  1985   *Out of Africa/Shadows on the Grass* (Harmondsworth: Penguin Books).
  1986a   'Babette's Feast', in *idem*, *Anecdotes of Destiny* (Harmondsworth:
          Penguin Books): 23-70.
  1986b   'The Blank Page', in *idem*, *Last Tales* (Harmondsworth: Penguin
          Books): 99-105.
  1986c   *Ehrengard* (Harmondsworth: Penguin Books).
Dinnerstein, Dorothy
  1987   *The Rocking of the Cradle and the Ruling of the World* (London: The
          Women's Press).

Drabble, Margaret
    1969   *The Waterfall* (London: Weidenfeld & Nicholson).
Dusinberre, Juliet
    1999   *Alice to the Lighthouse: Children's Books and Radical Experiments in Art* (Basingstoke: Macmillan, rev. edn).
Easterman, Daniel
    1994   *The Judas Testament* (San Francisco: HarperCollins).
Eilberg-Schwartz, Howard
    1994   *God's Phallus and Other Problems for Men and Monotheism* (Boston, MA: Beacon Press).
Evans, Nicholas
    1998   *The Loop* (London: Bantam Press).
Exum, J. Cheryl
    1995   'Feminist Criticism: Whose Interests Are Being Served?', in Gale A. Yee (ed.), *Judges and Method: New Approaches in Biblical Studies* (Minneapolis: Fortress Press): 65-90.
Fewell, Danna Nolan, and David L. Gunn
    1993   *Gender, Power and Promise: The Subject of the Bible's First Story* (Nashville: Abingdon Press).
Fisch, Harold
    1988   *Poetry with a Purpose: Biblical Poetics and Interpretation* (Bloomington: Indiana University Press).
Fohrer, Georg
    1968   *Introduction to the Old Testament* (trans. David Green; Nashville: Abingdon Press).
Freer, Coburn
    1972   *Music for a King: George Herbert's Style and the Metrical Psalms* (Baltimore: The Johns Hopkins University Press).
Freud, Sigmund
    1924   *Collected Papers. II. Clinical Papers; Papers on Technique* (London: The Hogarth Press and the Institute of Psycho-Analysis).
    1973   *Introductory Lectures on Psychoanalysis* (The Pelican Freud Library, 1; Harmondsworth: Penguin Books).
    1976   *Jokes and their Relation to the Unconscious* (The Pelican Freud Library, 6; Harmondsworth: Penguin Books).
    1985   *The Origins of Religion* (The Penguin Freud Library, 13; Harmondsworth: Penguin Books).
    1991   *On Metapsychology: The Theory of Psychoanalysis* (The Penguin Freud Library, 11; London: Penguin Books [German original 1915]).
Frye, C. Northrop
    1983   *The Great Code: The Bible and Literature* (London: Ark Paperbacks).
Fullerton, K.
    1924   'The Original Conclusion to the Book of Job', *Zeitschrift fur die alttestamentliche Wissenschaft* 42: 116-36.
Gibbs, Robert, and Elliot R. Wolfson (eds.)
    2002   *Suffering Religion* (London: Routledge).
Gill, Anton
    1989   *The Journey Back from Hell* (London: Grafton Books).

Girard, René
    1987   *Job the Victim of his People* (trans. Yvonne Freccero; London: The
              Athlone Press).
Goldin, Hyman E.
    1952   *Hebrew Criminal Law and Procedure* (New York: Twayne Publishers).
Goldman, Ronald
    1997   *Circumcision: The Hidden Trauma; How an American Cultural Practice
              Affects Infants and Ultimately Us All* (Boston, MA: Vanguard Publica-
              tions).
Goldthwaite, John
    1996   *The Natural History of Make-Believe: A Guide to the Principal Works of
              Britain, Europe, and America* (New York and London: Oxford
              University Press).
Gollaher, David L.
    2000   *Circumcision: A History of the World's Most Controversial Surgery*
              (New York: Basic Books).
Grant, Robert M.
    1997   *Irenaeus of Lyons* (London: Routledge).
Gray, Alasdair
    1995   *Five Letters from an Eastern Empire* (Harmondsworth: Penguin
              Books).
Greene, Graham
    1999   *Collected Essays* (London: Vintage).
Gubar, Susan
    1981   '"The Blank Page" and the Issues of Female Creativity', *Critical
              Inquiry* 8: 241-63.
Guberman, R.M. (ed.)
    1996   *Julia Kristeva Interviews* (New York: Columbia University Press).
Guest, Deryn
    1999   'Hiding Behind the Naked Women in Lamentations: A Recrimi-
              native Response', *Biblical Interpretation* 7: 413-48.
Gyllensten, Lars
    1967   *The Testament of Cain* (trans. K. Bradfield; London: Calder & Boyars).
Halperin, David J.
    1993   *Seeking Ezekiel: Text and Psychology* (University Park, PA:
              Pennsylvania State University Press).
Hanson, Anthony, and Miriam Hanson
    1953   *The Book of Job: Introduction and Commentary* (London: SCM Press).
Hartman, Geoffrey H., and Sandra Budick (eds.)
    1986   *Midrash and Literature* (New Haven: Yale University Press).
Heider, George C.
    1985   *The Cult of Molek: A Reassessment* (*Journal for the Study of the Old
              Testament*, Supplement Series, 43; Sheffield: JSOT Press).
Hesse, Hermann
    1965   *Steppenwolf* (trans. Basil Creighton; rev. Walter Sorell; Harmonds-
              worth: Penguin Books).
Hickey, Kieran
    2000   'A Geographical Perspective on the Decline and Extermination of
              the Irish Wolf *Canis lupus* — An Initial Assessment', *Irish Geography*
              33: 185-98.

Hoffman, Laurence A.
   1996   *Covenant of Blood: Circumcision and Gender in Rabbinic Judaism*
           (Chicago: University of Chicago Press).
Hughes, Ted
   1989   *Wolfwatching* (London: Faber & Faber).
Jabès, Edmond
   1996   *The Little Book of Unsuspected Subversion* (trans. Rosmarie Waldrop;
           Stanford, CA: Stanford University Press).
Jones, Steve
   1996   *In the Blood: God, Genes and Destiny* (London: HarperCollins).
Josipovici, Gabriel
   1998   *The Book of God: A Response to the Bible* (New Haven and London:
           Yale University Press).
Jossua, Jean-Pierre
   1995   'Pourquoi Judas?', *Revue de sciences philosophiques et théologiques* 79:
           549-51.
Jung, Carl G.
   1952   *Antwort auf Hiob* (Rascher: Zürich).
   1954   *Answer to Job* (trans R.P.C. Hull; London: Routledge & Kegan Paul).
Kafka, Franz
   1977   *Letters to Friends, Family and Editors* (trans. Richard and Clara
           Winston; New York: Schocken Books).
Kemp, Peter
   1974   *Muriel Spark* (London: Paul Elek).
Kendall, Carol
   1990   *The Gammage Cup* (New York: Harcourt Brace Jovanovich, reissue
           edition [first published 1959]).
Keneally, Brendan
   1991   *The Book of Judas* (Newcastle: Bloodaxe Books).
Kepnes, Stephen, Peter Ochs and Robert Gibbs (eds.)
   1998   *Reasoning after Revelation: Dialogues in Postmodern Jewish Philosophy*
           (Boulder, CO: Westview Press).
Kermode, Frank
   1979   *The Genesis of Secrecy: On the Interpretation of Narrative* (Cambridge,
           MA: Harvard University Press).
   1986   'The Uses of Error', *Theology* 89: 425-31.
Kierkegaard, Søren
   1970   *Journals and Papers*, II (ed. and trans. H.V. Hong and E.H. Hong;
           Bloomington: Indiana University Press).
   1983   *Fear and Trembling: Repetition* (ed. and trans. H.V. Hong and E.H.
           Hong; Princeton, NJ: Princeton University Press).
   1987   'The Diary of a Seducer', in *idem*, *Either/Or*, Part One (ed. and trans.
           H.V. Hong and E.H. Hong; Princeton, NJ: Princeton University
           Press): 301-445.
   1990   *For Self-Examination/Judge for Yourself!* (ed. and trans. H.V. Hong
           and E.H. Hong; Princeton, NJ: Princeton University Press).
Klein, Melanie
   1957   *Envy and Gratitude* (London: Tavistock Publications).

Kristeva, Julia
    1982   *Powers of Horror: An Essay on Abjection* (trans. L.S. Roudiez; New York: Columbia University Press).
    1993   *Les nouvelles maladies de l'âme* (Paris: Fayard).
    1994   *The Old Man and the Wolves* (trans. Barbara Bray; New York: Columbia University Press).
    1995   *New Maladies of the Soul* (trans. Ross Guberman; New York; Columbia University Press).

Landy, Francis
    1997   'Do We Want Our Children To Read This Book?', in Dana Nolan Fewell and Gary A. Phillips (eds.), *Bible and Ethics of Reading, Semeia* 77: 157-76.

Langbaum, Robert
    1964   *The Gayety of Vision: A Study of Isak Dinesen's Art* (London: Chatto & Windus).

Lanner, Laurel
    1999   'Cannibal Mothers and Me: A Mother's Reading of 2 Kings 6.24–7.20', *Journal for the Study of the Old Testament* 85: 107-16.

Lasine, Stuart
    1991   'Jehoram and the Cannibal Mothers', *Journal for the Study of the Old Testament* 50: 27-53.

Lerner, Gerda
    1986   *The Creation of Patriarchy* (Oxford: Oxford University Press).

Lesnik-Oberstein, Karín
    1994   *Children's Literature: Criticism and the Fictional Child* (Oxford: Clarendon Press).

Levenson, Jon D.
    1972   *The Book of Job in its Time and in the Twentieth Century* (The Le Baron Russell Briggs Prize Honors Essay in English, 1971; Cambridge, MA: Harvard University Press).

Lévi-Strauss, Claude
    1969   *Totemism* (trans. R. Needham; Harmondsworth: Penguin Books).

Lewis, Cecil
    1989   *The Gospel According to Judas* (London: Sphere Books).

Linafelt, Tod
    1995   'Surviving Lamentations', *Horizons in Biblical Theology* 17: 45-61.
    1996   'The Undecidability of *brk* in the Prolog to Job and Beyond', *Biblical Interpretation* 4: 154-72.
    2000   *Surviving Lamentations* (Chicago: University of Chicago Press).

Lopez, Barry Holstun
    1995   *Of Wolves and Men* (New York: Touchstone/Simon & Schuster).

Maccoby, Hyam
    1991   *Judas Iscariot and the Myth of Jewish Evil* (New York: Free Press).

Macherey, Pierre
    1978   *A Theory of Literary Production* (trans. G. Wall; London: Routledge).

MacLeod, Angus (ed. and trans.)
    1952   *The Songs of Duncan Ban Macintyre* (Scottish Gaelic Texts, 4; Edinburgh: Oliver & Boyd).

MacNeice, Louis
 1979 *Collected Poems* (London: Faber & Faber).
Magnus, Bernd, Stanley Stewart and Jean-Pierre Mileur
 1993 *Nietzsche's Case: Philosophy as/and Literature* (New York: Routledge).
Magonet, Jonathan
 1994 *A Rabbi Reads the Psalms* (London: SCM Press).
Maimonides, Moses
 1956 *The Guide for the Perplexed* (trans. M. Friedländer; New York: Dover Books).
Malterre, Elona
 1990 *The Last Wolf in Ireland* (New York: Clarion Books).
Martin, François
 1996 *Pour une théologie de la lettre: l'inspiration des Ecritures* (Paris: Editions du Cerf).
Mawer, Simon
 2005 *The Gospel of Judas* (London: Abacus).
May, Hal, and Deborah Straub (eds.)
 1981 *Contemporary Authors* (New Revision Series, 25; Detroit: Gale).
McCarthy, Carmel
 1981 *The Tiqqune Sopherim and Other Theological Corrections in the Masoretic Text of the Old Testament* (Orbis biblicus et orientalis, 36; Freiburg: Universitätsverlag; Göttingen: Vandenhoeck & Ruprecht).
McEntire, Mark
 1999 *The Blood of Abel: The Violent Plot in the Hebrew Bible* (Macon, GA: Mercer University Press).
Medawar, Peter
 1977 'Unnatural Science', *The New York Review of Books*, 3 February: 13-18.
Midgley, Mary
 2001 'The Problem of Living with Wildness', in Virginia A. Sharpe, Bryan Norton and Strachan Donnelley (eds.), *Wolves and Human Communities: Biology, Politics, and Ethics* (Washington: Island Press): 179-90.
Miles, Jack
 1995 *God: A Biography* (London: Simon & Schuster).
 2001 *Christ: A Crisis in the Life of God* (London: William Heinemann).
Mintz, Alan
 1984 *Hurban: Responses to Catastrophe in Hebrew Literature* (New York: Columbia University Press).
Morgan, Edwin
 1997 *Virtual and Other Realities* (Manchester: Carcanet).
Morpurgo, Michael
 2002 *The Last Wolf* (London: Doubleday).
Newton, Michael
 2002 *Savage Girls and Wild Boys* (London: Faber & Faber).
Nietzsche, Friedrich
 1994 *On the Genealogy of Morality* (ed. K. Ansell-Pearson; trans. C. Diethe; Cambridge: Cambridge University Press).

Ouaknin, Marc-Alain
    2000   *Mysteries of the Kabbalah* (trans. J. Bacon; New York: Abbeville Press).
Ozick, Cynthia
    1996   *Portrait of the Artist as a Bad Character* (London: Pimlico).
Paffenroth, Kim
    2002   *Judas: Images of the Lost Disciple* (Louisville, KY; Westminster/John Knox Press).
Page, G.
    1912   *Diary of Judas Iscariot* (Kila, MT: Kessinger Press).
Paillard, Jean
    1995   *Broder Judas: Om en märklig upprättelse av Iskariot* (Stockholm: Libris).
Panas, Henryk
    1977   *The Gospel according to Judas* (trans. Marc E. Heine; London: Hutchinson [Polish original 1973]).
Pardes, Ilona
    1992   *Countertraditions in the Bible: A Feminist Approach* (Cambridge, MA: Harvard University Press).
Patrick, Millar
    1949   *Four Centuries of Scottish Psalmody* (Oxford: Oxford University Press).
Pattison, George
    1987   'Jung, Kierkegaard and the Eternal Feminine', *Theology* 90: 430-40.
    1990   'A Drama of Love and Death: Michael Pedersen Kierkegaard and Regina Olsen Revisited', *History of European Ideas* 12: 79-91.
Pavlov, Ivan P.
    1927   *Conditioned Reflexes: An Investigation of the Physiological Activity of the Cerebral Cortex* (trans. and ed. G. Anrep; Oxford: Oxford University Press).
Percy, Walker
    1983   *Lost in the Cosmos: The Last Self-Help Book* (New York: Farrar & Giroux).
Pesch, Otto Hermann
    2000   *What Big Ears You Have! The Theologians' Red Riding Hood* (trans. Grant Kaplan and Linda M. Maloney; A Michael Glazier Book; Collegeville, MN: The Liturgical Press).
Pfeiffer, Robert H.
    1952   *Introduction to the Old Testament* (London: A. & C. Black).
Plotkin, Henry
    1995   *Darwin Machines and the Nature of Knowledge: Concerning Adaptations, Instinct and the Evolution of Intelligence* (London: Penguin Books).
Polanyi, Michael
    1962   *Personal Knowledge* (London: Routledge & Kegan Paul).
Pollack, Richard
    1994   *Signs of Life: The Language and Meanings of DNA* (London: Penguin Books).
Pritchard, James B. (ed.)
    1958   *The Ancient Near East. I. An Anthology of Texts and Pictures* (Princeton, NJ: Princeton University Press).

Rayner, William
    1969   *The Knifeman: The Last Journal of Judas Iscariot* (London: Michael
            Joseph).
Rickels, Lawrence
    1988   *Aberrations of Mourning: Writing on German Crypts* (Detroit: Wayne
            State University Press).
Rose, Jacqueline
    1984   *The Case of Peter Pan or the Impossibility of Children's Fiction* (London:
            Macmillan).
Rosenthal, Peggy
    1998   'Introduction', in Robert Atwan, George Dardess and Peggy
            Rosenthal (eds.), *Divine Inspiration: The Life of Jesus in World Poetry*
            (Oxford: Oxford University Press): xxvii-xliii.
Rutherford, Jonathan
    1992   *Men's Silences: Predicaments in Masculinity* (London: Routledge).
Sagan, Carl
    1996   *The Demon-haunted World: Science as a Candle in the Dark* (London:
            Headline Book Publishing).
Sattel, Jack
    1983   'Men, Inexpressiveness and Power', in B. Thorne, C. Kramarae and
            N. Henley (eds.), *Language, Gender and Society* (Rowley, MA:
            Newbury House).
Savelle, M.
    1967   *The Gospel of Judas Iscariot* (New York: Exposition Press).
Scarry, Elaine
    1985   *The Body in Pain: The Making and Unmaking of the World* (Oxford:
            Oxford University Press).
Schafer, C.
    1973   *The Sanhedrin Papers Including the Gospel of Judas* (New York:
            Vantage Press).
Schwartz, Regina
    1997   *The Curse of Cain: The Violent Legacy of Monotheism* (Chicago: Uni-
            versity of Chicago Press).
Seidman, Naomi
    1994   'Burning the Book of Lamentations', in C. Büchmann and C. Spiegel
            (eds.), *Out of the Garden: Women Writers on the Bible* (London:
            Pandora): 278-88.
Shlain, Leo
    1998   *The Alphabet versus the Goddess: Male Words and Female Images*
            (London: Allen Lane).
Skea, Ann
    1998   'Wolf-Masks: From Hawk to Wolfwatching'. Available online at
            <http://ann.skea.com/Wolves.htm>. First published in L. Scigaj
            (ed.), *Critical Essays on Ted Hughes* (New York: G.K. Hall & Co.,
            1992).
Spark, Muriel
    1955   'The Mystery of Job's Suffering: Jung's New Interpretation
            Examined', *The Church of England Newspaper*, 15 April: 7.
    1957   *The Comforters* (London: Macmillan).

1961   *The Prime of Miss Jean Brodie* (London: Macmillan).

1985   *The Only Problem* (London: Triad Grafton Books).

Staley, Jeffrey L.

1995   *Reading with a Passion: Rhetoric, Autobiography, and the American West in the Gospel of John* (New York: Continuum).

Stanford, P.

1997   'Jesus Christ's Smarter Brother', *The Guardian* 2, 25 February: 2-3.

Stavrakopoulou, Francesca

2004   *King Manasseh and Child Sacrifice: Biblical Distortions of Historical Realities* (Beihefte zur *Zeitschrift für die alttestamentliche Wissenschaft*, 338; Berlin: W. de Gruyter).

Steinberg, Leo

1996   *The Sexuality of Christ in Renaissance Art and in Modern Oblivion* (Chicago: University of Chicago Press, 2nd edn).

Steiner, George

1996   *No Passion Spent: Essays 1978–1996* (London: Faber & Faber).

Stonehouse, Julia

1994   *Idols to Incubators: Reproduction Theory throughout the Ages* (London: Scarlet Press).

Strange, K.H., and R.G.E. Sandbach (eds.)

1978   *Psalm 23: An Anthology* (Edinburgh: Saint Andrew Press).

Summers, Montague

1933   *The Werewolf* (London: Kegan Paul, Trench, Trubner).

Tatar, Maria (ed.)

1999   *The Classic Fairy Tales* (New York: W.W. Norton).

Terrien, Samuel

1954   'Introduction to Job', in *The Interpreter's Bible*, III (New York: Abingdon Press): 884-88.

Townsend, John Rowe

1995   *Written for Children: An Outline of English-Language Children's Literature* (London: The Bodley Head, 6th edn).

Tsvetaeva, Maria

1980   *A Captive Spirit: Selected Prose* (ed. and trans. J. Marin King; Ann Arbor: Ardis).

Urbrock, William J.

1981   'Job as Drama: Tragedy or Comedy?', *Currents in Theology and Mission* 8: 35-40.

Van Greenaway, Peter

1972   *Judas!* (London: Victor Gollancz).

Warner, Marina

1994   *From the Beast to the Blonde: On Fairytales and their Tellers* (London: Chatto & Windus).

1998   *No Go the Bogeyman: Scaring, Lulling and Making Mock* (London: Chatto & Windus).

Weiss, Meir

1983   *The Story of Job's Beginning; Job 1–2, A Literary Analysis* (Jerusalem: Magnes Press).

Wellhausen, Julius
    1871   Review of A. Dillman's *Hiob* (Leipzig: S. Hirtel, 1869), *Jahrbücher für deutsche Theologie* 16: 552-57.
Whedbee, J. William
    1977   'The Comedy of Job', *Semeia* 7: 1-39.
White, David Gordon
    1991   *Myths of the Dog-Man* (Chicago: University of Chicago Press).
Williams, Rowan
    2000   *Lost Icons: Reflections on Cultural Bereavement* (Edinburgh: T. & T. Clark).
Woolf, Virginia
    1989   *Congenial Spirits: Selected Letters* (ed. J.T. Banks; London: The Hogarth Press).
Wright, Christopher
    1987   *The Meaning of BRK 'To Bless' in the Old Testament* (Atlanta: Scholars Press).
Yerby, Frank
    1969   *Judas, My Brother: The Story of the Thirteenth Disciple* (London: Heinemann).
Young, Dudley
    1993   *Origins of the Sacred: The Ecstasies of Love and War* (London: Abacus).
Zim, Rivkah
    1987   *English Metrical Psalms: Poetry as Praise and Prayer, 1535–1601* (Cambridge: Cambridge University Press).
Ziolkowski, Theodore
    1972   *Fictional Transfigurations of Jesus* (Princeton, NJ: Princeton University Press).
Zipes, Jack (ed.)
    1993   *The Trials and Tribulations of Little Red Riding Hood* (New York: Routledge, 2nd edn).

INDEXES

INDEX OF REFERENCES

INDEX OF AUTHORS

Lightning Source UK Ltd.
Milton Keynes UK
06 August 2010

157987UK00001B/56/A

9 781905 048328